RITUAL AND EXPERIMENT IN MODERN POETRY

Also by Jacob Korg

George Gissing: A Critical Biography

Dylan Thomas

Language in Modern Literature

Browning and Italy

RITUAL AND EXPERIMENT IN MODERN POETRY

Jacob Korg

St. Martin's Press
New York

RITUAL AND EXPERIMENT IN MODERN POETRY
Copyright © 1995 by Jacob Korg

ISBN 0-312-12453-8

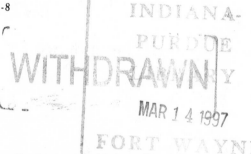

Library of Congress Cataloging-in-Publication Data

Korg, Jacob.
    Ritual and experiment in modern poetry / Jacob Korg.
        p. cm.
    Includes bibliographical references (p.) and index.
    ISBN 0-312-12453-8
    1. American poetry—20th century—History and criticism.
  2. Modernism (Literature)—United States. 3. English poetry—20th
century—History and criticism. 4. Experimental poetry—History and
criticism. 5. Modernism (Literature)—Great Britain. 6. Ritual in
literature. I. Title.
PS310.M57K67 1995
811'.5209—dc20   94-25159
                                        CIP

Book Design by Acme Art, Inc.

First Edition: August 1995
10 9 8 7 6 5 4 3 2 1

FTW
AHW5356

To Cynthia

TABLE OF CONTENTS

ACKNOWLEDGMENTS

I have had considerable help in working on this study, some of it casual (but no less valuable) from a number of sources. I have had useful suggestions from my colleagues, especially Professor Douglas Collins and Professor Paul Pascal of the University of Washington. I am, of course, deeply indebted to the many scholars and critics who have worked in the field of modern poetry and whose contributions are acknowledged in detail in my notes. The award of an Arts/Humanities Research Professorship from the Graduate School of the University of Washington enabled me to spend some time in England and to use resources there. Some of the research was carried on in the Bodleian Library, the libraries of the University of Washington, the British Library, the library of the Tate Gallery, and the library of King's College, Cambridge, to whose archivist, Dr. Michael Halls, I am especially indebted.

I am grateful to the *Journal of Modern Literature* for permission to use some material from an article published there as a portion of Chapter 1. Grateful acknowledgment is given to New Directions Publishing Corporation for permission to quote from the following works of Ezra Pound: *Personae* (copyright 1926 by Ezra Pound); *Selected Prose 1909-1965* (copyright 1960, 1962 by Ezra Pound; copyright 1973 by the Estate of Ezra Pound); *Ezra Pound's Poetry and Prose: Contributions to Periodicals* (Garland Publishing, copyright 1991 by the Trustees of EPLPT); *The Cantos* (copyright 1934, 1937, 1940, 1956, 1962, 1963, 1966, and 1968 by Ezra Pound).

Lines from Pound's translation of Confucian odes 275 and 291 are reprinted by permission of the publishers from *Shih-Ching: The Classic Anthology, Defined by Confucius*, by Ezra Pound (Cambridge, Mass.: Harvard University Press, copyright 1954 by the President and Fellows of Harvard College; copyright renewed 1982 by Mary DeRachewiltz and Omar Pound).

Grateful acknowledgment is given to New Directions Publishing Corporation for permission to quote from the following works of H. D.: *Tribute to Freud* (copyright 1956, 1974 by Norman Holmes Pearson); *HERmione* (copyright 1981 by the Estate of Hilda Doolittle and by Perdita Schaffner); *Collected*

RITUAL AND EXPERIMENT IN MODERN POETRY

1

Ritual, Experiment, Poetry

A poem is a rite: hence its formal and ritualistic character.
—W. H. Auden, *The Dyer's Hand*

All poetry is experimental poetry. —Wallace Stevens, *Opus Posthumous*

The novelist Bryher, looking back to the period of disillusionment that prevailed among British intellectuals after World War I, wrote: "The only thing left in which we could believe was art. It was to us what religion was to the Middle Ages, discovery to the Renaissance, and what science is becoming to the present day."[1] Bryher's analogues—religion, discovery, science—are significant. Many of the major modern poets, both English and American, courageously attempted to assimilate values from all three into their work, challenging the view that their first principles were incompatible with each other. Alfred North Whitehead described the cultural situation of the time in this way: "It seems as though, during the last half-century, the results of science and the beliefs of religion had come into a position of frank disagreement, from which there can be no escape." He added, however, "The clash is a sign that there are wider truths and finer perspectives within which a reconciliation of a deeper religion and a more subtle science will be found."[2]

Poets writing between 1910 and 1950 responded to this promise by employing resources drawn from the two procedures that epitomize the ideologies of religion and science: ritual and experiment. Yeats, Eliot, Pound, H. D., and David Jones, in varying degrees, brought ritualist and experimental elements together as part of their efforts to keep poetry abreast or ahead of their time. The result was not the reconciliation Whitehead hoped for, which is perhaps not within the power of poetry, but rather the invention of poetic modes capable of encompassing the breadth of thought and feeling he regarded as a context for it.

This conjunction of ritual and experiment, with its effects on diction, form, subject matter, and the basic conceptions of the nature of poetry, may be seen as one of the persistent themes of the modern poetic revolution. It played a part in the expansion and diversification of poetry, reflecting the conviction that, in Whitehead's words, "A clash of doctrines is not a disaster—it is an opportunity."[3] My study is concerned with the ways in which some of the major modern poets took advantage of this opportunity. The poets in my study were selected because their poems exhibit features of both ritual and experiment. But there are other commonalities among them. All, with the exception of David Jones, were to some extent influenced by Ezra Pound and his effort to encourage poetry that would do justice to the "heteroclite elements" of the modern mind. In the cases of Yeats and H. D., the influence was reciprocal: Pound learned from them lessons that he incorporated into his own poetry and teaching. All of the poets, with the exception of Yeats, suffered from some degree of mental illness for which they sought treatment. Eliot's sessions with Dr. Vittoz, Pound's years at St. Elizabeth's, Jones's breakdowns, and H. D.'s treatment by Freud all suggest that their thinking transcended the current notion of normality, and this might also be said of Yeats. Their efforts to join ritualistic and experimental resources may well be an aspect of violent rebellions against conventional thought that resulted in mental dislocation.

We must not forget, also, that the wars of the period exerted a powerful influence. The reactions of the poets varied from Pound's despairing protests to the exalted resignation of Yeats, who found a "terrible beauty" in the Irish rebellion, and the piety of Jones, who saw a sacramental significance in war. In spite of these differences, it seems safe to say that all felt in the unprecedented scope and fury of the twentieth century wars an emergent reality that transcended the expressive capacities of conventional language and conventional poetic forms.

I must concede, as a necessary preliminary, that neither a poem nor any literary work can be a ritual or an experiment in the original sense of these terms, for both are fundamentally actions external to language. In her study, *Ritual Theory, Ritual Practice,* Catherine Bell uses the term *ritualization* to mean forms of behavior borrowed from ritual that interact with the social and cultural environment; this is what is generally found in the poems we will be examining.[4] (Unfortunately, the counterpart term, *experimentalization,* is unemployable.) Such events as formal meals, graduation exercises, union meetings, and trials can be considered secular rituals. They are separated from ordinary actions, spring from unknown origins, recapitulate earlier enactments according to fixed rules, and embody tradition and communal agreement. The participants do not feel that they are in the presence of a supernatural reality, but they do pay tribute to an overarching belief or custom that the ritual is intended to substantiate, to something perhaps as vague as the spirit of the occasion. A poem, regarded as a secular ritual, expresses devotion to what the ancients personified as a muse—a poetic purpose or spirit, however that may be conceived. Specific rituals and experiments are rarely enacted in poetry, but language, form, subtext, or allusions may be borrowed from them and the world view they imply. By referring to experiment and ritual in poetry, I mean only practices derived from both as they are embodied in language and as they deviate from what is conventionally expected of poetry.

Both ritual and experimental elements are latent in every significant poem. But they acquired a contradictory aspect in modern poetry, where they appeared together overtly as models, subjects of description, sources of allusion, and, most significantly, as determinants of form, language, imagery, and rhythm, bringing their conflicting ideological implications into an intellectual environment that still echoed the science and religion controversy of the nineteenth century. Ritual and experiment stem from metaphysical systems that diverged at about the time of the Renaissance and have supported opposing traditions in Western culture ever since.

A comparison of the ideologies attached to ritual and experiment underlines the contradictions that confronted the modern poets who were attracted by both. They derived their ideas of ritual from sources as varied as the Cambridge school of classicists, especially J. G. Frazer, and such specialists in the occult as the Theosophical Society.[5] While some of these ideas have never achieved respectability, or have undergone much critical revision, they were nevertheless enormously useful to the modern poets. Although their view was later attacked, theorists of the modern period, led by Frazer, held that ritual existed prior to myth as a primary expression of belief. Because it is free of linguistic and narrative conventions, ritual offers a more immediate relation to transcendental reality than myth and, in defiance of postmodern doctrine, claims to bring permanent and absolute realities into presence.[6] It was Jane Harrison's view that myth was called upon to supply verbal explanations when the actions that constituted the ritual lost their meaning. Her study of Greek festivals shows that they originated as magical cults and acquired their associations with the Olympian deities only later.[7] The primacy of ritual is also clear from Mircea Eliade's point that ritual is the re-enactment of a beginning, of a step out of chaos. The myth is the story of such beginnings and "the rite makes the myth present."[8] Similarly, Owen Barfield calls the sense of collectivity achieved by ritual participants "not only pre-logical but pre-mythical"; it precedes even totemic representation and only later finds expression in language.[9]

Sacred rituals, in their prototypical form, undertake to dispel such illusions as time, space, matter, and change that conceal the permanence of real existence. Ritual has the general purpose of renewing a vision of the world and man that antedates the corrupting influences of later times. According to Eliade, "archaic man" regards ordinary life as an inferior counterpart of the moment in which the world came into existence, when the sacred archetypes of which all other things are imitations were created. These original divine creations are the true reality, possessing authentic Being. The only significant actions men perform are those that replicate them and make it possible to pass from inconsequential historic time into the realm of the permanently meaningful. "Through repetition of the cosmogonic act, concrete time . . . is projected into mythical time, *in illo tempore* when the foundation of the world occurred."[10] This repetition of the primary creative action, an "eternal return" to the real beginning of things, to the "ontological order of the archetype," is the function of ritual.

As the modern poets understood it, ritual regards ordinary objects and events as symbols of that absolute reality and proposes to mediate between this inaccessible realm and the audience. It affirms the continuity or cyclical nature of time, maintains that the fundamental needs and rhythms of life never change, and opens a line of vision between the past and the present by re-enacting ancient or mythic events. It operates within a rich, stable context of familiar association to release the tranquilizing power of tradition. In replicating the world's emergence from nothingness, an event whose true nature can never be known, the ritual implies that there is a limit to human cognition.

Eliade's analyses involve a number of archaic ideas that seem paradoxical to the modern mind. They show that only mythical, unverifiable concepts handed down from remote origins are "real," while immediate experience is illusory and worthless. Since the ritual is based on the conviction that only the sacred archetypes have true existence, the participant must achieve a state of identification with a sacred being. Hence, alterity is an essential element of the ritual; one becomes real only if one loses one's identity and becomes another, an idea given currency in modern poetry by Rimbaud's "*Je* est un autre" and Yeats's doctrine of the Mask.[11]

Every mass, wedding, or funeral, properly experienced, is to be identified with the primordial event of its kind as an affirmation that the present is continuous with the sacred past. This is an assurance to its participants that their spiritual needs and the remedies for them are the same as those of their ancestors and a demonstration that it is possible not only to communicate with the divine and the dead but also to stand in their presence. The objects and events of a ritual are, properly speaking, not mere signs but the embodiments of essences. These may be represented to the senses in material form, but they can be genuinely apprehended only through intuitive channels without, or even in spite of, empiric evidence. This component of mystery is a reminder that what can be known and expressed rests ultimately on supernatural authority.

A scientific experiment, like a ritual, is a formal, rule-bound action, but while ritual confirms beliefs that are already known, experiment tests what is doubtful, thrusting forward into unprecedented situations to generate new knowledge. Unlike ritual, experiment suggests that reality consists of differentiated situations that are best understood through direct observation. The individual experiment presents itself as an instance of this reality, taking observation and reason based on firsthand experience as its authority; speculation and imagination are not ruled out, but they must be verified by experience. The experimental consciousness does not deal with essences but with relationships. It is concerned not with fixing the nature of things but with understanding structures and influences. If the elementary psychological ingredient of ritual is faith, which generates calm, for experiment it is doubt, which generates activity. Neither the hypothesis the experimenter begins with nor the conclusion he reaches may be regarded as absolutes. Only doubt can preserve the independence of mind needed for escaping the bondage of involuntary assumptions and confronting the new and possibly unwelcome truths experiment may reveal. Skepticism, inquiry, and innovation are essential to the experimental spirit, which is content with provisional insights and which envisions a future of continuing change.

Thus, the twentieth-century poets who experimented with their art and also adopted ritual principles were attempting to accommodate what the Western world believed to be contradictory views of apprehending truth and shaping the sense of reality. The intellectual environment of the modern period offered much encouragement to this effort. During that time, the positivism that had dominated the science of the nineteenth century was meeting serious challenges. Numerous scientific thinkers, including Albert Einstein, Werner Heisenberg, Karl Popper, and Gaston Bachelard, as well as Alfred North Whitehead, supported a subjective and even a religious approach to science in general and to experiment in particular. The significance of scientific data, it was agreed, depends upon a paradigm or framework of basic ideas that is intuitively based and not readily distinguishable from religious belief, except that it is acknowledged to be provisional.

Many twentieth-century scientists were willing to believe that ideas that are purely theoretical, even if they conflict with physical evidence, may have a heuristic value and may eventually prove to be valid within a new theoretical framework. By recognizing the part that cultural forces, subjective reactions, and individual imagination play in science, and by acknowledging that "natural laws" are only partial and provisional readings of external reality, critics of positivism have transformed the advancing sciences into disciplines that approach the condition of the humanities. Many scientists acknowledged that, as Albert Einstein said, the fundamental laws of physics (and presumably of science in general) are "freely invented" and "fictitious" and that scientific thinking rests on intuitively accepted or even unconscious assumptions such as Gerald Holton's *themata* and Karl Popper's "basic statements."[12] Recent theorists such as Thomas Kuhn and Stephen Toulmin have shown that the fundamental principles of science, as well as its topics of investigation and its conclusions, must be regarded as provisional because they are influenced by contemporary interests.[13] Thus, it has become increasingly clear in science, as it has always been in the humanities, that the mind cannot look to the external world for its authority but must depend on the integrity of its concepts.

The philosophy of experiment has undergone a parallel modification. Karl Popper was willing to define scientific objectivity as doctrine that survives repeated experimentation by different investigators, a process he called "inter-subjective testing." Experiment, in his system, serves the purpose of deriving objectivity from subjectivity on a grand scale. The change from Plato's belief in certainty to Popper's consensualism has been traced by James Wayne Dye, who says, "If truth is established by the continuing and ultimate agreement of competent investigators, there just is no knowledge without social corroboration. . . . Truth is approached, asymptotically at best."[14] Accordingly, it became clear that the interpretation of experiments is "theory-bound," determined to a great extent by the experimenter's preconceptions and the intellectual climate of his time.

Paul Feyerabend, perhaps the most radical critic of mainstream science, even argues that the advancement of science requires freedom from reason and empiricism. He declares that many of the elements identified with religion and humanistic pursuits, such as propaganda, intuition, style, and beauty, are essential to the continuing vitality of science. Like many others, he recognizes that shifts in science have not been rationally motivated but are based on "aesthetic judgments, judgments of taste, metaphysical prejudices, religious desires, in short . . . *our subjective wishes.*" And he regards this as the most advanced and free form of scientific thinking. "*We need a dream-*

world," he says, *"in order to discover the features of the real world we think we inhabit* (and which may actually be just another dream-world)."[15] If scientific experimentation operates under conditions like these, it is not too much to say that it can be regarded as a form of cultural, social, and spiritual expression that has much in common with art, literature, and religion.

The works of the modern poets reflect the conflict Mircea Eliade describes between the historicist view of history as a linear sequence of unprecedented events which must be individually interpreted and the archaic or traditionalist belief that history conforms to a cyclical, repetitive plan determined in the original moment of creation. The poets were not alone in turning to ritual in modern times, for, according to Eliade, many people still take shelter from "the terror of history" in traditional attitudes, and the full meaning of the archaic world view is being unfolded by cyclical theories of historiography and economics. This renewal of old beliefs is not limited to social theory, for, says Eliade, "the work of two of the most significant writers of our day—T. S. Eliot and James Joyce—is saturated with nostalgia for the myth of eternal repetition, and, in the last analysis, for the abolition of time."[16]

Ritual elements entered modern poetry through two channels: the survival in modern forms of ancient practices, and the self-conscious adoption of ritual language and symbols. The language of poetry has a surplus of meanings that transcend referentiality; if these are assimilated to a purely imaginary moral vision, they become anagogic expressions of spiritual realities. From this perspective, ritual values are inherent in poetry itself.[17] But the modern poets embodied these values in their work on a more overt level by self-consciously emulating, echoing, and even quoting religious rituals.

For example, many passages of modern poetry take the form of prayers. W. B. Yeats wrote four poems titled as prayers and in "A Prayer for My Daughter" he praised ritual by asking, "How but in custom and in ceremony / Are innocence and beauty born?" In "Ash Wednesday," whose general tone is one of Christian devotion, T. S. Eliot invokes an unnamed sacred figure in ritualized language: "Blessèd sister, holy mother, spirit of the fountain, spirit of the garden, / Suffer us not to mock ourselves with falsehood." The despairing staccato lines of Eliot's "The Hollow Men" climax with a phrase from the Lord's Prayer—"For Thine is the Kingdom"—a fragmentary and apparently futile attempt at devotion. In David Jones's *In Parenthesis*, the anguish of the soldiers who are waiting to go on the attack and perhaps to their deaths is intensified by the interpolation "Responde mihi," which Jones identifies as a phrase from the Dominican Office of the Dead whose origin is the Book of Job's "Answer thou me."

Julian Huxley, the father of the idea that human ritual is related to animal behavior and that ritual serves survival purposes for both, also observed that it crosses over into art: "The arts involve ritualization or adaptive canalization of the creative imagination."[18] Such art forms as prehistoric cave paintings and carvings are thought to be connected with rituals; music, dance, and theater have clear affiliations with ritual, and critics often suggest that literature originated in ritual chants or in narratives intended to explain rituals. Alastair Fowler speculates that the poetic genres had their ultimate origins in rituals and numerous forms, such as the ode, the elegy, and the epithalamion are clearly linked to ritual.[19] Frazer's homeopathic and contact forms of sympathetic magic, the first operating through resemblance, the second through contiguity, correspond to metaphor and metonymy. Both ritual and poetry depend for their effect on the participant's ability to envision a reality beyond ordinary perception. Lyric poetry, in particular, focuses, like ritual, on a timeless moment of intense feeling that has a transformational effect, dividing a comparatively imperceptive past from a future of heightened awareness. Ellen Dissanayake has explained the close association of ritual and art in primitive societies by arguing that such pleasurable elements as singing and dancing were introduced to encourage participation in rituals. Activities that later developed into independent art forms thus performed the function of "enabling mechanisms" that insured the continuation of the rituals considered essential for communal survival.[20]

Ritual, as a "matrix" of cultural activities, is linked to art as well as to experiment in the theories of the anthropologist Victor Turner. His contention that "living ritual may be better likened to artwork than to neurosis" at once confirms David Jones's view that all creative work amounts to ritual and rejects Freud's theory that art is a neurotic symptom.[21] Turner has vigorously developed the ideas of the anthropologist Arnold van Gennep who, in his 1908 work, *Les Rites de passage,* first identified a phase of license and disorder which occurs in many initiation rituals as a "liminal" period. At this time, the novices, being on the threshold of initiation are, for the moment, between two realms: they are both sacred and outside the social order and therefore able to commit transgressions that are normally forbidden.

Turner describes Van Gennep's liminality as a time for play, discovery, innovation, challenge, and interrogation. "In short, parts of liminality may be given over to experimental behavior." He specifies that the experimentation he means is not scientific, but consists merely of temporary ventures into the unknown. It is only a part of a process that ultimately proves the need for order and thus serves the traditional purposes of the community.

However, it may also bring about change, for it "contains the potentiality for cultural innovation as well as the means for effecting structural transformations within a relatively stable sociocultural system."[22] Turner sees the "lost liminality" of traditional rituals being regained in the cultural activities of modern times and mentions the works of Joyce, Beckett, and surrealist painters as instances of the new emphasis on "the experimental and the ludic."[23]

The innovative potential Turner sees in liminality comes to the fore in phenomena he calls *liminoid*, secular versions of ritual liminality that would seem to follow the principle of Catherine Bell's "ritualization" and to provide a rationale for relating experimental science and experimental poetry. Liminoid phenomena are deviant activities occurring in the secular settings of industrial societies that do not ultimately support tradition, as liminality does. On the contrary, they "are not merely regressive, they are often subversive, representing radical critiques of the central structure and proposing utopian alternative models."[24] Unlike liminal behavior, which is mandatory and contained within the social structure, liminoid activities are truly radical. They appear in complex industrial societies at the margins and transitional points of social institutions, such as laboratories and universities, where originality, freedom, individuality, and serious playfulness are prized. Turner characterizes liminoid phenomena as "plural, fragmentary and experimental." Because it is, almost by definition, a departure from received ideas, experiment, in Turner's nonscientific sense seems, in fact, to be the defining characteristic of the liminoid, and one that justifies his linking the works of Beckett and Joyce with scientific experimentation.

Until comparatively recent times, productions that we now regard as works of art served some specific function in a religious, political, or social context and were made for that purpose. The idea of art as an autotelic phenomenon intended solely to give aesthetic pleasure is a late development. T. S. Eliot, recognizing this, asked, "At what point in civilisation does any conscious distinction between practical or magical utility and aesthetic beauty arise?"[25] Thus, the interest of the modern poets in ritual represents a return to roots that had only recently been lost, but it was a modified return. Auden, while defining poetry as a rite, nevertheless insists on its secular nature, distinguishing it from religious ritual on the grounds that the purpose of art is "to disenchant and disintoxicate" by telling truth and that spiritual purification is appropriate only for "religious rites." He describes the poetic rite as a structure in which the sense of the absolute, which he identifies with Coleridge's Primary Imagination, is expressed through the resources of the

Secondary Imagination. Art, he says, originates with a desire to express the sense of the sacred, but the poem transforms the sacred into the profane, adopting the formal aspects of the religious ritual while dropping its magical ones. "This rite, " says Auden, "has no magical or idolatrous intentions. . . . With God as Redeemer, it has, so far as I can see, little if anything to do."[26]

Geoffrey Hartman concurs with Auden in distinguishing art from ritual while maintaining that there is a relationship between them. He takes the view that art is an agency for generating a meeting between the sacred and the secular and that poetry, like art in general, projects a sense that it arises from some enigmatic preverbal origin allied with ritual. Emphatically denying that the sacred and the secular are incompatible with each other, in apparent contradiction to Durkheim, Hartman suggests that art "ambiguously" involves both, that its intrusions into the holy precincts of ritual purify the profane and demystify the sacred. "The secular," he concludes, "is the sacred integrated rather than degraded or displaced," and literature, through its efforts to express the ineffable, to raise language to the level of the transcendental, becomes part of "the sacred event."[27] Peter Bürger has observed that the aesthetic movement, which immediately preceded the modern period, produced a "sacral" art that was independent of religion. "Instead, art generates a ritual."[28]

Stéphane Mallarmé and David Jones, beginning from very different points of departure, agree in identifying the Mass as the supreme expressive form. Mallarmé, who wrote about religion as though it were art and about art as though it were religion, thought that the Mass, which he considered to be the prototype of all ceremonies, held some significance for the poet. Catholicism, though a derelict religion, must nevertheless have embodied the intimate and unknown secret of the people. "L'heure convient," he concludes, "avec le détachement nécessaire, d'y pratiquer les fouilles, pour exhumer d'anciennes et magnifiques intentions."[29]

Mallarmé regarded the poet's work as a ritual process. He attached symbolic significance to the inkwell, the page, the folded leaves of the book, and, above all, to the letters of the alphabet, which have the mysterious power to generate an infinity of meanings as they are combined. Even the knife used to cut the pages of the book, Mallarmé observed, is suggestive of ritual sacrifice.[30] Mallarmé's plans for his great work, the *Livre*, show that he meant his text to be read aloud as a theatrical performance combining music, dance, drama, and poetry in a complex ceremony. He felt that theater was capable of revealing ultimate reality and that "elle n'est pas sans analogie avec la messe."[31]

Ritual's aesthetic appeal rests on the fact that it addresses the senses. David Jones, with the Mass in mind, wrote that the Catholic church emphasizes "the body and the embodied," that it is committed "to sense-perception, to the contactual, the known, the felt, the seen, the handled, the cared for, the tended, the conserved; to the qualitative and to the intimate."[32] Ritual communicates through such physical acts as uncovering, uplifting, separating, combining, cutting, and touching, through the objects involved in these movements and the place where they are performed. These generate a nonverbal grammar of repetition, contrast, variation, transformation, and other effects that express relationships and gain coherence through the nondiscursive channel of form. Ritual language and ritualizing poetry replicate this coherence verbally. W. H. Auden, as we have seen in *The Dyer's Hand*, feels that all poetry emulates ritual, "hence its formal and ritualistic character."

Because they have so much in common with each other, ritual and literature, especially poetry, have been able to exchange functions at various historical periods. Ritual is mimetic; it is a fictional, imaginative replication of an action. It endows objects and actions of the profane world with sacred significance, transforming them into symbols. It expresses intuitive ideas that cannot be embodied in rational form and bases its associations on homologies, causalities, and identifications not recognized by rational thought but often conveyed in such poetic tropes as metaphor, metonymy, and catachresis. It accepts paradox and contradiction, as well as such apparently irreconcilable combinations of feeling as fear and love, awe and intimacy, pride and humility. It demands alterity, the capacity to adopt alien thoughts and feelings.

Both drama and fiction are capable of closely replicating ritual structures, but poetry embeds these structures in a rhythmic medium that stimulates the prerational capacities of the mind.[33] More significantly, poetry is one of the few forms capable of expressing communal consciousness left to our scientifically oriented culture. As David Ward explains, when ritual magic loses its effectiveness, "poetry is among the most conservative factors of cohesiveness, returning most easily to primitive ways of perceiving and organizing perception. . . . We allow, and even expect the poet to relate experience and emotions which in other contexts would be dismissed as madness: we have learned how to allow certain sceptical and critical reactions to lie fallow while the poet speaks, if he speaks well."[34]

Renato Poggioli has described "experimentalism" as one of the "primary characteristics" of avant-garde art and an expression of its desire to align itself with the modern scientific temper of its time.[35] While it may not be possible to characterize all of modern poetry as avant-garde, or to identify all of its experimentalism with science, experiment does seem to be a concept essential to the major works. The word invariably appears, sooner or later, in critical discussions of modern literature, often with scientific associations.

Before the modern period, literary experiment usually meant mere departure from convention. But some of the modern poets responded to the specifically scientific implications of experiment, adapting it to the expression of ideas that lay outside the conventional limits of poetry. Ezra Pound, especially, thought of the modern movement as a program of innovations under the control of quasi-scientific principles that ought to emulate the spirit and even the structural features of its scientific model. Free verse, typographical effects, mixed diction, unconventional tropes, varying meters, and unstable or indeterminate poetic voices are among the numerous resources the moderns used to distance themselves from poetic tradition.

In science, new concepts are justified either by establishing their continuity with basic statements, *themata*, or previous knowledge, or by creating wholly new frames of reference. Unless it seeks incoherence, poetry, also, even in its most radically experimental ventures, must employ and continue past understandings, even if these are as fundamental as the notion that the marks on the page are letters and that the letters, in some instances at least, form words. But experimental poetry may also entail a degree of indeterminacy that implies some new basis of understanding. To the modern poets literary experiment meant innovation in this nearly, but not quite, unlimited sense. Gillian Beer has aptly defined the modern use of the term "experimental" in relation to art as meaning "a free-ranging, exploratory, innovatory project often lacking or avoiding any determined conclusion."[36]

Most of the modern poets regarded experimentation as an imperative of their time. Cleanth Brooks has suggested that as the modernists came to regard the poem as an independent artifact in accordance with the principles of the New Criticism, "the process of composition has been conceived of as one of experimentation and exploration—a testing of insights against the funded experience of the race as contained in, and refracted through, language."[37] Lyndall Gordon's description of T. S. Eliot's effort to find "a formula" for transcendental vision in *Four Quartets* is a perfect model of the experimental process: "The successive poems," she says, "tell the story of Eliot's gradual discovery of this formula, starting—like a scientist—from a flash of intuition. With painstaking care, he goes on to test intuition against experience; the experience of his own life and the experience of others in other ages."[38]

But the poets in this study felt also the imperative of ritual. They shared the urgency Alfred North Whitehead expresses in his chapter on "Religion and Science" in *Science and the Modern World*: "When we consider what religion is for mankind, and what science is, it is no exaggeration to say that the future course of history depends upon the decision of this generation as to the relations between them."[39] The sense that the two are incompatible with each other is a comparatively recent development in Western history. They can be seen co-existing in ancient methods of divination, in the principles of magic, in alchemy and astrology, and even in the speculations of Sir Isaac Newton. Only after the Enlightenment did it appear that religious beliefs and the doctrines of rational empiricism seriously contradicted each other.

The countermovement, which began as early as the nineteenth century, gained authority in the modern period as the modern critics of positivism moved the advancing sciences into positions approaching the condition of the humanities by recognizing the part that cultural forces, subjective reactions, and individual imagination play in science and by acknowledging that natural laws are only partial and provisional readings of external reality. The affinities of religion with poetry had always been widely recognized. But the potential compatibility of poetic thinking with scientific thinking was an insight distinctive of the modern period, though anticipated in some degree by the seventeenth-century metaphysical poets.

By interlacing the principles of ritual and experiment in their works, the modern poets foregrounded a number of the connections and homologies very much emphasized by modern theorists. Both ritual and experiment are preverbal actions performed in rigidly demarcated spaces set apart from ordinary life that nevertheless claim to have determining influences on life, usually through a verbal or symbolic medium. Both are transactions with the unknown, although ritual sets aside the problem of cognition and adopts an attitude of unquestioning belief, while experiment proposes to penetrate and illuminate the unknown. Experiment, like ritual, requires imagination, the capacity to envision what is unseen and implausible. Like ritual, it is based on intuitively accepted metaphysical beliefs, though they are, of course, entirely different from the beliefs that ritual requires. Both transcend the accepted field of knowledge, and both are acts of renewal: ritual seeks to renew the spiritual life of the community, as experiment seeks to renew an aspect of its intellectual life.

2

The Language of Ritual and Experiment

The idea that the languages associated with ritual and experiment were distinct from each other was well established by the beginning of the twentieth century. In the Victorian period, Matthew Arnold had much to say about this division. Ruth apRoberts observes that he deployed a "concept of the two languages," which he called the scientific and the "humane": "The literal mode is that of science, moral maxims, creeds, dogmatic statements, newspaper reports; the metaphorical mode is the language of poetry (or art) and religion."[1] In *Science and Poetry* (1925) I. A. Richards went so far as to say that poetry, in its use of words, is the reverse of science, and he agreed with Arnold that the rise of science would intensify the need for poetic language capable of expressing feelings and emotions.

In *The Discourse of Modernism* (1982) Timothy J. Reiss has continued Arnold's two-language tradition by distinguishing the types of language he calls "analytico-referential discourse" or "experimental discourse" or "the discourse of experimentalism" on the one hand and "patterning discourse" on the other. The first is the ordinary reportorial language we mistakenly regard as a neutral, objective medium of public information and communication, which has been the dominant style of Western discourse, according to Reiss, since the seventeenth century. He explains its basis as follows:

> Analytico-referential discourse assumes that the world, as it can be and is to be known, represents a fixed object of analysis quite separate from the forms of discourse by which men speak of it and by which they represent their thoughts. . . . Equally basic is the assumption that the proper use of language will not only *give* us this object in a gradual accumulation of detail (referentiality), but will also *analyze* it in the very form of its syntactic organization. . . . The assumption of this coincidence of universal reason and general grammar was essential.[2]

This verbal mode cannot grasp things in their fundamental natures as totalities but is well equipped to understand them by accurately describing their attributes and relationships. Beginning with the premise that reality coincides with human reason and is fully knowable, experimental discourse undertakes to organize the world in accordance with human understanding. In this view, the arbitrariness of signs is an advantage, for it permits the free exploration of phenomena that would be impossible if names were identical with things.

Reiss calls this discourse "experimental" because it is related to the rise of experimental science. It is not to be identified with experimental poetry, but is, on the contrary, the norm poetic experiment rejects, the definitive, authoritative idiom it deviates from and subverts. Nevertheless, the common terminology reveals that the two share certain presuppositions and the same basic rationality. Modern poetic experiment, like its scientific model, regards reality as an appropriate subject of investigation and analysis. It regards contact with particulars as crucial, an attitude illustrated by W. C. Williams's "No ideas but in things," and Pound's "Knowledge resides in particulars," and deviates from customary usage in order to express new and precise perceptions. Its conviction that new forms of expression can give access to areas of thought and feeling that lie outside of common experience rests on the analytico-referential assumption that language can replicate the structures of reality. Hence, poetic experiment, while it constitutes a revolt against "the language of experiment," nevertheless may be said to have its roots in the same empiricism.

The responsibility assigned to the scientific portion of analytico-referential discourse was defined in an article published in 1868 by Ernst Mach, who argued that only empirically verifiable statements could be regarded as scientific. The view emerged that observable facts were illustrations of structures actually found in nature, that the scientific laws described these structures, and that knowledge of this kind was absolute.[3] Mach's view was confirmed in the early twentieth century by the "picture theory" of Ludwig Wittgenstein's *Tractatus Logico-Philosophicus,* which maintained that language, even though it does not resemble reality, can represent it clearly in the same way that a musical score clearly represents sounds to which it has no obvious connection. More general philosophic support came from the group of positivists called the Vienna Circle, who promulgated the rule that theoretical terms could be accepted in scientific statements only if they could be shown to correspond with actual phenomena.

The mode of expression that Timothy J. Reiss calls "patterning discourse" (the language of primitive, traditional, and religious communities and prescientific cultures in general), resembles the idiom of ritual. It is based on the belief that the universe is the creation of a divine mind and that all things in it are parts of a divinely ordained, harmonious, and unalterable pattern. Since every aspect of creation reflects the design of the divine intention, all things have the same ultimate meaning and can be considered to have a basic identity with each other. Language and thought are not merely structural parallels to the world but identical with it. They do not refer to reality as something external to themselves but embody it, sharing its attributes, so that the name of God is as sacred as God himself and to think of sinning is as evil as a sinful deed.

Patterning discourse grasps and presents things in their essential meaning, as wholes. The speaker is positioned as a part of a universal totality, able to articulate it because he shares its nature and it speaks through him. The discourse based on this view exploits resemblances and affinities that make no sense to the rational mind and generates meaning in ways that violate the scientific idea of order. The idea of universal design renders such concepts as causality and individual motivation meaningless and overrides the distinctions of time and place that rational thinking uses to organize its world. The power of this sort of discourse resides in its faith that the universe is a unity whose soul is manifested everywhere, so that all things are holy and capable of being associated with each other within the divine plan.

Reiss considers the two discourses and the modes of thought they represent absolutely incommensurate with each other, even maintaining that it is impossible for modern minds to adequately comprehend patterning discourse, with its multiple synchronic identities, because the linear and "objective" medium we employ cannot avoid distorting a radically different system of thought. "Any *definition* of the one in terms of the other is probably impossible," he writes. "Patterning functions at odds with analysis; if the two discourses function simultaneously . . . they subvert each other."[4] He maintains, nevertheless, that the rise of science cannot be understood without a sense of its roots in the discourse of patterning.

As Reiss's analysis makes clear, there is a sharp difference between the referential status of words as they are used within the two modes. In patterning discourse, the ancient conviction that there is a real relation between words and their referents prevails, and this relation often takes the form of absolute identification. Cassirer has explained this view as a characteristic of mythic thinking that immerses itself in an immediate reality to the exclusion of any other ideas so that consciousness is filled with it. The word denoting the thought is therefore merged with it, "consumed" by it, as Cassirer says. In the case of sacred ideas, the word becomes as sacred as the idea, acquiring powers that are considered magical. "Whatever has been fixed by a name, henceforth is not only real, but is Reality."[5]

The same view of language is found in medieval religious philosophy, according to Owen Barfield. Pursuing the argument that what we call "phenomena" are merely ideas that are communally accepted, Barfield cites Aquinas to show that phenomena must be realized through words: "The phenomenon itself only achieves its full reality . . . in being named or thought by man."[6] To the modern science-oriented mind, a thing seems most real when it is external to thought, but to the medieval mind, as to the mythic one described by Cassirer, nothing is real until it enters consciousness and is given a name.

This phenomenon is not confined to primitive societies but also appears in a long occult tradition that refers to Plato for its ultimate authority. Brian Vickers has shown how such beliefs as the divine origin of all things, the unity of spirit and matter, and the Hermetic idea of a transcendental reality corresponding to the physical world led Renaissance Neoplatonists to maintain that words and symbols were identified with their referents. Language was thought to be "natural," a divine creation, and the word was regarded as an aspect or essence of the thing it signified, a concrete talisman with magical power. Socrates, in the *Cratylus*, argued that the names of things are as natural as the things themselves, and the same unifying impulse led the Neoplatonists to interpret metaphors and analogies literally, so that their terms did not merely correspond with each other but were different names for the same thing.[7]

We see counterparts of this mystical identification of symbol and referent which is a prominent feature of ritual in much of the imagery of modern poetry, especially in the work of Mallarmé and Yeats. It is characteristic of the poetry of Dylan Thomas, who said that his images were to be taken literally and, when asked to explain the plot of a poem, said that "the plot is told in images, and images *are* what they say, not what they stand for."[8] Such imagery corresponds to religious ritual with its implication of presence and suggests that ritualization offered the modern poets a way of achieving immediacy by overcoming the Saussurean disjunction between signifier and signified.

It seems clear that the two types of discourse Arnold and Reiss distinguish from each other correspond in most respects to ritual and experimental language. Ritual might be described as what Reiss calls patterning discourse in its purest state, unadulterated by any communicative intention and meant only to encompass the sense of divine presence the participant feels in the world about him. The language of experiment, on the other hand, aspires to analytico-referential discourse, but it cannot achieve its referential purposes without resorting to metaphor.

In his study, *The Language of the Rite* (1974), Roger Grainger, while distinguishing sharply between the worlds of ritual and science as Arnold and Reiss do, nevertheless offers reasons for expecting ritual to generate language that expands ordinary usage in ways that would correspond with the aims of experimental poetry. In his main argument he says that "the rite exists to tell us about the limitation of the ability of natural science and logical reasoning to provide us with an adequate language for human existence."[9] The special virtue of the ritual is its capacity for giving substance to the vision of a complete and orderly universe that reflects divine intention. The knowledge it conveys is experiential, the kind of knowledge that cannot be thought, but only lived. "The rite is the language of embodied aspiration which becomes fact on becoming translated into ritual action."[10]

Grainger also describes rituals, in accordance with Freudian theory, as expressions of obsessive and irrational feelings that ordinary language cannot communicate.

> This alternative language provides the only way in which the deeply ambiguous experience can be transmitted and expressed. . . . the neurotic code which [the participant] employs is his own, designed to fit his unique message, it is how he feels driven to express himself, the only way he can understand himself, the truth about himself. . . . He is talking nonsense—but he is doing it sensibly, or he is behaving sensibly in doing it. After all, 'nonsense' is all he can talk; it is his message to the world of sense.[11]

Hence, religious rituals speak obscurely as a way of acknowledging that what they are saying cannot be rendered intelligible to the secular world.

Grainger also observes that the action which is the primary mode of expression in ritual is "non-propositional, precognitive, instinctive"; it is meant to convey a sense of existence which transcends that of ordinary social life, symbolizing "ideas . . . which cannot be expressed in any other way." Its purpose is "to create a tension out of which some new knowledge, some deeper and more intense understanding, can proceed. It is a laboratory, a melting-pot, an arena."[12]

The analogues that Grainger has chosen strongly suggest that ritual resembles scientific investigation in its capacity for bringing minds to new areas of thought and feeling. The reverse has also been argued. It has often been pointed out that scientific language has emotive and rhetorical aspects of the kind Grainger attributes to ritual.

A better understanding of the limitations of reference in scientific discourse had been developing before the modern period. This radical softening of nineteenth-century dogmatism recognized that the language of experiment has connotative and metaphoric powers and cannot avoid a degree of subjectivity. For example, Karl Pearson, a nineteenth-century critic of positivism, realized that the inadequate referentiality of scientific description was due not to a deficiency of language, but to a condition inherent in the nature of science, which defines our perceptions of things, not the things themselves. Because our world is a construction made up of such materials as sense-impressions, inferences, and "the consciousness of others," it is more meaningful, Pearson observed, to say that man dictates laws to nature rather than the reverse. Scientific terminology does not refer to anything that actually exists: "It asserts no perceptual reality for its own shorthand," writes Pearson, in a disclaimer that comes very close to Sir Philip Sidney's defense of the poet: "He nothing affirms and therefore never lieth."[13]

In its use of language, science is compelled to sacrifice a degree of referentiality for the sake of coherence. Thomas Henry Huxley warned that the abstractions used as signs by scientists were often reified in common use. He recognizes this limitation forcefully and somewhat impatiently in a lecture delivered in 1886: "The philosopher who is worthy of the name knows that his personified hypotheses, such as law, and force, and ether, and the like, are merely useful symbols, while the ignorant and careless take them for adequate expressions of reality." They are not, Huxley asserts, "real existences." They have "no greater value than the fabrications of men's hands, the stocks and stones, which they have replaced."[14] Later thinkers concur: Einstein and many others taught that the symbols recording scientific findings have no counterparts in reality but rather refer to products of the imagination. Ernst Cassirer has observed that science is distinguished from other forms of thought, not because it can dispense with signs, but because, "differently and more profoundly than is possible for the other forms, it knows that the symbols it employs are *symbols* and comprehends them as such."[15] As Northrop Frye has said, "All structures in words are partly rhetorical, and hence literary, and . . . the notion of a scientific or philosophical verbal structure free of rhetorical elements is an illusion."[16]

Frye's view is emphatically confirmed from a scientific perspective by Geoffrey Cantor, who concludes a study of scientific reports by declaring that such documents should be classified as fiction. He finds that they are generally intended to persuade and that there are often discrepancies between the actual course of an experiment and the published account of it. He calls such accounts "literary remains" and says that they are "a form of narrative . . . open to the kinds of analysis which can be applied to other literary genres." Scientific writing, he concludes, is a sophisticated form of rhetoric, "the most potent instrument of persuasion in our culture, which only *seems* to exclude the resources used in poetry, the pulpit and political oratory." When we realize this, "The mythic dimension of experimental discourse becomes apparent," says Cantor, and we cannot consider experimental results to be reports of truth; they are rather myths embodying particular values.[17]

Ritual normally communicates through metaphor, as the familiar instances of the wine and wafer in the Eucharist show. And metaphor, it has been argued, is an inescapable aspect of experimental language. Experiment itself, in which a single instance or group of instances is related to a general conclusion, has a distinctly metaphoric quality. Metaphor is a natural and widely used resource for expressing new insights and new emotions. Scientific and experimental investigation can hardly avoid depending on it in communicating new findings. Sophisticated thinkers like Thomas Henry Huxley have always realized that scientific terms must be figurative. "I suppose," he writes, "that, so long as the human mind exists, it will not escape its deep-seated instinct to personify its intellectual conceptions." The scientist confronted with new data must employ precedents as models in extending the field of knowledge so that "the key forms of thought and argument involved are metaphorical or analogical."[18]

Jacques Derrida, approaching metaphor in much greater detail, and from his postmodern point of view, warns that the metaphoricity of all language and all thinking has created a tradition of specious truths that must be demythologized. But even if the sometimes insidious tendency of metaphor to insinuate unexamined ideas is granted, it retains its value as a vehicle of emergent consciousness and remains an indispensable, if potentially misleading, agency of culture. Derrida supports metaphor, with its multiple implications, on the grounds that "Nature gives itself in metaphor," and that "metaphor. . . is what is proper to man." He refers to it as the power "to perceive resemblances and to unveil the truth of nature" and concludes that "the metaphoric and the proper" should not be considered as contraries, for they "have never done anything but reflect and refer to each other in their radiance."[19]

Max Black has provided a rationale for believing that metaphor can be a vehicle for new insights in his "interaction view," in which the two terms of a metaphor select, suppress, and borrow certain aspects of each other. The metaphor, then, is not merely a comparison but a conjunction in which the two terms are brought together to generate a new idea. It has a constitutive effect; it may be said to dictate, rather than to record, a conception of reality in a way that cannot be fully duplicated.[20]

Paul Ricoeur accepts Black's analysis of the way in which metaphors achieve meaning, but believes that as long as the two terms of the metaphor are conventionally conceived, their interplay cannot rise above the conventional level. He prefers Monroe Beardsley's theory, which bases the creative power of the metaphor on the fact that the logical absurdity of its literal meaning forces the reader to understand its words in a genuinely new sense, so that it becomes a "semantic innovation." This innovation, argues Ricoeur, generates a correspondingly novel context created by the interaction of the multiple meanings implied by the words of the metaphor, so that, unlike the metaphor of Black's theory, it transcends paraphrase.[21] The equivalent of the scientific model is not the individual metaphor, says Ricoeur, but rather the extended metaphor, which deploys a network of relationships comparable to the array of facts revealed in a scientific finding.[22]

The place of metaphor in scientific discourse has been strongly affirmed by Barry Barnes, who maintains that its use in science is inescapable because science is a "highly differentiated" aspect of general culture. "Creative, non-routine scientific activity," he writes, "becomes intelligible as an aspect of the universal human propensity to create and extend metaphors—a propensity so basic that without it not only would the existence of real cultural change be impossible, but also the existence of culture itself." As a consequence, "a theory is a *metaphor* created in order to understand new, puzzling or anomalous phenomena . . . . all research traditions develop their beliefs, and culture generally, through the deployment of metaphors; long term cultural changes are metaphorical extensions, or changes of metaphor."[23] In addition, the relation of the experiment to its hypothesis is metaphoric, an expression, in concrete terms, of an emergent idea.

In science, as in intellectual life generally, the metaphoric sense of terms and concepts becomes less visible with use, although it remains essential to the assimilation of new knowledge. Barnes shows that the scientific metaphor can produce new insights and transform existing ideas, for "The two sides of a metaphor can interact in a way inexplicable in terms of comparison," as Max Black says they do in rhetorical usage. As the expectations aroused by the metaphor are fulfilled, and the theory it formulates is confirmed, its nonliteral status recedes, and it becomes an accepted method of description. Barnes explains change in science as a process of associating problems with "key metaphors" drawn from existing principles and argues that general cultural forces exert a determining influence on science through these metaphors. Hence, "the understanding of creative science is always bound up with the understanding of metaphor; and understanding metaphor is essential to understanding all kinds of cultural change."[24]

Since scientific ideas can be communicated only in some symbolic form resembling words, and since these symbols have no exact counterparts in reality but are imaginatively generated, the distinctions between the discourses of science on the one hand and those of religion and poetry on the other become less sharp. As we have seen, scientific findings do not fully describe the external world but rather present data that require interpretation. Since this process, as many have argued, is under the partial control of cultural, historical, and subjective determinants, it is possible to regard experimentation as a means of interpreting reality analogous in some ways to the plot of a novel or the imagery of a lyric poem.

Claude Bernard, the prominent nineteenth-century theorist of scientific experiment, realized fully that experimentation might arouse emotions, as art and literature do. The knowledge and pleasure of discovery, he says, are elusive and soon disappear, becoming the scientist's "sole torment and sole happiness." And he adds, "Those who do not know the torment of the unknown cannot have the joy of discovery."[25]

Bernard's comment has obvious relevance to the spiritual background of the modern period, whose poets, besieged by scientific advances, social disorder, mental illnesses, and the unimaginable horrors of war, became "expert beyond experience." Bernard I. Duffey has explained the experimentalism of the modern lyric poem as the result of emotions that correspond with those Bernard attributes to the experimental scientist. According to Duffey, the modern lyric poet, operating without the guidance of Romantic beliefs and traditional ideas about time and the self, can make only indeterminate responses to the "unknown," the intrusive objects of the external world not subsumed by any concept of order. The personal encounter with externals becomes inverted, self-examining. As a result, says Duffey:

> The lyric becomes feeling experimenting with its object. . . . [It] becomes experimental . . . as it deals with an uncertainty, or, better, with a discontinuity of feeling from both an unidentifiable self and from any clearly defined occasion; [it becomes] . . . a great exploration of poetry itself as the emotional accommodation of the world and its experience.

As such a lyric self-reflexively tests its ability to plumb an enigmatic reality, it becomes an experiment undertaken, not for any distinct purpose, but "as an inescapable act of its own poetic being."[26] If poetic experimentation arose as an inevitable result of the spiritual conditions of the modern era, as Duffey convincingly maintains, the same might be said of the turn to ritual; it offered forms of belief and cognition in place of those that poetry had lost.

The poets of ritual and experiment looked to what Coleridge called the "synthetic and magical power" of the poetic imagination to achieve a deeper insight into the modern condition by overcoming the division between the two modes of expression. They employed the metamorphic and transfiguring capacities of language to challenge the view that their systems of thought were incompatible with each other. The advance they achieved, like the advance of modern poetry generally, was due not to successful new alignments of ideas—though this was a part of their effort—but rather to the vigorously imaginative expansion of their medium. As they ritualized and experimented with forms, language, tropes, and subjects, overcoming conventional distinctions and penetrating new areas of thought and feeling, they opened unrevealed dimensions of poetry and infused it with a new vitality.

3
—

William Butler Yeats

Yeats was more fully committed to ritual than any of the other modern poets. But the fanciful mysticism of his poems and plays gains unexpected authority from his quasi-scientific research into the occult, in which he insisted on proof, evidence, and precision.

It was Yeats's bitter opposition to the scientism he identified with Huxley and John Tyndall, and the threat he thought it offered to the life of imagination, that ultimately led him to the world of ritual. He had been a dreamy youth who liked to let his imagination wander freely, and resented the limitations imposed on it by science and rationality. One of his best early poems, "The Song of the Happy Shepherd," laments the passing of the ages of myth, and advises, "Dream, dream, for this is also sooth." He found confirmation of his imaginative energies and a channel for them when, at the age of nineteen or twenty, he became friendly with group of young men who were interested in mysticism and occult doctrines. They founded a Hermetic Society devoted to the study of magic, spirits, ghosts, supernatural manifestations, and such systems as Theosophy and Cabbalism. Yeats was a leader in these activities beginning in 1885 and he steadily extended his interest in them, becoming a member of the Theosophical Society in 1887 and joining a secret society called The Rosicrucian Order of the Golden Dawn in 1890.

These groups emphasized ritual. Yeats went through the seven initiation rituals of the Order of the Golden Dawn, fashioned his own symbolic implements according to prescribed procedures, and made intensive studies of its complex syncretic principles. Virginia Moore's account in *The Unicorn* shows that he was deeply occupied with ceremonial practices of all kinds for several years. As a result, he became familiar with the lore and practices of occultism and Hermeticism and with arcane symbology. In his *Autobiographies* he tells how the discovery of an abandoned castle on an island in the lake of Lough Key gave him the idea of making it a center for a religious order of his own and for performing "mysteries like those of Eleusis and Samothrace." For the next ten years, he writes, his chief aim was "a vain attempt to find philosophy and to create ritual for that Order."[1]

Yeats's belief in magic, occult teachings, and the existence of a transcendental world whose truths could be found in alchemy, astrology, Theosophy, Cabbalism, and many other esoteric disciplines became a lifelong conviction. His studies were intended to provide foundations for his poetry, which he thought of as a force allied to magic, and his work in both poetry and prose is saturated with visionary ideas based on the rituals of the occult.

The symbols of the complex initiation rituals Yeats underwent when he entered the Order of the Golden Dawn were borrowed from an eclectic background of ritual sources. Moore quotes Yeats as saying, in a draft version of his *Autobiographies*, that he wished his writings "to have a secret symbolical relation to those mysteries," and in fact, his poetic imagery is often rooted in ritual symbolism, and the speeches of characters in his poetic dramas resemble the dialogues of the participants in the Rosicrucian rites.[2] The meanings and forms of these symbols changed with Yeats's shifting attitudes toward poetry and ritual, but they remained embedded in his consciousness and in his writing.

Yeats shared the Hermetic view that the physical world is linked to a transcendental one and that it is possible to select and combine appropriate actions and words and employ them, through the energies of the mind or soul, to control supernatural forces. Behind the elaborate ceremonials he learned and practiced was a long arcane tradition whose persistence through Druid, Egyptian, pagan, Cabbalistic, Hermetic, Masonic, and other phases seemed to confirm the existence of a universal shared consciousness that he called the Great Memory or *Anima Mundi*. Morton I. Seiden believes that the mysteries of Eleusis, which dramatized death and rebirth and which were based on a pattern of the life cycle resembling the Great Wheel of Yeats's *A Vision*, were the chief model that Yeats had in mind in his quest for an archetypal and universal religious ceremony.

"Again and again," says Seiden, "his ritual dramas, like so many passages in *A Vision*, transport us all the way back to Eleusis and ask us to participate in an Orphic festival."[3] The Eleusinian rites were widely regarded as a fundamental source among devotees of the occult; the Rosicrucians used a formula from them to indicate the moment in their initiation rites when the candidate passed into their Order, and Yeats had them in mind in planning the ceremonies for his Lough Key community. Belief in the importance of the Eleusinian mysteries was not limited to spiritualist circles. The mysteries generated an arcane tradition that lasted throughout the centuries and became an important element of Ezra Pound's world view.

Ritual was Yeats's "artifice of eternity." It led to truths he considered eternal by deepening his intuitive associations and placing apparently familiar tropes in relationships that transcended their ordinary meaning as well as the limits of logical thinking. It offered him a symbolic vocabulary and a symbolic syntax. Such paradoxical concepts as rebirth through death, purgation through sacrifice or suffering, insight gained through ignorance or unconsciousness, and the importance of Presence as an entrance to the transcendental often form the basis for what Yeats is saying, especially in the later poems.

In his poetry, as in ritual, idealized "images" with charismatic power are preferred to inert realities: "I seek an image, not a book," says "Ille" in "Ego Dominus Tuus," and in "Among School Children," "Both nuns and mothers worship images." Such symbols of Yeats's iconography as the tree, the sword, the figure of the fool, the tower, the sun, the moon, gold, and silver appear both in the eclectic lore of the rites and in the Tarot pack that was used in them. The Rose, which suggests multiple concepts, such as nature, beauty, the feminine, and the principle of life, is paired with the Cross, which represents the contraries, forming the central emblem of Rosicrucianism. Images drawn from physical reality become stepping-stones to transcendental reality. In Yeats's poetry, "the image," as Helen Vendler writes, "while seeming transitory and mute, like the physical world, nevertheless in a mysterious way masters creation and becomes . . . an immortal thing."[4]

One of Yeats's most persistent themes, alterity, was supported by the Rosicrucian initiation ceremonies, which urged the candidate to evaluate himself from an impersonal point of view and employed masks of gods and animals to represent occult forces. Yeats drew on these to implement two strands of thought that became intricately entwined in his doctrines and his poetry: the tendency to self-examination and self-remaking and a preoccupation with dualities. The combination of the two emerged as the obligation to seek "the antithetical," the qualities or functions that faced one's own on the opposite side of the Great Wheel. The impulse to seek out his anti-self became one of Yeats's most obsessive concerns and one of the factors involved in the shifting styles that mark his development as a poet. His ideas on the subject are expressed at length in the essay "Anima Hominis" (a counterpart to the following "Anima Mundi"), in which he quotes from "an early diary": "All happiness depends on the energy to assume the mask of some other life, or a rebirth of something not one's self." He adds that we must "imagine ourselves as different from what we are, and try to assume that second self" if we are to exercise the "active virtue" of self-discipline.[5] The parallel with the personal experience of alterity offered by rituals, especially rituals of initiation like those of the Order of the Golden Dawn, is clear.

Yeats's symbol for the anti-self, the Mask, was a constitutive image in his thinking and became one of the four human "Faculties" in *A Vision*, which traces the Mask's changing values in every phase of the Great Wheel. In Yeats's primary phases, the Mask is not articulate but merely imitative, a controlled and limited entity. In the antithetical phases it becomes free, vigorous, and creative, but with the potential for destruction. Yeats saw in such great men as Keats, Walter Savage Landor, and Christ figures who followed the principle of the antithetical and he regarded the contest between the existing self and the Mask of an opposing character as a struggle essential to the artist and the source of great poetry. He declared that "all creation is from conflict," a restatement of Blake's "Without Contraries is no progression." "We make out of the quarrel with others rhetoric," Yeats writes, "but of the quarrel with ourselves, poetry."[6]

The Mask is described in *A Vision* as "a form created by passion to unite us to ourselves."[7] The speaker called "Ille" in "Ego Dominus Tuus" explains how this is done:

> By the help of an image
> I call to my own opposite, summon all
> That I have handled least, least looked upon. (157)

It seems clear that the Rosicrucian initiations, which employed masks as symbols of various spiritual states and encouraged the participant to seek a higher level of existence, have a direct relevance to Yeats's concept of poetry; the principle of alterity they embody corresponds to that "quarrel with ourselves" that he identified as the source of poetry.

There are some striking and unexpected correspondences between Yeats's doctrine of the Mask and Lacan's concept of the Other. For Yeats, the formation of the Mask consists of encompassing elements outside the self, such as the teachings of the past; according to Lacan, the living subject must begin its life as an articulate being by deriving a first signifier from the field of the Other. This concept, the Other, Lacan's *petit objet a*, is never defined, but it seems to consist of such ingrained unconscious patterns as the Oedipus complex. For Lacan, the inescapable relation with the Other has a threatening side, for, as in the Oedipus complex, it involves the subject in the dilemmas of sexual life and reproduction, which imply both the continuation of the species and the mortality of the individual. There seems to be something similar in Yeats's mind as he suggests that the antithetical self is achieved only by those who refuse to be deceived; "whose passion is reality." (It is perhaps not entirely irrelevant that Yeats translated both of Sophocles's

Oedipus tragedies.) The adoption of the Mask is at least partially a matter of facing painful truths, which enables the artist to profit from knowledge of "the darkness—the void."

Lacan specifies that the living subject suffers from two "lacks," as his translator puts it. The first arises from its dependence on the Other, the second from the inevitability of death. Yeats seems to have some feeling about this, for he anticipates both Lacan's word and the ambiguity he sees in the relation of self and Other in saying that spiritual unity is found when "the man has found a Mask whose lineaments permit the expression of all the man most lacks, and it may be, dreads."[8] It is tempting to conclude that these parallels are not merely fortuitous, but suggest that Yeats's immersion in the traditions of ritual gave him some early insights into patterns of speculation about mental processes that were to emerge later in the century.

According to Yeats, the members of the Rhymers' Club, which he frequented in the 1890s, felt that their beliefs were confirmed by Lionel Johnson's observation that "life is a ritual."[9] The system of A Vision, which was revealed to Yeats many years later, is an expansion of this idea. It expresses the conviction, drawn from Hermetic and Symbolist sources, that the physical world is linked through "correspondences" with a transcendental spiritual reality so that every object and event acquires symbolic significance. In the section of A Vision called "Dove or Swan," historical eras are identified with the phases of the Great Wheel, and actions acquire the status of symbolic gestures that enact the interplay of "faculties" and "tinctures" generated by the movements of Yeats's gyres until history as a whole becomes a vast ceremony whose repeated actions reflect a realm of transcendental truth.

A Vision had its source in Yeats's notorious experience with automatic writing. Beginning in 1917, and for a period of seven years, his new wife, as well as other assistants, supplied him with "scripts" transmitting the messages of spirit informants who addressed him, saying, "We have come to give you metaphors for poetry." These messages, recorded in dozens of notebooks and in an extensive card file, contained a vast range of images, occult classifications, mythic tales, and spiritualistic advisories, as well as observations about history, historical figures, and Yeats's friends and lovers, which must have seemed to him a revelation of the enormous store of wisdom latent in the collective soul, shared by all human beings, that he called the Great Memory. These experiences could only confirm the view he expressed after citing some cases as evidence that the ghosts of the dead reappear: "All about us there seems to start up a precise inexplicable teeming life, and the earth becomes once more, not in rhetorical metaphor, but in reality, sacred."[10]

In the first section of the original version of *A Vision* the Great Wheel was given a quasi-ritualistic origin. Michael Robartes tells the story of four Royal Personages from the Country of Wisdom who come to reveal the mysteries of human nature to a certain caliph by performing a dance. The dance is unintelligible, and the dancers are put to death. But a sage examines the marks of their footprints in the sand and from them draws the understanding the caliph desires, for the marks have formed the pattern that came to be known as the Great Lunar Wheel. In Yeats's work, the dancer is a symbol of the intuitive wisdom that knows the permanent truths beyond the reach of intellect and assimilates temporal events into the cyclical patterns of myth, so that it is impossible to separate the dancer from the dance. This association, together with the theme of sacrifice introduced by the execution of the dancers, gives their performance and the pattern of footprints it produced the primary and authoritative status of ritual; the interpretation that naturalizes them corresponds to myth.[11]

Yeats admired historical periods that emphasized formality, repetition, tradition, the antithetical, and the self-conscious effort to achieve alterity, because they seemed to qualify as ritualistic phases of the Great Wheel. He imagined that in the Byzantium of his poems, "history, religious, aesthetic and practical life were one," that its artists worked in a state of impersonal absorption, contributing works of all kinds to a single "vast design" that declared their consciousness of "their invisible master."[12] As "Meditations in Time of Civil War," "Symbols," and "Blood and the Moon" show, Yeats thought of his life in the tower at Thoor Ballylee as a life of this kind, for he attributed symbolic significance to every aspect of the place, from the "symbolic rose" on the grounds to the Japanese sword he kept on his table. In these years, between 1919 and 1922, says Richard Ellmann, "the Yeats touch turned all to symbol."[13] A life led from this perspective would, of course, resemble the performance of a ritual.

The late poem "Parnell's Funeral" describes a modern funeral as an ancient pagan ceremony. By associating the dead hero with the Apollonian or Dionysian archetype, and describing the funeral service as a sacrificial rite, Yeats treats the fate of Parnell as the recurrence of a mythic pattern capable of evoking barbaric, elemental emotions of communal grief and guilt and of opening the way to their purgation. Earlier Irish martyrs had been killed by "strangers," but the Irish themselves were implicated in Parnell's death, inaugurating an epoch in which, according to Yeats's doctrine of antinomies, their previous innocence was negated. "An age is the reversal of an age," so that with the death of Parnell, "all that was said in Ireland is a lie" (275).

The obscure imagery of the second stanza implies that Parnell's funeral is a ritual counterpart of some sinister and unrecoverable transcendental event.

Then, in the poem's second section, Yeats declares, through a cannibalistic metaphor, that Ireland would have fared better if the Irish leaders had eaten Parnell's heart, a reference to the primitive belief, still extant in such ceremonies as the Mass, that consuming the flesh of the hero is a way of acquiring his virtues. The poem's sacrificial imagery has a shocking effect as Yeats underlines its literal meaning by transferring it from a mythic to a contemporary context in the last two lines:

> Through Jonathan Swift's dark grove he passed, and there
> Plucked bitter wisdom that enriched his blood. (276)

Because Parnell, like Swift, was a leader who experienced the ingratitude of the public, he is identified with the Frazerian figure of the dying god who wins the Golden Bough that gives him the right to rule as priest-king but also dooms him to become the victim of ritual murder. The poem links ritual with actuality by using the conventional rite of the funeral to show that the death of Parnell is itself part of the great ritual of the cosmos, and to open the symbolic meanings that emerge when it is placed in that context.[14]

"Her Vision in the Wood" achieves this identification in a reverse direction, by having the speaker recognize that the figure she sees in the ritual of the dying god is actually that of her lover. The woman, who feels that she is too old for love, comes to the sacred wood and inflicts a wound on herself, apparently in the hope of achieving purgation through this sacrifice. But suddenly a wounded man is carried into the grove, accompanied by a troop of women singing a song that is both an expression of grief and a "malediction." Finding herself in the midst of a sacrificial ritual, the woman joins the song; but when the dying man looks into her eyes she realizes that the celebrants ("Those bodies from a picture or a coin") were carrying "no fabulous symbol there / But my heart's victim and its torturer"(270). Not only has the actuality of a real love relationship erupted in the middle of a rite, but the real speaker and the symbolic scapegoat have been identified with each other in dual roles of "victim" and "torturer," just as the self-inflicted wound of the woman has somehow evoked the mythical wound of the man.[15] In this way the intensely contradictory emotions embodied in the sacrifice are mirrored in the unhappy relationship of the lovers.

Phase Fifteen of the Great Wheel, which is described in *A Vision* as "a phase of complete beauty," a state of the soul ideal for reverie and the creation of art, seems indistinguishable from the ritual state of mind. (Yeats mentions only poem, painting, or reverie, but the application to ritual is obvious.) In it, thought is an end rather than a means; contemplation and desire are united;

all that is loved has "bodily form"; and all forms are beloved, but without desire, for the lover is resigned to his separation from them. Troubling contradictions are resolved in the universal perceptiveness of a soul asleep in an "immovable trance."[16]

Some of Yeats's most famous and most intense poems invoke this spiritual condition by ritual means. The imagery of "Byzantium," for example, strongly suggests some ceremony of mystic possession and spiritual renewal. "Flames that no faggot feeds, nor steel has lit" refers to an eternal sacramental fire at the center of some ceremony whose participants undergo purification, "Dying into a dance, / An agony of trance." As "Spirit after spirit!" they surge over the Emperor's golden workshops, mounted on dolphins and accompanied by the sound of gongs, images borrowed from the symbology of the Golden Dawn. The second stanza of "Vacillation" clearly sets the scene for the rebirth of the dying god of whom Attis is a prototype. The rape in "Leda and the Swan" corresponds to primitive rituals of bestiality in which the union of human and animal life reflects the unity and sacredness of all life. "All Souls' Night," which, like "Leda and the Swan," first appeared as a part of *A Vision*, has the form of a secular ceremony, as Yeats sets out two glasses of wine and summons the ghosts of dead friends, who are invited to drink "the wine-breath" while mortals drink the wine itself, thus enacting the correspondence of material and transcendental worlds. "The Second Coming" is a variant on this pattern, a ritual whose sacred intentions are reversed by the arrival of an opposing historical cycle, so that "the ceremony of innocence" calls up out of the Great Memory not a god, but a monster.

"The Second Coming" also offers a startling confirmation of René Girard's theory of the origin of ritual. According to Girard, sacrificial ritual is a mechanism for transforming the threat of communal violence into a benign influence by "generative violence" that imitates past, unsanctified violence in a controlled manner. But if the imitation is too close, or is otherwise unsatisfactory, it loses its sacred character, and the initiates become "monstrous doubles" who incorporate both good and evil.[17] In Yeats's poem the "ceremony of innocence"—that is, baptism, an imitation of drowning—has been transformed by "the blood-dimmed tide" of war into an actual drowning. Since the ritual has gone wrong, its consequence is the monster with lion body and human head, whose appearance will not end the anarchy of the widening gyre but perpetuate it.

Yeats, under the influence of the Irish rebellion and World War I, seems to have anticipated Girard's view that sacrificial ritual is an antidote to violence. It is apparent in the poems that ritualize his life in the tower at Thoor Ballylee, which were written during the Irish Civil War, and in "Easter, 1916," where he finds, in the deaths of friends killed in the Easter Rising, "a terrible beauty," as if they illustrated the "generative violence" Girard attributes to sacrificial rites. Initiation and ritual murder are the commonest types of ritual in Yeats's poems and plays. Both of these, according to Girard, are meant to protect the community against dissolution, the first by formalizing potentially destructive processes of change, the second by ending indiscriminate violence.

Many of Yeats's shorter poems, as well as parts of the longer ones borrow some of the qualities of ritual performances, though they do not embody ritual. They are in the present tense; they employ invocations, questions, or exclamations; and they witness some mystic transformation, so that they approach the condition of deeds or enactments rather than mere expressions of feeling. Yeats's imagery, though it often seems conventional or even banal, may bear profound spiritual connotations derived from a ritual source. In "Coole Park and Ballylee, 1931" Yeats, after a mainly objective description of the lake on Lady Gregory's estate, exclaims "Another emblem there!" and compares it with the soul. It was the habit of ritual that led him to see everything as symbolic, so that his images ring with overtones of elusive significance.

Yeats's ritual consciousness is displayed most conspicuously in his plays, whose ritual elements are derived from both pagan and Christian rites as well as the Noh theater of Japan. "The theatre," he wrote in 1899, "began in ritual, and it cannot come to its greatness again without recalling words to their ancient sovereignty."[18] But he did not approach this ideal in his own work until 1916, after Ezra Pound had introduced him to the Japanese form of drama called Noh. With "At the Hawk's Well" he initiated a phase of his playwriting that employed masks, songs, dances, musicians present on the stage, and other adaptations from Noh, as well as actions centering on the death and rebirth of a god. As Andrew Parkin observes, the concentrated, symbolic form of Noh, which employs one character and very little action to dramatize a single spiritual insight, closely resembled the rituals Yeats had been composing for his Lough Key order. "Just as Yeats saw his drama as ritual," writes Parkin, "we may see his ritual as striving towards drama."[19]

Morton I. Seiden has argued that many of Yeats's plays follow the pattern of the Orphic mysteries.[20] By presenting such ritual actions as sacrifice, miracle, and resurrection in the form of understated, stylized, distanced performances with evocative passages of music and dance, Yeats clearly intended to address his audience's intuitive resources. The play form renews what is often lost in the mechanical performance of prescribed rituals: the sense that the action of the ritual makes a difference and effects a transformation. Yeats's emphasis on the antinomies of the Great Wheel prevents his audience from surrendering passively to the idea of salvation and opens the imagination to the complexities of the Great Memory.

By embedding traditional patterns in those of the cosmic ceremonial represented by the Great Wheel of human history and bringing the ironies inherent in the dichotomies of his system to bear on them, Yeats employs ritual elements to go beyond the traditional meaning of ritual. This effect has been closely examined by Parkin in his analysis of "A Full Moon in March," which, he says, extends the pattern of Yeats's earlier dance-plays to present "ritual within ritual."[21] The play is about a Queen who observes the ritual of an annual singing contest at the time of the March full moon, which is the time of resurrection and also corresponds to the fifteenth phase of the Great Wheel. The contestant whose song most movingly expresses his love for the Queen will become her husband and take over her kingdom. The repulsive Swineherd who appears as the contestant says that he does not care for the kingdom, but that the Queen's gain will be a night of love. Angered by his insulting language, she does not allow him to sing, and orders that he be beheaded. Nevertheless, the head sings after its separation from the body. Sacrifice and rebirth have therefore taken place, in accordance with the traditional pattern. The Queen now yields to her dead suitor, and expresses love for him by picking up the head, dancing with it and kissing its lips. The renewing effect of the sacrifice is diverted by this second ritual into a union of the dualities represented by the Queen and the Swineherd: high and low, soul and body, sacred and profane. The fifteenth phase of the Great Wheel represented by the full moon of the title is a time of complete subjectivity, when all the faculties or aspects of the soul come together; and the relation of the Queen and the Swineherd seems to enact such a union. The Queen's paradoxical behavior seems to reflect Yeats's belief that "we free ourselves from our obsessions that we may be nothing. The last kiss is given to the void."[22] The point that the actions of the characters transcended the sacred limits of ritual is suggested in the refrain at the end, which repeats that what they sought was "desecration and the lover's night".

Yeats's sense that there is a void beyond ritual saves his ritualized poems from uncontrolled mysticism and enables them to resist the skepticism of their time. He once declared that his dramas were "the ritual of a lost faith," affirming their resemblance to sacred ceremonials, but also acknowledging that their original meanings and the sources of the emotions they recall and renew have been forgotten. For Yeats, there is "agony" in the sacred "trance" as well as deliverance. Perhaps for this reason he does not demand an uncritical acceptance of the messages of visions and dreams but rather treats them as aspirations whose worth must constantly be tested. Here, surprisingly, the principles of experiment appear.

In spite of his hostility to science and his dependence on subjective experiences, Yeats had a strong empiric bent. When he belonged to the Theosophists, he undertook what he called "a series of experiments" to see whether certain results predicted in their literature would actually take place. After the experiments failed, he was told that Theosophists were required "to believe what they could never prove."[23] He left the group not long afterward and turned to the Rosicrucians, because he believed their claims that their methods were systematic and verified by long experience. In 1924 he joined the president of the Society for Psychic Research to investigate supernatural manifestations in France, undertaking an inquiry into spiritualism primarily in order to obtain proof of life after death that would convince the skeptical but also because "his intellect refused to abdicate."[24]

Yeats constantly sought corroboration, coherence, and supporting evidence for the arcane doctrines in which he was immersed. The great project of automatic writing that was the source of *A Vision* was thoroughly experimental in spirit, and while it cannot be called scientific, Yeats's handling of his material was systematic, critical, and precise. In his later years he read scientific works by A. S. Eddington, Bertrand Russell, and Alfred North Whitehead to see whether he could snatch support for his views from the enemy. He valued evidence that would persuade minds still hemmed in by rationality and welcomed rational verifications of occult tenets. His elliptical review of Western art in "Under Ben Bulben" acknowledges that "measurement began our might." This strand of experimentalism emerges in his poetry in the form of occasional ironies and moods of despair generated by encounters with realities outside the world of imagination.

Yeats's potential skepticism is illustrated in "Vacillation," a dialogue whose poems alternate between assertions of the power of myth and mystic vision and acceptance of death and "responsibilities." The Soul urges, "Seek out reality, leave things that seem," by which it means the reality of dogmatic religion. The poet, who fears that this course would silence him, accepts the truth of miracles, but answers that "Homer is my example and his unchristened heart." The power of a pagan mind free to confront experience directly overrides the attractions of religious commitment. Spokesmen for this general point of view, including lovers, beggars, and Crazy Jane, are often heard in Yeats's poems.

The imagined or ritualized situations of the poems often begin with moments of frank realism. "Prayer for My Daughter" is occasioned by a violent storm; the voyage to Byzantium is undertaken as an escape from a country that is not for old men; and in Byzantium itself there are streetwalkers and drunken soldiery just out of sight. Having dignified Parnell as a counterpart of Orpheus or Apollo in one poem, Yeats writes others in which the statesman is praised because "he loved his lass" or in which he confronts a poor man with the reality of his condition: "Ireland shall get her freedom and you still break stone" (309).

Science plays an essential, if unsympathetic, role in Yeats's drama of antinomies. In his system, experimental science and imagination are locked in a Blakean pattern of contraries necessary for progression, mutually correcting each other, living each other's life and dying each other's death. "Science," he wrote to T. Sturge Moore,"is the criticism of Myth. There would be no Darwin had there been no Book of Genesis, no electron but for the Greek atomic myth; and when the criticism is finished, there is not even a drift of ashes on the pyre. Sexual desire dies because every touch consumes the Myth, and yet a Myth that cannot be so consumed becomes a spectre."[25]

In Blake's myth, the "spectres" are the ineffective, tormented shadows that result when man's faculties have been divided from each other. To prevent this, supernatural concepts must be "consumed" or confirmed by empirical verification. In *The First Book of Urizen,* "Science" appears as something beneficent, a dark curtain erected by the Eternals to protect Enitharmon from the void. And at the close of *The Four Zoas,* as Urthona regains his unity, he rises

In all his ancient strength to form the golden armour of science
For intellectual War. The war of swords departed now,
The dark Religions are departed & sweet Science reigns.

The passage seems to envision a time when the conflicts of divided man are replaced by a productive interchange between reason and intuition that brings about the fall of superstition and the emergence of religious beliefs corresponding with scientific principles.

Yeats's version of this consummation is the belief that science will ultimately verify myth and unite with it. Speculating on the possibility that empirical evidence might some day be found to support reincarnation, he writes, "All our thought seems to lead by antithesis to some new affirmation of the supernatural. . . . The belief held by Plato and Plotinus, and supported by weighty argument, resembles the mathematical doctrines of Einstein before the experimental proof of the curvature of light."[26] Science will vindicate the pioneering insights of the imagination by showing that matter is controlled by spirit. Science will not be conquered by imagination, but assimilated into it.

This respect for empiricism is an important component of Yeats's poetry. His commitment to myth and ritual might otherwise have been less acceptable in a period of scientific progress. It renders his images at least partly intelligible on the basis of common experience even if their ritual context gives them a significance that transcends the rational. The resistance of ritual to intellectual formulation differentiates it from myth and legend, an attribute it shares with art. Yeats fully appreciates this symbiosis. He observes that the more a poet sets knowledge aside and devotes himself to art, "the more does the little ritual of his verse resemble the great ritual of Nature, and become mysterious and inscrutable."[27] The remark embodies the belief, elaborated in his use of the Great Wheel to reflect the pattern of history, that "Nature," or physical reality itself, is a ritual; that ritual is enigmatic; and that a poet who is immersed in his art will emulate ritual and its mysteries in his poetry.

Yeats's theories of the occult are often stated assertively in his prose writings, but in his poetry they are saved from ridicule by his view that the poet withholds final commitment to any particular form the changing realities of the world might take. In his poetry, his feeling for the antithetical, his view that every form contains the seeds of its contrary, intervenes to produce in one class of poems the clear, sharp imagery and colloquial discourse of the material world, and in another, suggestiveness, mystery, and a sense of transcendental reality. In many poems of the latter type the two are combined, and tinges of irony, skepticism, or pessimism accompany their occult themes.

Ritual and experiment might be regarded as instances of Yeats's antithetical tinctures, forms of scientific and imaginative thought that oppose each other but nevertheless share each other's existence, creating the conflicts within the soul that are not resolved until some final unity worthy of belief is achieved. As a "little ritual" imitating the great ceremony of Nature, Yeats's poetry moves toward that mysterious unity by drawing the balances and homologies of the physical world into ritualized patterns that claim the power of magic. Yeats identified poetry with magic as a force capable of revealing the cosmic pattern of which man formed a part. His belief in magic enabled him to stand aside from both science and religion. But it might also be seen as a discipline that combines the ritual resources of religion with the experimental methods of science. Ritual stimulated and disciplined his imagination, gave him access to a repertory of symbols that tradition had made particularly evocative, and supported his visionary experiences. But it was the antithetical aspect of his character, one allied to the experimental spirit, that urged him to ground occult doctrines in the material world, to test and explore supernatural manifestations, and to see the cosmos as a coherent whole. The struggle within him between these forms of the subjective and objective phases of his Great Wheel was the animating force of his poetry, the self-reflexive "quarrel," as he said, of which poetry was made.

4

T. S. Eliot's Early Poems

T. S. Eliot's effort to overcome the dissociation of sensibility is a major instance of the confrontation between ritual and experiment that took place in modern poetry.[1] He tended to regard "realism" and "liturgy" as contraries, and if we identify the occasional realism of his early works with the empirical spirit of experiment, we can see that the conjunction of ritualism and experimentation in these poems was a significant expression of the dualism he sought to unify. Before his official entry into the Church of England in 1927, Eliot experienced a period of tension between the need for faith and an inability to accept contemporary forms of it.[2] His doctrinal shift was paralleled by a changing balance, in his poetry, between the experimentalism of the modern period and the spiritual and poetic resources of ritual. A. D. Moody observes that after writing *The Waste Land* Eliot moved toward a union of the natural and the divine, seeking "a dynamic form to enact the progression from nature through mind to the realm of grace—a single and complete rite for that passage through the looking-glass."[3]

Eliot was not immune to what Michel Serres has called a "powerful myth," the influence of science. In a letter to Norbert Wiener, written at the time when he was immersed in the philosophic questions of his thesis on Bradley, Eliot was ready to say, ". . . the world of natural science may be unsatisfying, but after all, it is the most satisfactory, as far as it goes." In this letter, he went on to develop the duality that was to mark his thinking for a long time by saying that while "Reality," or materialism, and "Value," or the appreciation of beauty, were opposites, neither was entirely absent or separable from the other, or complete in itself.[4]

Eliot's early poetry, in fact, has a convincing quasi-scientific objectivity. Much of the imagery and tone of his first volume, *Prufrock and Other Observations*, supports the detachment claimed in its title. Its ironies reflect his view that scientific knowledge had its place but could not fulfill the philosophic role assigned to it by Bertrand Russell and I. A. Richards as a source of moral authority. In a 1927 review of Richards's *Science and Poetry*, Eliot acknowledged that "belief" in science was as compelling as religious belief but denied Richards's implication that science invalidated the "religious, ritual or magical view of nature upon which poetry has always depended." Eliot had insisted on the importance of this relation not long before, when, reviewing two books by anthropologist W. J. Perry, he asked, "Is it possible and justifiable for art, the creation of beautiful objects and of literature, to persist indefinitely without its primitive purposes . . . ?" In his review of Richards's book he observed that Richards's agnosticism surrendered one of the two ways of thinking that Eliot himself could still employ; he must have meant by these two the religious and the scientific.[5]

His early essays exhibit this dualism, for they often rely on ordinary empirical and logical arguments intertwined with the respect for intuitive power that was to dominate his later thinking. "Tradition and the Individual Talent" (1919) admits in its first paragraph that in England tradition requires the support of "the reassuring science of archaeology" and closes by acknowledging the authority of rational investigation.[6] Eliot's idea that the meanings of works in the literary canon are slightly shifted by the appearance of new works would probably not have occurred to him without the example of the history of science, where new discoveries change what has been known in the past but also form a continuation of it. Especially striking is his pronouncement that the work cannot merely repeat what has been done before, for if it did, "it would not be new, and would therefore not be a work of art."[7]

As Carol T. Christ has observed, Eliot's cultural tradition is "independent of historical agency"; it reflects a desire "for a unifying structure to reveal itself independently of the will of any single participant." And while the structures Eliot had in mind are cultural and religious traditions, Christ further observes that this desire resulted in "the most radical experiments" combining formal innovation and traditional ideas.[8]

In Eliot's view, the "depersonalization" required for writing poetry involves the detachment and freedom from personal emotion associated with science, and in fact, says Eliot in "Tradition and the Individual Talent," enables poetry to "approach the condition of science." What is especially telling in this essay is the analogy of the catalyst. By aligning the action of the poet's mind upon his experiences with that of the shred of platinum as it promotes the formation of a compound, Eliot implies that there are intelligible affinities between poetic creation and the workings of nature revealed by science. But the ritual consciousness is also present in this early essay, for Eliot declares that the poet's work is a "continual surrender of himself as he is at the moment to something which is more valuable . . . a continual self-sacrifice," that is, a ritual act, motivated by a respect for tradition that resembles religious devotion.[9]

The quasi-scientific tone is also heard in "The Function of Criticism," written four years later, in 1923, which maintains that criticism should be systematic, that it should rely on some external authority, that it should cultivate a "sense of fact" and employ comparison and analysis rather than interpretation. When Eliot concludes that such criticism aims at "the possibility of co-operative activity, with the further possibility of arriving at something outside of ourselves, which may provisionally be called truth," his notion of criticism becomes nearly indistinguishable from the intersubjective testing of scientific investigation.[10]

It is possible to identify, then, at least three aspects of experimental thinking that survive in Eliot's poetry, side by side with his ritualism. These are innovation, empiricism, and contingency; or, to paraphrase: the need for new expressive forms to match the order of history, respect for the testimony of personal experience as distinguished from traditional authority, and a recognition of the provisional nature of knowledge. When we observe that these are conventionally opposed to the values ordinarily associated with the ritual consciousness that nevertheless prevails in much of Eliot's poetry, we can sense the paradoxical nature of his poetic achievement and the modernism of which it is a part.

In concluding his chapter on Eliot's attraction to primitivism, William Skaff writes, "Eliot wrote three long poems which *are* rituals. Eliot the poet performs through poetry the same rite that the ritualistic structure would dictate a religious celebrant to perform."[11] Early evidence of Eliot's commitment to ritual appears in the paper he read at a Harvard seminar in 1913 defending the mystical insight of primitive ritual. He argued that the meanings of rituals are always concealed from their participants and that anthropologists cannot learn their real purposes because the modern mind is compelled to interpret them rationally, on the basis of its own inappropriate metaphysics.[12] Scientific thinkers make distinctions unknown to the primitive mind and assume causalities and motivations intelligible to themselves, says Eliot, but "you cannot dissolve the imaginative and emotive element in invariable terms."[13] In the introduction to his mother's *Savonarola* in 1926, he reiterated points he had made in this paper: that interpretations of rituals usually cannot explain their origins, that the meanings of a ritual are uncontrollably variable, and, most significantly, that a rite may have originated before the concept of meaning itself was understood. In short, ritual is a primary, aboriginal phenomenon that defies analysis. F. R. Leavis, in *New Bearings in English Poetry* (1932), detected these attitudes in *The Waste Land* and showed that Eliot's anthropological knowledge generated an interplay between the primitive and scientific approaches in the poem. He accurately formulated Eliot's view that scientific study revealed the fertility rituals as efforts to achieve "harmony" with nature, but it also stripped sexuality of its moral and emotive qualities, rendering it the sterile experience described in the poem.[14]

The profound respect for prehistoric intuitive powers displayed in the Harvard seminar paper led Eliot to a sense that the modern world needed a greater participation in religion and its ceremonials. He felt that poetry could recover the lost truths of man's relation to nature which had been expressed through the totemism, animism, magic, and the paradoxical associations found in primitive rituals. He wrote approvingly of Stravinsky's *Sacre du Printemps* with its admixture of sexual rhythms and allusions to primitive religion and remarked in the same article that Frazer's *Golden Bough* might be read as "a revelation of that vanished mind of which our mind is a continuation." In a 1923 review he declared, "All art emulates the condition of ritual. That is what it comes from and to what it must always return for nourishment."[15]

However, the speakers of Eliot's early poems fail with both ritual and experimentation. The two dramatic monologues "The Love Song of J. Alfred Prufrock" and "Portait of a Lady" exhibit minds scanning themselves in efforts to sustain a sense of selfhood and to overcome their isolation through social rituals. In each case the quest ends in indeterminacy. The utterly conventional social forms, the sterile tea parties, the concert by the "latest Pole" are all hollow modern substitutes for once meaningful communal activities, anticipations of a theme that is to become dominant in *The Waste Land*.[16] The experimental spirit is not absent, but moribund. The speakers envision new kinds of behavior but fear to try them. Prufrock's mind is full of questions "Do I dare? . . . how should I presume? . . . And how should I begin?" and he feels that there is time for "visions and revisions," intuitive insights followed by intellectual modifications, yet he makes no attempt to act (4-5). If he dared to approach the "overwhelming question," he would experience a counterpart of Lazarus's resurrection, but he foresees that, like everything else he has to offer, the answer would be ineffective in his thoroughly conventional context. According to David Ward, Prufrock's "disappointing . . . sexual experiment," anticipated with religious fervor ("I have wept and fasted, wept and prayed" [6]), embodies a fear of the union of the sexual and the spiritual that he thinks he desires.[17]

During the turbulent decade preceding his work on *The Waste Land*, Eliot seems to have undergone a conflict between a will to believe in some absolute and the testimony of his senses, which revealed a world of urban squalor, war, and marital unhappiness.[18] Such early poems as "Preludes" and "Rhapsody on a Windy Night," which register profound pessimism about contemporary spiritual life in remarkably graphic imagery—also a feature of "Prufrock"—provide no basis for faith. The poems of Eliot's 1920 volume continue in this mode by treating religion in disillusioned and sarcastic tones, occasionally criticizing contemporary religious life by depicting corrupt religious ceremonies. The esthetes with foreign names mentioned in "Gerontion" seem guilty of performing some social ritual that treats Christianity as a merely cultural phenomenon, turning the spring, the time of the Resurrection, into "depraved May" with its "flowering judas." Hence, they are devouring "Christ the tiger" in a double sense: as a parody of the Eucharist and as an act of destruction.[19] The satire of "Mr. Eliot's Sunday Morning Service," furthermore, is directed against "sapient sutlers of the Lord" who are performing a ceremony that the poet finds empty of spiritual significance because it is limited to traditions that have no basis in primitive beliefs.

The Waste Land is an experimental poem that is thoroughly permeated, in all its dimensions, by ritual values. The fact that Eliot intended to name the whole poem "The Burial of the Dead" as a parallel to the service in the Anglican Book of Common Prayer suggests that he thought of it, at one point at least, as a ritual performance.[20] Its central image, the waste land, links it to one of the important functions of ritual, as Mircea Eliade describes it. According to Eliade, waste land is seen by the archaic mind as a chaos that antedates creation, and it can be transformed into cosmos, brought into reality, and given form only by a ceremony that replicates the original act of creation. In *The Myth of the Eternal Return*, as we recall, Eliade mentions Eliot, together with Joyce, as one who "is saturated with nostalgia for the myth of eternal repetition, and, in the last analysis, for the abolition of time," a feeling powerfully expressed in both *The Waste Land* and *Four Quartets.*[21]

In *The Waste Land* Eliot draws the belief that ritual symbolism has an ultimate magical reference to sexuality and fertility from Frazer's theme of sacrifice and resurrection and Jessie L. Weston's analysis of the Grail Romances, *From Ritual to Romance*. This reworking of the Grail story as a failure of ritual is an allegory of the modern spiritual situation. The shallowness of modern life is rooted in the trivialization or degradation of ancient customs, illustrated by such modern phenomena as the Tarot deck, which uses ancient sex symbols, and the unmarried lust of the typist and the clerk. Weston believes that the Perilous Chapel was a heathen temple that challenged the piety of Christian knights, but in Eliot's poem it is the deserted ruin of a decayed faith. If we accept the implications of Frazer's and Weston's anthropology, the despair of Eliot's poem arises from a sense that in losing touch with the symbolism of the ancient agricultural ceremonies, the modern world has forfeited the relation to natural processes embodied in them. But Eliot's emphasis on ritual, as becomes more apparent in later poems and plays, is also directed at other values, including humility, order, religious awe, and an escape from history to the mystical "peace that passeth understanding."

The burden of guilt and the need for purgation through suffering so often emphasized in Eliot's poetry are generally attributed to the Christian version of the myth of the dying god and the doctrines associated with it. But the nameless horrors and fears that spring up out of the quiet corners of daily life in his poems seem to have some other source. His allusions to "horror" and "terror," to "fear in a handful of dust," to "dry bones that can harm no one" suggest that the need for penitence originates in something more concrete than Frazer's sympathetic magic or the Christian doctrine of original sin. Lyndall Gordon has observed that the unpublished "Love Song of St. Sebastian," which describes scenes of self-flagellation and murder, echoes Eliot's interest in a number of Renaissance paintings of martyrs pierced by arrows. The poem itself exhibits an inchoate sense that violence is linked to sanctity. Gordon calls these instances of violence "a ritualized attack on the flesh."[22] Eliot's agonized vision of the spiritual life, and the imagery that often accompanies it have a suggestive correspondence to the episode of the surrogate victim in the theory of ritual later developed in René Girard's *Violence and the Sacred.*

Eliot died seven years before the publication of Girard's book, but he might have found Girard's theories congenial. It is true that there is no place for the supernatural in Girard's system, while Eliot's belief in a higher power is, of course, fundamental. But there is a crucial resemblance, for our purposes, in the emphasis both place on the centrality of religious ritual.

Girard vigorously rejects theories, such as Frazer's, that describe rituals as re-enactments of seasonal changes or personal spiritual development, maintaining that all ritual stems from ceremonial sacrifice, a term that, theorists often remind us, means "to make sacred." At a remote time which may be hypothetical, but is no less real in the consciousness of the group, Girard says, uncontrolled violence among groups or individuals threatened to destroy the community. This contagion of destruction was halted when the community fixed responsibility for it on one individual—the traditional scapegoat—and channeled the violence against him in a controlled and approved sacrificial ceremony. The victim had to be a surrogate, not a member of the warring groups, but a neutral from the outside or the margins of the community, such as a slave or a domestic animal, for otherwise it would be impossible to secure unanimous agreement to the sacrifice.

This was the primeval ritual action. It established a new era of peace in which the community could progress and prosper on the basis of the unanimity it had achieved. In this way, "reciprocal violence," which was purely destructive, was replaced by "generative violence," which became the source of communal unity and ultimately of religion and culture. The scapegoat figure is both the demon and the god of this scenario, for while he bears the guilt for the community's initial state, he also becomes the source of its blessings, and an object of worship, thus undergoing resurrection.

According to Girard, all religious rituals, without exception, are related to this pattern, though inversions and modifications may make it difficult to recognize. He claims that the phenomenon of ritual sacrifice is of supreme importance and universal application: "All religious rituals spring from the surrogate victim, and all the great institutions of mankind, both secular and religious, spring from ritual."[23]

As we have seen, it is often observed that the origins and significance of rituals are unrecoverable and that the myths developed to explain them are mere rationalizations. The reason for this, according to Girard, is that the real nature of the event being re-enacted must be suppressed if the ritual is to retain its effectiveness. "Violence will come to an end only after it has had the last word and that word has been accepted as divine. The meaning of this word must remain hidden, the mechanism of unanimity remain concealed. For religion protects man as long as its ultimate foundations are not revealed. . . . The only barrier against human violence is based on misconception."[24]

This diabolically plausible theory has special relevance to ritualization in modern poetry. Girard observes that certain aspects of ritual "always involve a *lesser* violence proffered as a bulwark against a far more virulent violence." Acute critics have noted that poetry, even when it is conventional, and not ritualized, performs this ritual function. Roman Jakobson has defined poetry as "organized violence committed on ordinary speech," and Wallace Stevens maintains that the nobility of the poetic imagination is "a violence from within that protects us from a violence without."[25] The parallel implies that poetry functions like ritual in converting chaotic and destructive energies into positive forms. More specifically, it reminds us that the modern poets did much of their best work in the shadow of war and that a wide range of poems, including Yeats's poems about the Irish rebellion, Eliot's *Four Quartets*, and Pound's *Mauberley* and *Pisan Cantos* refer directly to the reciprocal violence of Girard's pattern as fact, not as metaphor. Girard's theory strongly suggests

that the poets' consciousness of the uncontrolled violence of their time is at
the root of their concern with ritual.

We have only to recall that Eliot lived through two great wars to see how
The Waste Land and *Four Quartets* are connected with Girard's theory of
reciprocal violence. It seems as if Eliot, unconsciously anticipating Girard's
rationale, turned to ritual as an antidote to the war's anarchic violence as well
as to the dangerous impulses he sensed within himself. From this point of
view, *The Waste Land* appears as both an effort at personal redemption and a
reply to the war, assigning to ritual the role Eliot himself had assigned to the
"mythic method" employed in Joyce's *Ulysses*: "a way of controlling, of
ordering, of giving a shape and a significance to the immense panorama of
futility and anarchy which is contemporary history."[26] Seen in relation to a
period racked by war, its apparently reckless disregard of the poetic conventions corresponds with Wallace Stevens's characterization of poetry as a
protective violence.

There is only an oblique allusion to war in *The Waste Land*, the speech of
Lil's friend, but "Coriolan" refers to war directly and provides a subtext for
The Waste Land's emphasis on ritual by counterposing war and ritual sacrifice
in a way that exactly fits Girard's pattern . The first part of "Coriolan" consists
of the remarks of a crowd witnessing the military procession that arrives at
a temple. "Then," says the poem, abruptly, " the sacrifice." But the people are
entranced by the eagles and the trumpets, indifferent to the sacrifice, without
respect for religion. The frustrated "statesman" in the second part hopes for
freedom from bureaucratic perplexities "If the mactations, immolations,
oblations, impetrations / Are now observed" (88). The first of these three
actions are variants of religious sacrifice. The speaker anticipates Girard by
seeing ritual as the only way of averting the destruction of society threatened
by war and by identifying the debased social condition that Girard calls the
"sacrificial crisis"—that is, the neglect of ritual.

Martyrdom is a persistent thread in Eliot's thinking. It appears in "Prufrock,"
where the protagonist faces drowning and identifies himself with the decapi-
tated John the Baptist, as well as in Eliot's requirement, in "Tradition and the
Individual Talent," that "self-sacrifice" and "continual extinction of personality"
are aspects of the artist's commitment.[27] And while he adopted Frazer's rationale for the religious value of sacrifice, the element of moral obligation with
which it is invested in his work is actually closer to Girard's view. Eliot, like
Girard, is conscious of the balance of good and evil in human nature that makes
spiritual redemption possible, and both regard the sacrificial ritual as its
essential mechanism. The affinity of Eliot's ideas with Girard's is startlingly
exposed in a line from the opening chorus of part II of *Murder in the Cathedral*,

where Girard's theory of sacrificial ritual is epigrammatically stated: ". . . war among men defiles this world, but death in the Lord renews it" (201).

Themes of death and violence are never completely absent from *The Waste Land*. They are sometimes connected with the "dead land" of the second line and sometimes appear in such images as the rape of Philomela, the dead body of Phlebas, and even the living dead on London Bridge. The cruelty of April in the poem's opening line has been variously interpreted, but a speech from *The Family Reunion* explains that spring is the time for the sacrificial rituals performed to encourage the growth of crops: "Spring is an issue of blood / A season of sacrifice," says Harry, and he goes on to wonder whether it is not also a season when the ghosts return. The blank card in Madame Sosostris's pack, indicating something she is not allowed to see, suggests Eliot's understanding that the origins of rituals are always unknown. This mystery haunts the blanks, ellipses, and unanswered questions of the poem and the mystique of religion itself. The poem reads,

> (Come in under the shadow of this red rock),
> . . . I will show you fear in a handful of dust. (38)

The secret concealed in this enigmatic imagery is revealed in the early poem "The Death of Saint Narcissus":

> Come under the shadow of this gray rock. . . .
> I will show you his bloody cloth and limbs
> And the gray shadow on his lips . . . [28]

It is the body of the surrogate victim, the St. Sebastian figure of some martyr, whose "flesh was in love with burning arrows." In this Girardian context, the "fear" of the final poem is not merely the fear of death but the fear aroused by the understanding that spiritual deliverance requires the sinner to accept the sacrifice symbolized by the sacred corpse.

Girard's "sacrificial crisis" occurs when a civilization fails to appreciate the value of ritual violence because it cannot distinguish it from illicit violence. When this vital distinction between what is forbidden and what is sanctioned disappears, other distinctions are cancelled, hierarchical structures and the values they embody are eroded, and general social disorder follows. Thus, the egalitarian ideal of modern society leads to a situation in which "coherent thinking collapses and rational activities are abandoned. . . . all values, spiritual or material perish," an era of anarchic violence returns, and "in the final stage of a sacrificial crisis the very viability of human society is put into question."[29]

The cause and the symptoms of spiritual sterility depicted in *The Waste Land* are remarkably like those described by Girard. In it, Eliot aligns scenes of license in a chaotic society indifferent to moral authority with the failed ritual of the Grail legend. Ritual sacrifice is closest to the surface of *The Waste Land* at the opening of "What the Thunder Said," with its allusions to the Passion, but the deaths of such innocents as the figures on the Tarot pack, "the drowned Phoenician sailor," "the Hanged Man," and Phlebas are considered spiritually productive. The same ambivalence seems to be attached to the dead body in Stetson's garden. The public knowledge of the death and burial—the friend refers to it conversationally—and the expectation that it will "bloom" suggest that some sacrificial rite anticipating resurrection has taken place. Both characters have been at war, yet they now enjoy the deathlike peace of city life, and it seems as if the buried corpse has played some part in this change. Nevertheless, the potential reappearance of the corpse is threatening, if we follow Girard, because it will expose the hypocrisy of which Stetson and the reader are both accused, that of gaining their deliverance at the expense of a surrogate victim.[30]

There is little overt violence in *The Waste Land*, but where it appears, it is invariably linked with sexuality. "Sexuality," declares Girard, explaining attitudes that modern thinkers refuse to face, "is impure because it has to do with violence. . . . It is a permanent source of disorder even within the most harmonious of communities."[31] The scenes involving sex in Eliot's poem are not mere instances of impropriety. Even when they do not involve force, they convey the uneasy sense that some principle of order basic to the peace of the community is being attacked. The sexually provocative Grishkin in "Whispers of Immortality" creates a "feline smell" in public, and "Rachel *née* Rabinovitch" in "Sweeney Among the Nightingales" forms part of a disreputable scene that causes the speaker of the poem to link the nightingales he hears singing near a convent with a classic event of violence: the murder of Agamemnon by his vengeful wife. In an even darker comment on sex, "The Hollow Men" declares that "Between the desire / And the spasm. . . . Falls the Shadow." If this feeling were to be openly expressed, it might take the form of Girard's statement that there is a natural tendency to shift between sex and violence, which would explain why the sacred sexuality connected with fertility rituals is benign, like the generative violence of sacrifice, but the unlicensed lust of casual encounters is dangerous, as illicit violence is.

According to Girard, the marriage ceremony is no less free of subliminal violence than other rituals. The fluid relation of sexuality and violence suggests an identification of marriage with sacrifice, and Girard cites records of primitive wedding ceremonies that involved combat or human sacrifice.[32] In a fragment of unpublished verse Eliot significantly rhymes the union of husband and wife with the knife of sacrifice in a listing of things equivalent to Resurrection.

The room in which the married couple appears in "A Game of Chess" is furnished as if it were the setting for some degenerate form of worship, with its confusion of marble, statues, candelabra, jewels, perfumes, and artificially colored fire. The debased ritual that takes place in this setting is, of course, the predictable round of middle-class life, a counterpart to the proletarian ritual of the pub closing in the next scene. Both are empty, unthinkingly repetitive forms of behavior that shape people's lives without purpose or meaning. The hidden aspect of the middle-class marriage emerges, however, when the husband is commanded by his wife to "think," and he summons up an image of unredeemed death: "I think we are in rats' alley / Where the dead men lost their bones"(40).[33] All of this contributes to the feeling one has, in reading this passage, that the husband harbors a suppressed wish to murder his wife in an act of unsanctified violence.

When, during his encounter with the hyacinth girl, the husband says he is "looking into the heart of light, the silence," he is using a phrase subtly connected with a ritual theme. "Heart of light" alludes to Conrad's *Heart of Darkness* and to the passage that Eliot intended to use as an epigraph until Ezra Pound vetoed it, Kurtz's deathbed exclamation: "The horror! The horror!" The horror Kurtz remembers is, of course, that of the cannibalism and sexual orgies that we suppose to have occurred during the African rituals in which he took part, that is to say, the generative violence of Girard's theory. The idealistic humanism Kurtz seems to have adopted at one time would, of course, regard them as "horrors," but if we follow Girard, they are also sources of deliverance and sanctity for their communities. Hence, Eliot seems to be anticipating Girard in reversing Conrad's metaphor, attributing "light," that is, an aspect of sublimity, to rituals of the kind Kurtz witnessed. While he can hardly have been in control of this connection, there is reason to believe that Eliot would have approved of it, for his remark, "Poetry begins, I dare say, with a savage beating a drum in a jungle . . ."[34] takes us back to Kurtz's barbaric ceremonies.

The Waste Land might be regarded as an extreme example of Roman Jakobson's definition of poetry as "organized violence committed on ordinary speech," with its parody and dismemberment of admired works, its "Jug jug" and "Weialala" passages, and its violations of syntax and printing conventions. It might be seen, metaphorically, as an altar where language, like the surrogate victim of Girard's theory, is sacrificed in order to counteract a greater violence, the vagueness and banality that the modernists thought were destroying literary language. When it is applied to the poem's treatment of language in this way, Girard's theory helps us to accept the abrupt ritualistic conclusion of a text that has all along been demonstrating the failure of ritual.

By reverting to pre-Christian religious feeling and to the germinal language of Sanskrit, the three repetitions of "Shantih" have the effect of a ritual gesture that is at once enigmatic and irresistible. The shift from the despairing recitation of fragmentary quotations to the Sanskrit word that means "the Peace that passeth understanding" certainly seems unmotivated, but it makes sense if we take the view that the language of Eliot's poem is going through a sacrificial ceremony. Eliot's closing "fragments," torn from their texts, and presented in an apparently incoherent sequence, might be seen, like the deviations in the early parts of the poem, as linguistic victims of the generative violence that Girard considers essential for spiritual deliverance. "Shantih" conveys the message that the foregoing has indeed been meant to plunge the reader into the oceanic experience of ritual by making a sacrifice of the mythical and cultural accretions of faith.

While Eliot eventually came to reject any scientific ideas that might conflict with religious feeling, experimental principles, stripped of their specifically scientific implications, continued to influence his poetry (as well as his criticism), in conjunction with the ritualism he advocated. For in spite of its responsiveness to tradition, *The Waste Land* is the classical expression of a modernism that was at least partly inspired by contemporary science. Its enigmatic presentation corresponds to the scientific revelation that the physical world is not what it seems but rather consists of structures that surpass imagination. It reflects indeterminacy, for it has remained impossible to classify, and such fundamental questions as whether it expresses hope or despair, or whether it is the speech of a single speaker, remain unsettled. According to the modernism of Joyce, Pound, Wyndham Lewis, and Eliot himself, the work of art is something artificially crafted, distinct from nature, impersonal, autonomous, and intricately structured, all qualities admired in contemporary science and technology and abundantly exhibited in *The Waste Land*. While the experimentalism of Eliot's poem does not conform to scientific standards, its selectivity and eclecticism are experimental in spirit. Its juxtapositions and parallels violate conventional expectations in order to reveal unrecognized affinities, very much as experimental interventions expose hidden natural processes. Its unraveling and reworking of previous literary forms through parody and fragmentation is entirely in the spirit of such figures as Einstein, Ernest Rutherford, and Werner Heisenberg, who were transforming accepted conceptions of ordinary reality.

There is, of course, no question that Eliot's poem was sensationally novel. Graham Hough wrote as late as 1960, "There is no other poem of any significance remotely like *The Waste Land*."[35] And, in fact, Eliot's work challenged established poetic practices on nearly every front. It seemed to lack unity; its fragments, many of them incomplete or asyntactical, are difficult to reconcile with a containing form; it employs a baffling paratactic structure; and its complex intertextuality claims relationships with many earlier works in different national traditions, compelling the reader to participate in a re-reading of literary history.

Eliot's notes are helpful, but they also present a challenge of their own. Since they have become an integral part of the poem, as Eliot admitted, they have transformed the poem into a hybrid of verse and prose, forms that are associated, respectively, with ritual and experiment, and correspond loosely to the "patterning" and "analytico-referential" discourses that Timothy J. Reiss considers incompatible with each other. The poetic text, even when it is superficially referential, really embodies some emotion or state of mind. For example, the ostensibly reportorial account of the typist's seduction is followed immediately by:

> (And I, Tiresias have foresuffered all
> Enacted on this same divan or bed. . . .) (44)

a parenthesis that applies to the poem as a whole. The reader surrenders to the language of the verse, shares both the feelings expressed and the confusion they create, and analyzes only to gain further immersion. On the other hand, the notes (with some interesting exceptions) adopt an objective, impersonal mode of discourse based on an attitude and, indeed, a world view that conflicts with any that might be derived from the verse. In contrast to the timeless, disjunctive, and chaotic world of the poem itself, the notes employ a transparent academic code to project a complacently historicized world of intelligible relationships.

Like many experimental discoveries, *The Waste Land* escapes complete understanding on the basis of current hermeneutic methods and points toward some future state of knowledge when it may become fully intelligible. It recalls Eliot's objection that the scientific efforts to interpret ritual were inadequate because of the assumptions on which they were based. What was needed, he said, was not a rejection of "science," but a science with new assumptions. This concept looks forward to the paradigm theory of Thomas Kuhn's *Structure of Scientific Revolutions*, which states that newly discovered facts force a change from time to time in the accepted theories, or paradigms that guide scientific research, and to Karl Popper's assertion that experiment has the function of opening the door to alternative theories by refuting accepted ones. Eliot's poem, which still eludes assimilation into the current cultural paradigm, continues to bear the aspect of an experiment, an act rather than a statement, a venture whose validity has not been finally assessed.

After *The Waste Land*, Eliot moved into a new region of poetry and feeling. His belief in the value of rational inquiry as a cultural force ebbed as his mind progressed toward his conversion of 1927 and the mysticism of *Four Quartets*. He came to express skepticism and even contempt toward science, and the harmful effects of technological advances is one of the major themes of his poetry. As one of the choruses from *The Rock* asks:

Endless invention, endless experiment
Brings knowledge of motion, but not of stillness. . . .
Where is the wisdom we have lost in knowledge? (96)

His growing orthodoxy led him to distance himself from the modernism in which he had been immersed and took him toward a goal where ritual rather than experiment would serve his poetic purposes. As a result, his works of the 1920s—"The Hollow Men," "Ash Wednesday," *The Rock*, and *Murder in the Cathedral*—approach ritual, with their incantatory rhythms, stylized speeches, repetitions and antiphonal construction, and, above all, their powerful religious feeling.

"The Hollow Men," writes David Ward, "is consciously verse designed as ritual."[36] As Ward interprets it, the mindless rituals of the Fifth of November alluded to in the epigraph and the child's chant parodied in section V reflect the superficiality of earthly life. The lyrics about "dream kingdoms" assembled from a number of fragments written at different times and originally assigned to a figure named "Doris" express, Ward feels, the futile desires of those who are spiritually hollow. He acknowledges, however, that the potential ambiguity of the deliberately limited vocabulary may justify a contradictory interpretation.

Evaluating the role of ritual in the poem may resolve this ambiguity. The poem's theme is the afterlife, the kingdom of death. The "hollow men" of its opening are, presumably, still on earth; their "life is very long," and they know nothing about life after death. The speaker of the following three sections seems better informed and can speculate about the various forms the "kingdom" of death can take. However, the "Shadow" of death intervenes to correct the illusions men have about the afterlife, and with the ritualistic words from the Lord's Prayer, "For Thine is the Kingdom," the various "kingdoms" or ideas of death imagined earlier are assimilated into or canceled by a humble attempt to surrender to the true one. But here the indeterminacy of experimentalism arises to produce the broken, hesitant sentences of the penultimate stanza, which seem unable to complete either the banal statement about life or the noble tribute of the prayer: "For Thine is / Life is / For Thine is the" (59). And finally, a profane ritual answers the religious one with "This is the way the world ends," an ironic imitation of a child's chant.[37] It seems then, that "The Hollow Men" exploits the enigmatic images, rhythms, and repetitions of the ritual mode to display the ineffectiveness and trivialization of ritual in the modern world.

David Ward recognizes the mingling of our two thematic elements in "Ash Wednesday" when he says that the opening words are an exploration, "as if experimenting with a ritual which is not yet authorized by custom and usage."[38] This ritual would involve the transformation of earthly love for a "lady" into spiritual devotion, a parallel to the experience Dante records in the *Vita Nuova*, one of the poem's many sources. But it is also a ritual that involves sacrifice, and it fails—a situation which recalls Girard's sacrificial crisis.

It is clear from part II, which was originally published as an independent poem called "Salutation," that a sacrifice has taken place, whatever the leopards and the organs they devour may symbolize. As Grover Smith has observed, the leopards "are also agents of purgation. . . . they have eaten up the old life, leaving the scattered bones to wait for symbolic resurrection."[39] When God asks, "Shall these bones live?" he is asking whether the sacrifice is, in fact, to have the spiritual efficacy that Girard attributes to generative violence. But the victim asks for commemoration in flattering and subservient language, and the answer is, of course, negative. The "dissembled" speaker is left to the dilemmas of earthly values, where love satisfied brings even greater torment than love unsatisfied, and to a forgetful indifference, projected through the precise, pacing rhythms of the section's final verse paragraph: "And neither division nor unity / Matters. This is the land. We have our inheritance" (63). I read these lines as an ironic parody of the passage from Ezekiel 45:1 giving directions for the layout of the temple of the New Jerusalem ("Ye shall divide by lot the land for inheritance"). The inheritance in the poem is a barren, earthly complacency, however, rather than the faith reflected, though not encompassed, in the liturgical rhythms of the verse and in the Biblical symbols of bones, Virgin, and Garden the speaker has mentioned hopefully.[40]

The fifth section begins with the assertion, in repetitive, obsessive language, that the unspoken secular "word" is a preliminary requirement for hearing the divine "Word"; if we transpose this into Girard's terms, it means that deliverance cannot come until the ritual sacrifice is respected. This explains why the ineffective sacrifice is followed by nightmare visions and the sense of loss, why the voice that speaks for "children at the gate / Who will not go away and cannot pray" asks the "veiled sister" to communicate for them with a divine power the children cannot hope to reach. The ritual phrases here are merely quotations, not acts of devotion. The rich religious diction and imagery of the poem as a whole, drawn from the Bible, Dante, church services, and other sources, reflects a state of deliverance that the speaker knows about but cannot enter. He cannot pray directly, but he can, as at the close of part I, ask others to pray for him.

"The Hollow Men" and "Ash Wednesday" reflect a stage of spiritual development in which the mind seeks to break out of the desert of immediate personal experience into the realm of faith, but it cannot find an adequate form of worship: "Lips that would kiss / Form prayers to broken stone"(58). They illustrate Bernard I. Duffey's concept of the "experimental lyric," a poem that foregoes the support of a definable persona and a definite theme in order "to convey its experience of an enigmatic world."[41] By confronting the language of personal lyric with ritual quotations and allusions, Eliot achieves a Bakhtin-like dialogue between individual and communal feeling. In this context, neither idiom retains its original significance but is shaped by its contact with the other; ritual expressions are usually broken or parodied under the ironic pressure of worldly knowledge, and the anguished poetry of love or personal loss acquires a religious dimension. Neither attitude is rejected; there is an effort to encompass contradiction: "Teach us to care and not to care"(67). This ambiguous spiritual position is embodied in the departures from convention with which these poems uproot secure beliefs. If the ritual passages strongly imply the possibility of escape through a revelation that will resolve the contradictions, the poems do not presume to articulate it. Like much of Eliot's poetry, they use the interplay of contrasting voices to convey the anguish of spiritual indecision.

The experimentalism of these early poems is a reflection of science's new attitude toward knowledge as Gaston Bachelard expresses it in *Le nouvel esprit scientifique* (1934): "L'essence même de la réflexion, c'est de comprendre qu'on n'avait pas compris." The objective thinking of the laboratory, says Bachelard, differs from subjective thinking by looking forward to further insights. At the end of each day in the laboratory, he writes, the scientist repeats, as an article of faith, the sentence, "Demain je saurai."[42]

Ritual and experiment do not overcome their incompatibility in these poems, in spite of Eliot's effort to achieve an integral world view that neither could convey in isolation. The resources of ritual and experiment are, indeed, used to press toward a totality that lies beyond logical thought and beyond the limitations of language. By bringing them together, Eliot may have meant to overcome the limits of "Reality" and "Value," as he described them in his 1915 letter to Norbert Wiener. He called upon a formidable and baffling array of avant-garde innovations to fulfill one of the central ambitions of modernism, that of achieving a form of expression that will at once surpass the past without rejecting it and sanction the future without dictating it. Instead, however, such experimental techniques as parody, fragmentation, parataxis, and multilingualism focus on the spiritual failure of contemporary civilization. They augment the tone of despair with which these early poems view the decline of the religious faith mirrored in their ritualized passages. The poem of Eliot's middle age, *Four Quartets*, reflects a new stage of his thinking as it achieves a more measured and meditative response to the dilemmas posed by the juxtaposition of themes of the inward spiritual life and experiences of external reality.

5

Four Quartets

I find it hard to believe that a poem of mine
which sells nearly 12,000 copies can be
really good.

—T. S. Eliot, on "The Dry Salvages"

While there are many ways of reading *Four Quartets*, a dialectic structure comes into view if it is read as a series of experiments testing each of the sites it describes to see whether it is a setting appropriate for ritual. It is a dialogue of voices debating the truth of the epigraph from Heraclitus, "The way up and the way down are the same," which takes the two paths as referring to spiritual insight and physical experience respectively, and seeks to unify them through responses to specific places. What Ronald Bush has said of "Burnt Norton" applies to the sequence as a whole: "To read it is to feel the pull of two elaborate belief systems."[1]

Eliot believed that the two systems, which are normally considered incompatible with each other, can be complementary. In discussing religion, he affirmed that the ultimate goal is a matter of feeling and intuition, but he also invoked the criteria of "intelligence" and "sense of fact" that he insisted on in his literary criticism. The "experimental" nature of his religious thought appears in such comments as "The Christian thinker proceeds by elimination and rejection. He finds the world to be so and so; he finds its character inexplicable by any non-religious theory."[2] *Four Quartets* follows this method. Beginning with his perceptions or memories of specific localities, Eliot asks whether each is a place where the spirit can leap from the foundation of physical experience into communion with the transcendental. As we will see, the last, "Little Gidding," seems to satisfy this requirement, so that the sequence has the form of a spiritual quest that ends successfully.

Each *Quartet* is an effort to convert responses to the world into ritual. Helen Gardner begins her discussion of the poem's sources by declaring that "The major sources of *Four Quartets* are experiences,"[3] and Lillian Feder augments this by writing that the poem is essentially a "private exploration," an effort to locate "consciousness of the supernatural within the human mind."[4] A. D. Moody has outlined this progress from experience to the supernatural by specifying four stages in Eliot's religious thinking: experience, "knowledge" (the assessment of experience), wisdom (the assessment of knowledge), and, finally, the vision of a "higher reality."[5] The first two stages belong to the experimental method, the latter two to ritual. While Moody presents them as sequential steps, the four stages are mixed and alternated in tones, rhythms, and vocabularies, as if they were scrutinizing the poet's experience from different points of view, in a project resembling, on a smaller scale, Browning's *The Ring and the Book.*

The paratactic structure of the individual poems of *Four Quartets* tends to conceal the relationships among them. We can therefore best examine the interaction of ritual and experiment by moving horizontally through the sequence, examining three of the modes or topics which appear in each of its sections, and then tracing the concept of "pattern." These topics are: first, experiences, especially experiences of places but also psychological episodes, including the imagined scene of the rustic dance and the visit of the compound ghost as well as the recollections of river and sea in "The Dry Salvages"; second, the problem of time, which underlies the interpretation of nearly all the experiences; and third, the problem of poetry and language.

These themes display a more intelligible continuity as they are followed through the *Quartets* than is apparent within the individual poems themselves. To each of them the poem brings the resources of both ritual and experiment, employing such apparently antithetical perspectives as the physical and the visionary, time and the timeless, immediate experience and abstract speculation, and referential speech and suggestive silence. It exhibits reluctance to accept either side of these dichotomies as final, moving between them with its varying voices in a hesitant and intermittent rhythm as it tests the validity of the poet's reactions. It ultimately arrives at the conviction that the spirit has only a limited capacity for apprehending the unity of time and entering into the ritual consciousness.

Eliot is initially attracted to the places of the *Quartets* for personal or historical reasons, but he subsequently sets each within a transcendental perspective that questions the relevance of time and place to basic spiritual issues, so that reports of immediate experience and expressions of visionary insight sometimes alternate and sometimes merge with each other. Each setting is an instance of the blending of objective and subjective perception that is the principle of Eliot's objective correlative and much of his poetic imagery.

After its opening passage of meditation (a passage originally written as a speech for *Murder in the Cathedral*), "Burnt Norton" recalls Eliot's visit to the deserted garden of a Gloucestershire mansion, a real-life event that frames the contest between physical and visionary perception. The poet senses that he has entered a place full of ghostly presences, never clearly identified. His intuition reaches a climax of mysticism as the sunlight creates the illusion that the empty pool is full of water and that the sacred lotus of Eastern creeds is floating in it. The phrase "heart of light" aligns this vision with the moment of ecstasy the husband of *The Waste Land* experiences in the presence of the "hyacinth girl."

But material reality asserts itself: as a cloud wipes the sunlight away, the poet thinks he hears the mocking laughter of children, and the thrush seems now to reject, rather than to invite him. In this way the mystical and empirical elements of the experience come together to support the opening assertion that past and future are united in the present. But this extraordinary perception of the unity of time is ephemeral and indefinite. It does not lead to a spiritual illumination, but only to a sense that the conditions for one are possible. As Derek Traversi has said, it offers not metaphysical truths, but only "an increase in *consciousness*, a sense that the normal limitations of time have been for a moment suspended," bringing past and present together "by an intuited simultaneity which *may* indicate something about their true nature."[6] The tentative meaning of the experience, however, is that time cannot be redeemed and that past and future appear ludicrously sterile.

The doctrine of time has a similar pessimistic implication in a parallel treatment of place, the passage about the underground station in part III of "Burnt Norton." There is no light to create an illusion of mystical insight, only a twilight in which past and future, the immobility of empty fancies and superficial movement, like that of the awaited train, are united in a debilitating timelessness. Nevertheless, these moments and places of contact with depressing realities have their value; they offer the sense that the ritual past and the experimental future are united in an eternal present.

Since the village of East Coker was the home of Eliot's English ancestors, there is an obvious surface truth to the observation he makes about this third experience of a place, "In my beginning is my end." But there is, of course, a more general significance in this collapsing of time, for "East Coker," like the passage about the autumn garden of "Burnt Norton," is about an escape from the temporal into the timeless. Movement and lack of movement are equated with each other, as images of process and verbs of action and motion are balanced against significant moments of "silence" and "waiting." The passing van is a visible counterpart of the changes the village must endure in the dimension of time. The rustic marriage ceremony the poet envisions is a merely secular ritual, a social custom. Its archaic spelling shows that it belongs to a time that has passed, and it participates in temporal rhythms. Because it reflects human and natural desires, not supernatural authority, it does not rise above the level of "Eating and drinking. Dung and death"(124). Nevertheless, it ultimately leads to the desired condition, for its dancing is to become the "stillness" of faith, just as birth into the world of time leads to dying into the transcendental world.

"The Dry Salvages" begins with a contrast between the domesticated, if unpredictable, river and the alien sea. The Mississippi River and the island group off the New England coast are transformed into mystical symbols of divine power. The tolling of the bell-buoy knits past and future together in a version of time known only to the sea, a timelessness that transcends the consciousness of the women who are pinned to the present as they wait for their men to return. As in the other places, realistic imagery and visionary intuition are brought together to penetrate the spiritual levels of experience.

The movement between physical and visionary experience that occurs in these scenes ends inconclusively until each of the first four poems in the sequence moves to its other themes of time and language to seek a plane on which they can be reconciled, but the setting of "Little Gidding," an old religious community, offers a promise of transcendence. Because the physical features of the site combine contradictory attributes—sun flaming on ice, with paradoxical cold at its heart—they leap outside of possible experience into a region beyond physical perception, creating the timelessness of "midwinter spring" and "zero summer." This suspension of the laws of opposition "stirs the dumb spirit" to the sense of cosmic unity in which contradictions disappear, so that, as the passage concludes, "the intersection of the timeless moment / Is England and nowhere. Never and always"(139).

While the attention to externals characteristic of experiment is needed in "Little Gidding," as in the other poems, the search for knowledge is inappropriate here; only ritual consciousness, kneeling and prayer will do. We realize here that "prayer is more than an order of words," more, in fact, than anything that can be known. The limitations felt in the other observations of place have been overcome, and "Little Gidding" seems to bring us to the verge of "the vision of a higher reality," the fourth stage of Eliot's religious thinking as Moody has described it. This is the only place in *Four Quartets* where the poet can say,

> You are not here to verify,
> Instruct yourself, or inform curiosity
> Or carry report. You are here to kneel
> Where prayer has been valid. (139)

As we have just seen, the experiences of "place" in *Four Quartets* invariably raise the issue of time and become tests of the process of passing from a specific time, marked by a specific place, to the timeless consciousness of cosmic vision. The goal to be attained is formulated in the "still point" passage of part II of "Burnt Norton"; it is a form of mystic consciousness that defies location in time and place. But the wheel-like image suggests that the visionary "still point" is embedded in the temporal "turning world" at its axis or pivotal center, so that "only through time is time conquered." The function of places in *Four Quartets* justifies the added insight that only through place is place conquered.

The beautiful brief lyric of part IV of "Burnt Norton" links the autumn garden with this insight by returning to the moment when the cloud dispelled the illusion of the lotus pool and asking, through a garden language of imagery, whether time will end in death. It replies by merging the metaphors of the wheel and the kingfisher's wing, identifying the afterimage of the ephemeral light glancing from the bird's wing with the "still point" of unconditional reality at the center of the physical world.

> After the kingfisher's wing
> Has answered light to light, and is silent, the light is still
> At the still point of the turning world. (121)

In this way, physical experience offers a sense of the paradoxes that lie beyond experience.

This vision is not available, however, in "East Coker," where entropy seems to prevail until the last few lines. The country scene reflects decay, the heroes of the temporal world advance into darkness, and we are told that experience cannot teach much that is of value. The images of the lights going down in the theater and the stalled underground train may be regarded as marking the borders between the world of experience and the ineffable realm that is to be attained only after the contradictions of darkness and light and stillness and dancing have been resolved.

The first verse paragraph of "East Coker"'s part V, where Eliot reviews his career as a series of futile but necessary efforts at valid expression is, in effect, a continuation of the despairing meditation on poetry in part II. But while the earlier part finds only continual deception in the changing patterns of experience, and counsels humility as the "only wisdom," the second counters this pessimism in its last paragraph by joining the episodes of daily life and the "deeper communion" of love into a single paradoxical mingling of time and timelessness that promises continuity and improvement, a condition that overcomes the inertia of mere renunciation and accepts the temporal as a stage in the process of salvation.

It accomplishes this by reversing and thus rendering positive the language and images of the earlier part of the poem. The "patterns" in constant motion in part II now form a stable, if more intricate, design of life and death. The "purgatorial fires" anticipated in the wounded surgeon lyric have now become the vital energies of daily life. The onrush of time at the opening of the poem makes the village a scene of rapid growth and decline, but age brings

> . . . a time for the evening under starlight,
> A time for the evening under lamplight. . . . (129)

These are durable moments, one in the presence of the cosmos, the other in domestic security, that contrast with the processes of growth and decay previously associated with "time." Of the "old men" dismissed with contempt in part II, we are now told that they ought to be "explorers," taking part in the movement toward the "deeper communion."

The final sea image continues this theme by subtly suggesting that the transcendental is embedded even in forbidding actualities. The watery waste that appears as an "empty desolation" to human beings is full of other life and other voices. In spite of its desolate aspect, it opens out as part of the journey to grace, contrasting sharply with the actual settings of "East Coker," the heat of the lane near the village, the dark theater, and the claustrophobic underground train. These reversals are summed up in the final line: the pessimistic "In my beginning is my end" of the opening is reversed into the triumphant "In my end is my beginning" at the close.

While the time measured by the river and sea in "The Dry Salvages" is alien to human consciousness, it is not the timelessness of mystic vision. It is, on the contrary, temporality intensified, the endlessness mourned in the sestina that follows, a merciless duration that occasions human suffering. The sestina finds only pain and destruction in real time, symbolized by an ocean that throws up wreckage and bones, where fishermen do work that will turn out to be profitless. The suggestion that its effects can be neutralized by prayer, a ritual entry into timelessness, is weak enough. As "The Dry Salvages" progresses, it speculates on the possibilities of reinterpreting experiences through memory or selection, but concludes that none of this will offer escape from time.

The final part of "The Dry Salvages" begins by contrasting degenerate expressions of supernatural belief with the genuine timelessness that only the saint can perceive. The closest approach most of us can make to this are certain epiphanic moments of actual experience, but Eliot, while identifying these with incarnation, nevertheless asserts that they must be completed by formal religious observances, a consummation that does not actually occur. As the meter changes to the rhythm of a liturgical chant and the language shifts to a language of paradox, we hear of a place where an "impossible union" is actualized, a spiritual condition admittedly denied to "most of us," who must follow the mode of continuity. Eliot is describing the sequence of passing through time to the timeless, through the inspirational moments of life to the ritual experience that takes us beyond life. But this goal is not attained; instead we are forced to return to the world of time, whose best hope is to keep aspiration vital in the life we know.

The contradictions we have noted in the description of Little Gidding tell us that here at last the poet has come to a place where consciousness can escape entrapment in time. The site acquires the aura attached to centers of pilgrimage, which, according to Mircea Eliade, are variously seen by the archaic mind as places where heaven, hell, and earth come together, as the navel of the earth, or the scene of creation, places of "absolute reality" where the sacred can be confronted.[7] There are other places, says Eliot, that are "the world's end," but he fixes the nearest firmly as "Now and in England." He adds, however, that the intersection of time and the timeless to which the closing passage of "The Dry Salvages" aspires makes time and place meaningless; the intersection is "England and nowhere. Never and always."

The dimension (or, rather, nondimension) of timelessness essential to salvation seems to be confidently entered at last in the final passages of "Little Gidding" as the poem maintains that it is impossible to distinguish beginnings from ends, or death from life, that any action is a step toward some death that is really a beginning. "We die with the dying. . . . We are born with the dead" (144) is a brilliant declaration of the vitality of tradition that takes us back to Eliot's earliest critical pronouncements.

One remarkable aspect of *Four Quartets* is its investigation, in a thoroughly experimental spirit, of the capacity of language to express transcendental experiences. The investigation is carried out not only in prosaic discursive passages that are often conversational in tone, but also by testing specimens of poetry. These are mainly of two types: artificially heightened, trope-laden passages of an intellectual strain, which are ineffective, and a visionary language of paradox that acknowledges the inability of language to convey transcendental truths.

The second section of each of the five sequences opens with a self-conscious, mannered exhibition of the poet's art whose artificiality sometimes suggests a lack of seriousness. Most of these lyrics are succeeded by contrasting passages that repudiate them more or less directly, establishing a dialectic of style and performing an inquiry into the power of poetry to convey spiritual experience that takes experimental form.

The "Garlic and sapphires" lyric uses fanciful imagery to repeat the message about the unity of time in the lines immediately preceding:

What might have been and what has been
Point to one end, which is always present. (118)

But the message is undermined by the plainness of the following passage ("At the still point of the turning world"[119]). Here we have a deliberately unsuccessful effort at achieving Timothy J. Reiss's "patterning" language, whose paradoxes and referential emptiness end with an acknowledgment of their irrelevance to time and place, the dimensions that Kant regards as the basic conditions of cognition. Even though, as Ronald Bush has observed, the "still point" passage is marked by a certain unwelcome self-consciousness, it offers a reply to the strained and extravagant lyric, which arrogantly attempts to express the inexpressible.[8]

The idea is clarified in the wonderful imagery of the "Words move . . . " passage, which also explains the rationale of the organization of Four Quartets. The Chinese jar creates an illusion of the motion it does not have; the feeling of the violin note extends into the ensuing silence. Similarly, words themselves, when they are set into a proper "pattern," can infuse the spaces and silences between them with relationships that suggest meanings beyond their referential power. In the same way, the physical experiences of part III of "East Coker," such as the sound of rivers and the sight of lightning generate "ecstasy," not as direct experiences, but only in relation to "the agony / of death and birth."

"East Coker" continues the interplay between two kinds of language by offering two mannered and spuriously "poetic" lyrics in order to dismiss them in prosaic sequels, and the discussion that follows the "Late November" lyric casually dismisses poetry in general, as well as wisdom. The "wounded surgeon" lyric of part IV elaborates a mordant allegory of the spiritual life whose tone is hard to identify; the medical imagery might be seen as mocking the modern, scientific idea that spiritual suffering is merely a clinical problem, while the last two stanzas express the paradoxes of sin and salvation. The final stanza outlines the irony of the self-deception in which the hospital patients consume flesh and blood as food, ignoring the vulnerability of their own flesh and blood. But the idea of the Eucharist comes to their rescue in the last line. Flesh and blood consumed sacramentally is an acceptance of Christ's sacrifice, and because the ritual is a pathway to grace, we credulously believe we are saved in spite of our ignorance. The extravagant metaphysical style of this lyric is convincingly repudiated in the following passage, however, where the poet dwells on the futility of his craft.

The conversation in "Little Gidding" with the "compound ghost" of earlier poets warns that salvation is not to be found in what language has to offer, for the reward of poets who devote their lives to it is an old age of painful remorse. David Ward has identified this scene with rituals in which priests tell of meetings with spirits carrying messages from some other world and has pointed out an echo of the Lord's Prayer in the ghost's speech: ("pray they be forgiven / By others, as I pray you to forgive / Both bad and good"[141]).[9] The magical, and specifically Christian character of the encounter is established by the image of the German bomber as a "dark dove." This startling identification of a weapon of destruction with the Holy Ghost and the messenger of the Annunciation seems entirely perverse. But it suggests that Eliot is thinking of war somewhat as David Jones did—as part of the timeless ritual of history—and is seeing its evil and suffering as indispensable prologues to an ultimate deliverance.

The tone of the passage about the ghost is matter-of-fact and nearly casual, an ease, as the poet says, that causes wonder in the face of its supernatural and oracular material. The ghost warns his auditor that the poet's old age is likely to be a time of painful remorse, but he does suggest an alternative, passing judgment on experiment and ritual in the process. In declaring that "last year's words belong to last year's language," and repeating Mallarmé's formulation of the poet's mission ("to purify the dialect of the tribe"), the ghost describes the modernist emphasis on change and renewal. These efforts are futile, but the ghost adds that they can be redeemed, "restored by that refining fire / Where you must move in measure, like a dancer"(142). Thus, poetic experiment can be validated by ritual consciousness.[10]

The repeated fire imagery associates fire with ritual language as a bridge between mortal and divine conditions. The references to tongues of fire suggest that fire speaks a sacred and unintelligible language that articulates transcendental reality, like the "tongues" generated by Pentecostal fire. The fire brought by the bomber in the lyric of part IV also has the form of "tongues" that "declare" the path to redemption. It is also a sacrificial fire that brings deliverance by consuming surrogate victims, performing the neglected sacrifice mentioned in the lyric of part II ("The sacrifice that we de-nied"[140]). This sacrifice is more specifically implied through the allusion to the myth of Hercules in the "shirt of flame" in part IV. Hercules, tormented by the fiery shirt of Nessus, ended his suffering by dying on a funeral pyre, thus transforming himself into a deity, in accordance with Girard's pattern. Hence, the "fire and fire" we cannot escape are the suffering of daily life on the one hand and the redemptive suffering of ritual sacrifice on the other.

The last verse paragraph of "Little Gidding" illustrates the assimilation of historical experiences into a timeless pattern by employing liturgical language and rhythm and paraphrases of a mystical text by Dame Julian of Norwich. Here, memory transforms the historical events of the English Civil War into symbols. This transformation can be achieved only when language is transcended, and the collaboration of the secular and the sacred in bringing this about is superbly conveyed in a political image as the conflicting parties are said to accept "the constitution of silence."

The impressive formulation of excellent style in part V as a communal dance tells us that even when it is perfected, poetic language can do no more than take part in the movement toward the silence of nonexistence and timelessness. That movement re-appears in the final verse stanza as a part of the consummation that is articulated at the end of the poem. "Exploration" is essential for the rediscovery of the secrets hidden in familiar things, a repetition of the advice given to "old men" at the end of "East Coker."

It is possible to feel that the last lines of the poem do not do justice to the austerity of the holy life. This condition is described in two contrasting idioms: Dame Julian's patterning language of mysticism and the compara-tively conventional poetic imagery of the knot, the fire, and the rose, which seems to seriously miss "simplicity." Perhaps these are put side by side to demonstrate the inability of language to articulate the transcendental, to show that it is firmly rooted in the temporal world and can rise to elegance but cannot express the ineffable realities encountered in ritual.

Reiss, we recall, termed the idiom that preceded analytico-referentiality "patterning language" on the ground that it reflected a conception of reality as something fixed and permanent. If we read *Four Quartets* as a quest, it is possible to say that its goal is a realization of this concept.

Eliot's emphasis on "pattern" is an aspect of his sympathy with ritual. In "The Music of Poetry" he explains that the words of a poem achieve significance through their relation to each other rather than in a directly referential way and can form "a musical pattern of secondary meanings." His observation that "the poet is occupied with frontiers of consciousness beyond which words fail, though meanings exist" refers to transcendental significance, which can arise only in spaces left vacant of rational significance. Contradicting the view that set forms seem to be disappearing in modern poetry, Eliot asserts that "the tendency to return to definite, and even elaborate patterns is permanent."[11] Hence, he says in part V of "East Coker":

> Only by the form, the pattern,
> Can words or music reach
> The stillness. . . . (121)

"Pattern" is a collaboration of movement and stillness, for in the last verse paragraph of "Burnt Norton," where the theme is introduced, we are told, "The detail of the pattern is movement," but the "end of movement" is enduring and unchanging love. This form, the poem specifies, must be fixed; words that "will not stay in place" cannot last, and the trouble with "knowledge derived from experience" is that the current of changing events constantly creates new and impermanent forms. This effect intensifies as we grow older, so that the wisdom attributed to old age becomes worthless.

This loss can be remedied, however, by a sense of tradition. The discursive passage of part II of "The Dry Salvages" dwells on the fact that experience, when kept in memory, ceases to be a "sequence" in time and becomes instead a stable form with a different meaning from the one originally attributed to it because it is based on the accumulated experience of generations. The speaker suggests that this new meaning is a transcendental one conditioned by the memory of "something that is probably quite ineffable"(133). The anguish of guilt so prominent in *The Waste Land* is set aside and the value of accepting the ritual sacrifice as a means of redemption is explained in the dry, matter-of-fact tone of a lecture. Personal guilt would, indeed, lower the worth of the sacrifice by transferring its pain to the feelings of the sinner. What is called for here is the recognition that the effective agent is the sinner's lasting memory of the victim's pain. This idea is dramatized in the superb images of the river and the rock, which remain what they always were, enduring, familiar and generally unheeded, like the memory of "something that is probably quite ineffable."

As the passage proceeds, it becomes increasingly clear that this "something" is an influence like that of Girard's ritual sacrifice. In looking back toward the terror of primitive life, says Eliot, we come to discover that moments of suffering occurring to others are permanent, while the memories of our own suffering do not last because they are overlaid with subsequent experiences. We might extend this into a Girardian view by suggesting that knowledge of the agony of others survives as the productive agony of the sacrificial victim, not as the enervating guilt of the survivor, and becomes part of a permanent pattern in that form.

Part III of "Little Gidding" explains that the transient patterns of life can be transformed into a permanent one by "detachment," which is carefully distinguished from "indifference." Through this depersonalization, a theme continued from Eliot's early essays, personal experiences are transformed and put into a new context, presumably one determined by permanent metaphysical truth, so that, as part V of "Little Gidding" declares, "history is a pattern / Of timeless moments"(144).

The language of timelessness appears sporadically throughout the sequence. The reflection that closes part III of "East Coker" paraphrases a passage from St. John of the Cross expressed in the "patterning" language of religious mysticism, whose paradoxes view the world as a divine creation in which opposites are identical with each other and tell us that the spiritual life must proceed by contraries, transcending both rationality and the expressive capacities of language. A different but related religious idiom appears in "The Dry Salvages," where the request for prayer adopts conventional attitudes and formulas less effective as poetry than as expressions of spiritual commitment. The justification for language of this kind appears in "Little Gidding," where prayer reaches beyond words to communicate with the dead in language that transcends that of daily life.

In these linguistic sacrifices the poet surrenders his own expressive powers in favor of the numinous language of something more important, collective worship. But most of the poem speaks through the objective correlatives of physical experience and approaches spiritual awareness through idioms arising from lower states of consciousness whose relation to truth is indirect and contingent.[12]

A. D. Moody grants *The Waste Land* and *Four Quartets* the status of rituals that perform "the same basic rite," transforming the temporal world into a permanent pattern. But he distinguishes sharply between them. He considers *The Waste Land* to be self-centered and negative, missing the communal effect rituals achieve, while he feels *Four Quartets* to be a far more successful "religious ritual" in which the poet, conscious of the world's general sinfulness, rather than merely of his own, transfigures immediate experiences into parts of a permanent spiritual pattern. "The poem," he says, "offers itself as a religious ritual for the time—as *the* ritual by which a foundering civilisation might be recovered." But Moody also declares that both poems "begin and end in the realm of experience, and bring themselves always to the proof of immediate experience."[13] It seems to me that this adherence to the realm of experiment, where externals play a determining part, mitigates the ritual effect of the poems and enhances their status as secular works. In evaluating poems as ritualizations, we should bear in mind Auden's warning that "catharsis is properly effected, not by works of art, but by religious rites."[14] Eliot would have agreed. He was skeptical of devotional poetry and felt that it was dangerous for the poet, as well as for the reader, to turn to poetry for religious fulfillment.

Material that he at first planned to include in *Four Quartets* but rejected suggests that Eliot had these dangers in mind and decided against trying to raise his poem to the level of ritual. The first draft of the ghost's speech in "Little Gidding" promises that recollection of things "of least and most importance" will ultimately confer "the final gift of earth. . . . One soil, one past, one future, in one place." But the poet replaced this assurance with the speech on old age, with its acknowledgment of the power of time. Surviving notes show that he intended to conclude "East Coker" with the line "To be reunited and the Communion," and to end "Little Gidding" with "Invocation to the Holy Spirit," and he wrote a passage for "Little Gidding" that ended with an adaptation of a prayer from an Anglo-Catholic manual. None of these drafts appears in the final versions.[15] As if to confirm his withdrawal from a definitive acceptance of ritual finality, he added the line "Old men ought to be explorers" to the manuscript of "East Coker" in pencil.[16] The theme is extended with the prediction that we shall continue exploration until we discover in the places where we started a sense of their ultimate significance within the transcendental pattern.

The poem is not written in the "patterning language" that presents itself as part of a divine creation but rather, as I have noted, in a variety of idioms ranging from the sacred to the mundane. Instead of the feeling of timelessness we would expect in a ritual text, *Four Quartets* offers potentiality, provisional insights, responsiveness to changing conditions, and the shock of the unexpected and unexplained, all those indeterminacies inflicted on us by the inescapable passage of time. While its innovations of language and form are less radical than those of *The Waste Land*, it expresses, in a more resigned and positive tone, the same dissatisfaction with what can be said and the same need to look to the future.

As Derek Traversi has astutely observed, the poem finds it impossible to live in what I am calling the ritual consciousness. "Since time and change are the laws of our being . . . the prolongation of the moments of ecstasy which seem to take us outside the temporal world would cost man nothing less than his life."[17] The assurance, timelessness, and stable pattern of the ritual consciousness are only aspirations expressed in a poem where the inquiry and change made necessary by a condition "between un-being and being" are the realities. Since the forms of experience are constantly changing, we must change with them, content with whatever satisfactions secular life can provide. But since experience is irrelevant to the life of the spirit, it cannot deliver ultimate significance. *Four Quartets* is a poetic demonstration of the validity of Browning's injunction in his "Essay on Shelley": ". . . the world is not to be learned and thrown aside, but reverted to and relearned."[18] It is the expression of a poet who experiences a powerful yearning for the transcendental but realizes that it can be pursued only by penetrating the opacities of the natural world and by enduring the twilight realm of doubt and inquiry.

"The great poet," wrote Eliot, "in writing himself, writes his time."[19] It is, therefore, not a betrayal of his religious convictions for Eliot to balance his religious intuitions with the experience of externals as he does in the dialogic structure of *Four Quartets*. His poem reflects the dilemmas and aspirations of modernism: It aspires to ritual but accepts the testimony of the material world, speaking in secular time to prepare the way for the salvation it cannot offer itself. Written about fifteen years after Eliot became a communicant of the Church of England, it reflects a deeper ritual sensibility while echoing the experimentalism of his early period. The two themes are both more subdued and more fully integrated with its general structure, creating a mood that might be described as a fervent acceptance of limits. They display a degree of collaboration that transcends what is seen in Eliot's early poetry, a collaboration that enables him to deliver his most mature account of his spiritual quest.

6

Ezra Pound's Early Poems

... the Confucian universe as I see it is a universe
of interacting strains and tensions.

—Ezra Pound[1]

Religion seems to have been an original element in Ezra Pound's concept of poetry. Though he seldom went to church, and was not affiliated with any official religion, Pound took both ritual and the general idea of religion seriously. He told Henry Hope Shakespear, his future wife's father, that he objected to a religious wedding ceremony primarily because the official clergy were not sincere, but also because he had no respect for the institutional church. "I have some religion," he declared, but it was not at all what Mr. Shakespear would approve. "I should no more give up my faith in Christ than I should give up my faith in Helios or my respect for the teaching of Confucius."[2] It is reported that while he was at St. Elizabeth's hospital later in his life, he performed the rituals of several religions, finding "the rites of celebration, reverence and rejoicing of all religions to be intracompatible."[3] This conviction that all religions share similar foundations is a pronounced and lasting feature of Pound's entire canon.

Pound's immersion in mystic and esoteric writings and the effect of these on his early poetry have been thoroughly analyzed by both Akiko Miyake in *Ezra Pound and the Mysteries of Love* and Demetres P. Tryphonopoulos in *The Celestial Tradition.*[4] He had taken an interest in the occult even before he left the United States, and when he lived in London he came under the influence of a number of people who were absorbed in esoteric doctrines. Comments made at about the time the *Cantos* was started (1915) show that Pound both approved of mysticism and also tried to find a rational basis for it. In defining "a god" as "an eternal state of mind" he was perhaps following Jane Harrison, who writes, in her study of Greek religion, that "there were no gods at all," only "conceptions of the human mind, shifting and changing colour with every human mind that conceives them."[5] And in formulating the object of religious worship as an "intimate essence of the universe," he proposed a metaphysical foundation free of supernatural or dogmatic elements. As Pound developed these principles in the 1921 "Axiomata," he supported the validity of mystic intuitions on psychological grounds as the responses of limited human consciousness to an "intimate essence" beyond its understanding.[6] He also justified the variety of world religions and authorized a freedom and flexibility that approaches agnosticism: "Belief is a cramp, a paralysis, an atrophy of the mind in certain positions"(SP, 49).

Pound's nearly indiscriminate syncretism is hospitable to almost all religions and the one feature that seems to be central to all of them, the cord running through the holes in the coins, is ritual. Pound wrote in a 1939 article, "The other rites [of the pagan religions, besides those relating to overt sex] are the festivals of fecundity of the grain and the sun festivals, without revival of which religion cannot return to the hearts of the people" (SP, 70). In a letter to Henry Swabey, he wrote: "RITUAL, good, it shd lift the mind to contemplatio."[7] He felt that ritual provided a channel to the fundamental truths of the spirit recognized by nearly all religions, a conviction which borders on the supernatural without quite surrendering a rational basis. According to Miyake, Pound shared the view, inherent in such rituals as the Greek mysteries and the Chinese rites of ancestor worship, "that even the powers from heaven depend on man's will to support them in rituals. The celestial powers, in return, will support man in his advancement to perfection."[8]

Displaying a fastidiousness that recalls Stephen Dedalus's fear of pretending a devotion he did not feel, Pound insisted that ritual must be accompanied by sincerity. He wrote, in his letter to Mr. Shakespear: "I think, seriously, that the spiritual powers are affronted when a person who takes his religion seriously complies with a ceremony which has fallen into decay." The religion that Pound took seriously was polytheism. In the catechism "Religio," published anonymously in the New Freewoman in October 1913, polytheism is offered as a basis for ritual—"This rite is made for the West."

Many of the poems in his first volumes, through the Ripostes of 1912, like the poems being written by H. D. at the time, employ the deictics of the prayer, hymn, or litany and take the form of praise or supplication addressed to a transcendental being, whether this figure is the Christian God, a pagan deity, or a lover idealized in the tradition of amour courtois. At this time, Pound favored prescribed forms such as "Villonauds," elegies, aubades, sonnets, and troubadour forms because they demarcate areas of common understanding, s ritual itself does. He says of the obscure troubadour poems called *trobar lus* that they speak "to those who are already expert." And he adds: "They re good art as the high mass is good art. . . . the second sort of canzone is ritual. It must be conceived and approached as a ritual."[9]

The first poem of *A Lume Spento*, "Grace Before Song," addresses the "Lord God of heaven," asking that the poems may find a responsive audience. Its most ignificant feature to one tracing Pound's poetic use of ritual is the image he ses in saying that God "with mercy dight / Th'alternate prayer wheel of the ight and light / Eternal," portraying the cycle of day and night, and therefore he movement of the universe, as a ritual event. It recalls the implication ontained in Yeats's view that history itself is a ritual, a repeated turning of the Great Wheel. Pound's reference to the Tibetan prayer wheel in this early poem trangely foreshadows the old poet's use in the later cantos of the rituals of the Na-khi people, who observed a religion related to Tibetan Buddhism.

"Salve O Pontifex!" also from *A Lume Spento*, suggests that already, at this very early date, Pound regarded the Eleusinian rites that were to form one of he structural elements of the *Cantos* as the primary source of poetic tradition. By addressing Swinburne, who was one of his models, as "High Priest of acchos," Pound casts him in the role of a priest of Eleusis, for "Iacchos" was he name by which Dionysus was addressed in the Eleusinian ceremonies. The poem speaks of "the secrets of inmost mysteries" and of the return of Persephone, a central figure of the mysteries, who is also the subject of Swinburne's "Hymn to Proserpine." In Pound's poem, Swinburne's poetic accomplishment, the making of "paeans" and "canticles," is interwoven with priestly functions, as if the two were hardly distinguishable from each other.

Pound's commitment to paganism surfaces in a number of the lyrics published in *Lustra* (1916). "Surgit Fama" ("Rumor Wakes") has Hermes telling the poet, "Once more in Delos, once more is the altar a-quiver," as though celebrations in the birthplace of Artemis and Apollo are to be renewed. Some of these poems reflect Pound's persistent belief that sexual symbolism played a part in ancient ceremonies that were essentially fertility rites. This assertion s often impudently directed against the prudishness of his contemporaries: "Dance the dance of the phallus / and tell anecdotes of Cybele! . . . (Tell it to Mr. Strachey)." The figures of female dancers, who may be ritual priestesses or idealizations of the feminine principle, move gracefully through some of the poems, which also allude to gods, Muses, and sacred sites of the ancient world. Pagan ritual even serves the irony that is a prominent tone in this volume. "Tempora" (which seems to be about H. D.,"the Dryad") quotes a woman asking that her poems should be published, a demand Pound pretends to mistake for the ritual cry,"Io! Io! Tamuz!" addressed to Adonis.[10]

The place of the Eleusinian mysteries in Pound's thinking will be taken up in detail in connection with the *Cantos*. But the point is worth making here that his sense of their importance developed gradually from a very early period. Akiko Miyake has convincingly argued that Pound's ideas about the influence of Eleusis were derived primarily from his reading of a five-volume work by Gabriele Rossetti (the father of Dante Gabriel) in the British Museum in the summer of 1906. Rossetti's *Il Mistero dell'Amor platonico del Medio Evo* elaborately develops the thesis that troubadour poetry descended from the Eleusinian ritual, and Pound may have been drawn to it by its chapters on Arnaut Daniel and other troubadour poets.[11]

Leaping over many centuries, Rossetti asserts that certain secret mysteries of North Africa and the Middle East, which had, according to the French authority he quotes, "un gran rapport avec la purification et les épreuves des mystères d'Eleusis," emerged in the medieval period as a cult of Amor in the allegory of the *Roman de la Rose* and the obscure language of Arnaut Daniel and other Provençal practitioners of *trobar clus*.[12] As Miyake shows, one of Pound's first critical essays, "Interesting French Publications," written in 1906, reflects his recent reading of Rossetti's book. The essay includes a review of two books by the French Rosicrucian, Joséphin Péladan, whose ideas seem to be derived from Rossetti's work. One of these, *Le secret des troubadours*, says nothing about Eleusis, but the other, *Origine et esthétique de la tragédie*, identifies the Eleusinian mysteries as the source of drama (instead of the Dionysian ritual favored by the Cambridge anthropologists) and asserts that tragedy embodies the covert doctrine of the ritual in a form that is disturbing, but not understood. Pound might well have found illumination in Péladan's view that pagan worship and its icons were easily transmittable both to the Christian liturgy and to secular cultural life and wrote approvingly of the importance Péladan attributed to the Eleusinian mysteries.[13]

Pound adopted as his own the theory that the body of troubadour poetry, with its emphasis on the senses, was a survival of pagan mysticism in "Psychology and Troubadours," first published in October 1912 and incorporated into later editions of *The Spirit of Romance.* Apparently following Rossetti, Pound asserts that the Hellenic spirit had come to the surface again in Provence as a secret religion based on "Hellenistic mysteries" and that the troubadour songs replaced the gods with lovers, adapting the religious music and language the poets had learned in the monasteries to songs about love. As Pound puts it, the troubadours "lost the names of the gods and remembered the names of lovers."[14] In this way, the pagan worship of Demeter and Persephone was reborn in the medieval worship of the idealized lady. Eleusis is not named, but in the brief statement "Credo," which appeared many years later in December 1930, Pound says flatly, "I believe that a light from Eleusis persisted throughout the middle ages and set beauty in the song of Provence and of Italy." "Terra Italica," published the following year, suggests that the Eleusinian rite provides a "key" to medieval thought (*SP*, 53, 54-60). Inconsistently, however, Pound also adheres to the ancient tradition that the secrets of Eleusis are hidden. "The mysteries are *not* revealed," he writes in a 1939 letter, "and no guide book to them has been or will be written."[15]

In 1913 a number of important events in Pound's poetic career seemed to conspire to emphasize the relation of ritual and poetry. In September he met the widow of Ernest Fenollosa, who gave him the notes on Chinese and Japanese literature compiled by her husband which led, among other developments, to Pound's study of the Noh drama. The comments by Pound and Fenollosa accompanying the translations of the volume *"Noh" or Accomplishment* (1917) attribute the origin of Noh to three ritual sources: court ceremonies of the Shogunate, god-dances of the Shinto rites, and sacred Buddhist pantomime. In its modern form, Noh retained a strong ritualistic character: it was highly stylized, depended on action rather than words (the choruslike narrative, Fenollosa speculates, was a secondary development), evoked emotion through a unified impression, and often employed supernatural elements, such as the ghosts of dead lovers.[16]

In the same month as the meeting with Mrs. Fenollosa, Pound met Allen Upward, who had contributed some Chinese-style lyrics to *Poetry* and who was the author of two books Pound later reviewed with enthusiasm, *The Divine Mystery* and *The New Word*. Pound's observation that the rational and the magical are interchangeable reflects Upward's view, in his introductory chapter to *The Divine Mystery*, that modern scientific study is uncovering new meanings in religious traditions whose original authority has disappeared and his contention that modern minds must find suitable interpretations for the enduring truths embodied in the old religions.

Pound's review of *The Divine Mystery* begins by quoting Upward's first three paragraphs, which describe a "Wizard" capable of sensing the influences of an "invisible environment" inaccessible to science or religion, a figure that is a prototype of Pound's ideal of artists as "antennas of the race."[17] Observing that "it is easier to change theology than ritual," Upward refers to Eleusis to show how a sacrificial rite meant to insure fertility of the soil by sympathetic magic can change its meaning as theology progresses.

Pound admired Upward's views, which paralleled Rossetti's and Péladan's ideas about the continuity and development of religious belief, and was to refer to him several times in the *Cantos*.[18] He had the mistaken impression that Upward's study undermined the validity of current religious practices by tracing them to prehistoric sources or "superstitions." What Upward actually said was that the barbaric origin of beliefs such as transubstantiation did not "discredit" them and that he hoped his book would "refresh" them, an anticipation of Pound's principle of "make it new."[19]

Upward's method may fairly be described as a rational approach to irrational material, but in this prewar period Pound also encountered an influence that took him over the border of rationality into the occult: the influence of Yeats. Pound's early poems, with their dreams, visions, and evocations of dead figures show that he was ready to believe in occult phenomena, at least metaphorically, before he came to England.[20] By 1913, when Yeats and Pound spent the first of their three winters at Stone Cottage, Yeats was a veteran of both the Theosophical Society and the Order of the Golden Dawn, and his profound commitment to ritual was based on a firm belief in magical and spiritual forces. He read occult literature at Stone Cottage, and while Pound complained that the older poet bored him with talk about it, he was nevertheless moved to follow Yeats's reading in his usual energetic fashion and to accept some of the poetic resources suggested by the esoteric texts. [21]

In spite of their ebullient originality, Pound's early poems contain little experimentation and no consciousness of science. But the essays he wrote during this period show that his ideas about poetry owe nearly as much to the influence of science as to that of religion. In the preface to *The Spirit of Romance*, dated 1910, Pound declares that "Art . . . is not, and never will be, a science," but by 1912 he is ready to say, "As the abstract mathematician is to science so is the poet to the world's consciousness. . . . Both are scientifically demonstrable" (*SP*, 362). And in 1913, he declares, "The arts, literature, poesy, are a science, just as chemistry is a science." And, after numerous analogies involving science: "The touchstone of an art is its precision."[22]

A critic Pound looked upon as a guide, Ford Madox Ford, justified his insistence on realism by referring to scientific principles, declaring that the arts had a "scientific" function, and employing scientific analogies, a practice Pound adopted in these early essays and reviews. As Ian F. A. Bell has shown, the change may also be at least partly attributable to the influence of a book Pound reviewed in 1910, *The Science of Poetry and the Philosophy of Language*, by Hudson Maxim. which suggested or confirmed a number of Pound's early poetic doctrines.[23]

Maxim, a self-taught American Jack-of-all-trades, had turned from science to poetry after making a fortune as the inventor of smokeless gunpowder and as a government consultant in the field of explosive weaponry. He accounts for his interest in poetry by the fact that "poetry and gunpowder were born about the same time." Believing that poetry had originated in numerous cultural functions, including religious ritual, he nevertheless undertook to show that "the principle of poetry . . . requires only simple scientific method for its elucidation."[24]

Maxim saw a parallel between the law of the conservation of energy and the need for economy of expression in poetry, a doctrine that became one of Pound's basic rules of Imagism and came to dominate American poetry for years. Ian F. A. Bell relates Pound's doctrine of the "luminous detail," a significant particular that leads to a general insight, to Maxim's reference to the scientist's ability to reconstruct prehistoric animals from the slight clues given by a few bones. Pound first expounded this crucial element of his poetic in an essay published about a year after he had reviewed Maxim's book.[25]

Evidence of Maxim's influence on Pound (and that of the contemporary scientific revolution) occurs, paradoxically enough, in an article that sets out to correct Maxim's definition of poetry—without naming him or his book. In his 1912 essay "The Wisdom of Poetry," Pound declares that the poet perceives intuitively what the scientist later confirms empirically, a link between the method of the poet and that of the scientist that became a permanent feature of his poetic. Maxim's "Poetry transforms the abstract to the concrete, the intangible to the tangible," is a statement in reverse of Pound's views that the poet's particulars imply general ideas that transcend the particulars themselves, and that the artist seeks the enduring truths behind transient phenomena. The essay closes with Pound's first use of a favorite analogy: that the poet speaks in a kind of algebra that is related to particulars in the same way that an equation is related to a geometric form: "What the analytical geometer does for space and form, the poet does for the states of consciousness." In spite of this acceptance of scientific abstraction as a poetic model, Pound resists a commitment to dogmatic scientism. He places the poet as an "agnostic" conscious of his ignorance who does not deny "the formulae of theosophy" (SP, 361). Like Maxim, Pound was eager to claim scientific validity for poetry, but he was also unwilling to surrender the authority stemming from mystical tradition.

In this way, Pound came to believe that the precision of science and the mysticism of poetry were not only compatible but also complementary.[26] Underlying many of his critical assertions is the further implication that poetry is capable of reconciling their conflicting claims. Many of Pound's critics, however, see only contradiction here. Robert Casillo, in a hostile comment that nevertheless recognizes the force of both ritual and experiment in Pound's poetics sees a "persistent conflict" between Pound's desire "to return to Nature by means of myth and ritual, and his support of movements committed to technological advancement and renovation and the control and domination of Nature."[27]

Pound himself saw no contradiction between the two ways of thinking and seems to have felt, consciously or otherwise, that every poem is, by its nature, both a ritual and an experiment. The two sensibilities appear side by side in such essays as "Psychology and Troubadours" and "The Serious Artist." Pound professed to believe that such concepts as electromagnetism and radio-activity were merely modern ways of formulating the spiritual influences of the "invisible environment" postulated by Upward. The theme is a central strand of his thinking. As late as 1938, in *Guide to Kulchur*, Pound draws a parallel between the Eleusinian ceremonies and the mysteries of science on the ground that both are accessible only to a privileged few. Ian F. A. Bell describes Pound's idea that science confirms ritual, linking traditional and contemporary thought with each other, in this way: "Myth and art ritualized the potency of valuable experience and knowledge and made it new through repetition in their own time, a repetition sealed, as it were, in organic continuity by the researches of contemporary science."[28] Or, to elaborate, science confirms the underlying identity of the spiritual and physical worlds that ritual claims to demonstrate.

The idea of experiment was perhaps the most productive element Pound adapted from science. In *Active Anthology* (1933) he writes: "Willingness to experiment is not enough, but unwillingness to experiment is mere death . . . the claim is that without constant experiment literature dies. Experiment is ONE of the elements necessary to its life" (*SP*, 397-98). In *Guide to Kulchur* he declares that he belongs to "a generation of experimenters."[29] The poetry he wrote before and after his arrival in London in 1908 exhibits personal originality within fairly conventional limits, but the developments that came a few years later, Imagism and Vorticism, represent principled efforts to achieve a poetic revolution.

Pound characterized some of his favorite medieval poets, including Cavalcanti, Arnaut Daniel, and Dante, as experimenters, and his readiness to accept experimentation is suggested by the distinction he makes, in a 1911 essay, between "symptomatic" and "donative" works. (The former reflect what is known about the thought of their time, while the latter uncover unknown distinctions and harmonies by subjecting the *Zeitgeist* to "discriminations.") He finds in Daniel's twelfth-century poetry "discriminations" that anticipate the Renaissance, qualities that, he says, might even be identified with the "scientific spirit" (*SP*, 25-26, 27-28).

The experimental values that Pound aimed to transpose from science into poetry were innovation, the capacity for renewing and reshaping ideas; objectivity, embodied in precision and impersonality; and contemporaneity, acceptance of the scientific cast of modern thought, or, as he puts it in "The Serious Artist," which appeared in *The Egoist* in 1913, "a communication between intelligent men." He did not, of course, borrow from science the principle of verification—the widespread acceptance of experimental results—but, on the contrary, thought the appreciation of experimental work was limited to an élite.

Experimentation alone, however, does not constitute great art. "The rights of experiment," writes Pound, "include the right to be unsatisfactory . . . wanderings in search of truth have their rights."[30] He places it among the methods the poet must use but warns that mere novelty is insufficient and that the achievements of tradition must be kept in mind. In "The Serious Artist," which was occupied with the scientific objective of achieving greater accuracy, particularly in the expression of emotions, he declares that the "patient testing of media" that amounts to experimentation "savours of the laboratory"; it is a subject for the "specialist" and the "dilettante" rather than a source of poetry. Nevertheless, he defends Joyce's extravagances by saying, "There is a time for a man to experiment with his medium."[31]

The Imagist movement that Pound led is less important as a school that produced a certain number of exquisite small poems than as the source of a set of influential principles and practices that reflected Pound's commitment to both ritual and experimental values. These are especially well unified in the early poems of H. D., although they may not be apparent when they have been successfully fused, for, as Renato Poggioli has said, "creation annuls and absorbs experimentation within itself."[32]

The experimental spirit of Imagism is exhibited in its use of free verse forms, typographical effects, asyntactic constructions, impersonality of tone, and directness of presentation, and in the precision and objectivity of the tropes that are the core of its doctrine. All of these, it must be remembered, departed radically from conventional ideas of poetry. It might even be suggested that the free-standing image, stripped of comment or explanation, is like the result of an experimental procedure, open to the interpretation the observer brings to it.

But experiment, as Pound said, is "not enough." His well-known definition of the Image as the presentation of "an intellectual and emotional complex in an instant of time" that gives "freedom from time limits and space limits" suggests that the Image encompasses a mystical and transcendental

dimension, offering, as William Pratt has said, "a moment of revealed truth."
According to Christine Froula, "Imagism . . . may be understood as a
quasi-theological effort to distill the very essence of poetry . . . an 'absolute
and 'perfect' coincidence of language and poetic idea."[33] The affinity of the
Image with ritual effects emerges strikingly when we reflect that Pound's
formulation closely resembles the Joycean epiphany, a secularized version
of a phase of Christian and pagan ritual.

The effectiveness of ritual, as we have seen, depends on its enigmatic
nature and a shared dedication to some common value. Similarly, the Imagist
poem transforms its readers into a privileged circle of those who accept it
not for what it may be saying but rather for the poetic principles it embodies.
Imagist doctrine praises directness of presentation, but the concrete objects
that constitute its imagery generate waves of indefinite suggestion. In this
way, they avoid overt symbolism, yet project significance.

> O fan of white silk,
>> clear as frost on the grass-blade,
> You also are laid aside. [34]

The parallel in this poem, "Fan-Piece, For Her Imperial Lord" from *Lustra*
(1916), a translation by Pound from the Chinese, is blunt and abrupt. The
attributes of the image—whiteness, coldness, and clarity—speak directly.
But the relation of these qualities to the situation of the speaker is a matter
of intuition that is incapable of proof or demonstration. Further, the fan
acquires a status resembling that of a ritual object as the poem addresses it
as if it were a responsive participant in the drama of feeling. Hugh Witemeyer
has termed this combination of the concrete and the suggested a "visionary
empiricism."[35]

In his study *In the Arresting Eye*, which is mainly devoted to refuting the
claims of Imagist theory, John T. Gage notes several aspects of Pound's
theories that are associated with ritual. Among these are the idea that the
sequential nature of language can be neutralized by the superposition of
images, an effect that creates an impression of simultaneity and timelessness;
and the belief that the word and its referent can be identified with each other
(a belief, we recall, that is characteristic of traditional religions and ritual
language).

In addition, Gage maintains that the Imagist poet cannot escape relying
on some common—and prior—basis of understanding with the reader that
impairs the effect of novelty and freedom claimed by Imagist theory. The
Imagist doctrine urges the poet to confront the object in a detached manner,

but Gage declares that images cannot avoid embodying some rhetorical intent: "Images . . . were meant to be arguments."[36] In spite of Imagist claims to directness, and the view of some critics that there is a scientific tone to its emphasis on precision, Gage argues that a record of emotions and ethical attitudes cannot be objective, for the very act of recording them implies that they are valuable. The disappearance of the speaker may create an impression of objectivity, but the choice of language and materials unavoidably implies some point of view, some value judgment. Imagist accuracy of presentation is, of course, intended to carry conviction, and Gage argues that convictions imply ethical attitudes, so that the nominal objectivity of the poem is forfeited.

Gage's negative arguments make it possible to connect Imagist doctrines with ritual consciousness. But James Longenbach's claims of a visionary component in Pound's theories are advanced in a positive spirit. According to Longenbach, Pound kept to himself a secret "Doctrine of the Image" whose traces can be seen in scattered critical texts and letters. Images, according to this doctrine, were glimpses of the trans-sensuous world that would come into full view after death, hence, intimations of the immortality of the soul. The concept is obviously indebted to Yeats's symbolism and infuses the apparently objective trope described in Imagist criticism with the supernaturalism of Pound's earlier poetry.[37]

The Imagist virtues seem to contradict each other precisely because they are associated both with experiment and with ritual. On the one hand, suggestion, metamorphosis, and an enigmatic inarticulateness that calls for communal understanding create a ritual mode. The Imagist poem treats the object as though it were a fetish with inexpressible magical qualities. On the other hand, Imagist doctrine extols clarity, objectivity, precision, impersonality, and innovation, values motivated by a quasi-scientific spirit and by the conviction that "the arts, literature, poesy are a science." As H. D.'s poems show, the successful Imagist or Imagist-inspired poem can resolve these theoretical contradictions.

Pound's shift from Imagism to the movement he called Vorticism was primarily a response to the technological and scientific advances of the pre–World War I period. But his statements about Vorticism blend religious and scientific convictions together to such an extent that critics have been able to claim both cultures as its source. The vortex that Pound and Wyndham Lewis devised as a logogram for the movement has been said to incorporate both. Ian F. A. Bell has found significant predecessors of it among the Greek philosophers, the mathematical theories of Descartes, and modern physicists. Akiko Miyake, on the other hand, believes that Pound derived it from passages in Plotinus and Dante about the descent of the soul and associates it with the mystic rose of ideal beauty in the *Roman de la Rose*.[38]

Vorticism flourished primarily in the graphic arts; although Vorticist principles influenced the shaping of the *Cantos*, there is little Vorticist poetry. The best example is no doubt "The Return," which Pound associated with Vorticist sculptures by Jacob Epstein and Henri Gaudier-Brzeska as an example of "objective reality." Its superiority to other attempts at Vorticist poetry, such as "The Game of Chess," is due to the balance achieved by its experimental treatment of materials suggestive of ritual. These divine figures were once, it seems, objects of worship, shod with the winged sandals of Hermes, and "souls of blood" even intimates that the ceremony involved sacrifice. Yet the poem's clipped, fragmentary images and free verse break new ground and demand that the traditional elements be understood in a new way, a merging of experimental form and ritual content that parallels the early poems of H. D. and anticipates some passages of the *Cantos*.

Hugh Selwyn Mauberley is Pound's most assertive preliminary move toward the experimentalism of the *Cantos*. Its innovative features are obvious. It is the first of Pound's poems that corresponds to the "modern poetic sequence" defined by M. L. Rosenthal and Sally M. Gall, "a grouping of mainly lyric poems and passages, rarely uniform in pattern, which tend to interact as an organic whole." It is a form whose disconnected units, varying in tone and style, betray emotional "pressures" that seem to demand resolution. It depends for its unity on "felt relationships" among "centers of intensity." The aim of this "liberated lyrical structure" is "neither to resolve a problem nor to conclude an action but to achieve the keenest and most open realization possible."[39] These features, according to Rosenthal and Gall, while they are found in certain Victorian works as well as in the major modern poems, are clearly experimental.

The departures that mark *Mauberley* as a conspicuously experimental work are its striking instability of voice, form, and tone; its detachment; its intertextuality; and its nonprogressive structure. Structure of this kind, which will be seen again in the *Cantos*, has been accurately described by Hugh Witemeyer (in connection with another poem by Pound) as comprising "an aggregation of units, locally unrelated, but contributing in each case some new dimension to the total meaning of the sequence. It is a dialectic structure which juxtaposes conflicting values between poems and within poems without arriving at a definitive synthesis."[40]

Although *Mauberley* is often considered an autobiographical reflection of Pound's experiences, the reader can never be sure who is speaking. The individual segments seem to come from scattered sources, some of them indefinable, with a variety of seemingly incompatible moods and intentions. Caustic irony is followed by a tone of devotion bordering on sentimentality; direct discourse is puzzlingly followed by verse that is primarily illustrative. What we have here is T. S. Eliot's "depersonalization," the characteristic modern rejection of the traditional concept of individuality. In spite of its expression of feelings that are obviously Pound's, the wide variations of style and mood seem to be bent on eradicating the idea of the author and on denying that the successive poems emerge from a single point of view or even from a single consciousness. The poem's numerous quotations and allusions seem to turn over the task of expressing its ideas to various literary and cultural traditions.

This sense of emotional detachment emerges more directly in the ironic treatment of social life, the tight-lipped quatrains imitating those of Théophile Gautier, and the constant resort to pastiche, as Pound enlists other writers to speak for him. Even the most headlong expression of feeling, the passage in *Mauberley* condemning war,

Some quick to arm,
some for adventure
some from fear of weakness,
some from fear of censure. . . . (*Personae*, 190)

is not a spontaneous outburst, but, as John Espey has shown, an echo of a passage from the Greek poet, Bion.[41] This detachment is strengthened by the vocabulary of quasi-scientific terms imitative of Jules Laforgue that projects a stiff, distancing irony:

The wide-banded irides
And botticellian sprays implied
In their diastasis

Which anaesthesis, noted, a year late. . . . (*Personae*, 200)

The poem does not move ahead in a narrative or discursive progression. Instead, it has the sort of organic form that Rosenthal and Gall identify as a characteristic of the modern poetic sequence. Its two parts and the lyrics that close each of them are best seen as contrasting with each other. The poor but virtuous "stylist" contrasts with the meretricious "Mr. Nixon," and two women, a bank-clerk's wife and the Lady Valentine, are paralleled as sexually defunct. In this way, the different parts of the poem comment on each other silently, without overt links, each element being offered as a "luminous detail"

or scientific specimen objectively presented. Enclosed within this aggres-
sively experimental structure, however, is regret for the loss of traditions
centered on ritual. The text laments that "we have the press for wafer, /
Franchise for circumcision," in a direct allusion to superseded ceremonies.

John Espey and others have observed that there is a strong sexual under-
current in the sequence, ambiguously suggested by such images as Mauberley's
"tool / The engraver's" and his "new found orchid" and more directly by the
reference to Milesian tales and the sexual passivity of the women. Akiko
Miyake's study of the symbols Pound borrowed from the Eleusinian tradition
discloses that this sexual imagery supports a submerged theme, the importance
of fertility rituals. The "Envoi" that closes the first section idealizes a lover, an
expressive mode that Gabriele Rossetti and Pound took to be a disguised form
of Eleusinian worship. The regret for the disappearance of "Dionysus / Phallic
and ambrosial" links sexuality and divine power, as Pound thought the Eleusinian ritual did. Thus, the Eleusinian rite's sacred marriage enters the poem as
a theme contrasting with the sterility of the modern world.

When it is approached in this way, *Mauberley* may be seen as a demand
for the preservation of ritual and its values expressed in experimental styles.
But Pound's experimental virtuosity dominates the case for ritual, nearly
effacing it. The urban tone and milieu of the poem do not sort well with the
agricultural concerns of the ritual element. We do not see the effect of one
mode undermining the other, which Timothy J. Reiss has noted in some
works, but rather feel a certain incongruity between the assertive modernism
of its form and the atavism of its ritual subtext.

Pound's assimilation of so many varied and inconsistent theories in his
pre-*Cantos* years was to determine the disjointed and eclectic nature of his
long poem. Its discordancies are rooted in his efforts to combine the scientific
empiricism exemplified by the unwavering attention to physical objects
counseled by the naturalist, Louis Agassiz, with the mystical sensitivity to
invisible forces described by Yeats and Upward that occupy much of his early
poetry and criticism. Such conflicting pairs as Swinburne and Ford Madox
Ford, Maxim and Confucius, electromagnetism and Eleusis poured into his
vigorously receptive mind and into his theories of poetry. This early work
displays his characteristic tendency to challenge conventional ideas of contradiction for the sake of perceiving some larger unity or fundamental
resemblance that others had missed. His commitment both to ritual and to
experiment is a prominent element of that pattern. In his early poems they
are already engaged in an uneasy relationship, one that lasted for nearly sixty
years of the poet's productive life and that had much to do with shaping both
the successes and the failures of the *Cantos*.

7

The Cantos

Language, colour, form, and religious and civil
habits of action are all the instruments and materials of
poetry.
                                  —Shelley, *A Defence of Poetry*

L'acqua ch'io prendo già mai non si corse.
[The water I take was never before traversed.]
                                  —Dante, *Paradiso*, Canto 2

Pound intended the *Cantos* to be a spiritual epic embracing a unified world
view. In Canto 116, one of the last to be written, he refers to his aspiration
in undertaking his "poem of some length":

To make Cosmos—
To achieve the possible—[1]

Ritual and experiment are among the disparate elements he brought together
in his effort to create a harmonious vision that would override the dichotomies in the field of modern thought, where he saw "Man drunk with god,
man inebriated with infinity, on the one hand, and man with a millimetric
measure and microscope on the other."[2] Speaking to an interviewer after
more than forty years of work on *The Cantos*, a poem that, as he said, excluded
nothing simply because it didn't fit, Pound explained the difficulty of
completing it by saying: "The modern mind contains heteroclite elements.
The past epos has succeeded when all or a great many of the answers were
assumed. . . . The attempt in an experimental age is therefore rash."[3]

Ritual has a prominent position in this experimental effort. Pound brings
together the ceremonies of widely scattered cultures, identifying their common
origins in the worship of nature and their common aim as a utopian deliverance.

In doing this, he employs the poetic method he called "subject-rhyme," the juxtaposition of materials with a common motif or form. Taking advantage of the fact that the rites of different cultures often resemble each other, Pound uses subject-rhyme to link the Eleusinian mysteries and their offshoot, Provençal poetry, with Renaissance despots, Chinese emperors, American founding fathers and the Na-khi people of Tibet. The method is not only a basic structural element of the poem but also Pound's way of introducing order and intelligibility into the vast panorama it surveyed.[4] Pound considered ritual to be a more fundamental basis of moral value than the various religions. As Jean-Michel Rabaté has said, Pound believed that "Rites . . . fulfill a more essential role than religions, because they effect the connection, the *re-ligere*, the harmonisation of the human world with the divine world."[5]

But if he was to succeed in modernizing the ritual consciousness, Pound needed resources other than those of occultism. In an effort to enable ancient ritualistic intuitions to coexist with modern skepticism and indeterminacy, he turned to the principles of the "experimental generation," as he calls it, whose literary revolution he had led between 1910 and 1930. This was the generation of T. S. Eliot, H. D., James Joyce, Wyndham Lewis, and William Carlos Williams. "Experiment," Pound wrote, "aims at writing that will have a relation to the present analogous to the relation which past masterwork had to the life of its time."[6]

Through this convergence of religious and quasi-scientific modes of expression, Pound hoped to create a poetic genre capable of encompassing the apparent contradictions of the modern cultural scene. What was needed was not an atavistic return to a ritualistic past but a renewal that would match the advances of modern thought. Ritual and myth form a vital core of the *Cantos* and bind some of its great patterns together. But they are only parts of a vast poetic design that employs personal observations, historical summaries, economic arguments, documentary insertions, new verse forms, and graphic effects to create relationships between traditional religious concepts and contemporary secular themes.

Many critics believe that the *Cantos* follows the Eleusinian pattern of descent, lustration, and salvation and that Pound's use of such mythical visits to the underworld as those of Odysseus, Aeneas, and Dante has as its prototype the descent of Persephone dramatized in the Eleusinian rite. Some have maintained that Eleusis is an essential part, if not the root, of the world view that forms the background of the *Cantos*. Demetres P. Tryphonopoulos has treated the poem as a "palingenetic" initiation ritual following the form of the Eleusinian ceremony, which was to be the epic of "a New Age prophesied by occultists at the turn of the century."[7]

Daniel D. Pearlman describes Odysseus's offer of blood to the shade of Tiresias in Canto 1 as an act of renewal that circumvents the passage of time. It is also, of course, a sacrificial ritual. Leon Surette observes that by beginning the *Cantos* with this scene, Pound had decided on "the adoption of the Eleusinian ritual of spiritual death and rebirth in the form of a *journey* to the Underworld." Odysseus's actions here "parallel the central ritual acts of the hierophant at Eleusis." Pound's "synoptic Eleusis," that is to say, his version of the rite, says Surette, is "the imaginative heart of the poem . . . the metaphorical structure which has prevented it from flying apart."[8]

Akiko Miyake's *Ezra Pound and the Mysteries of Love* is essentially a detailed elaboration of this idea; it sets out to show that the ritual pattern unifies the poem as it is replicated in such individual episodes as the story of Sigismondo Malatesta and the deeds of Chinese emperors. "Seeing the whole *Cantos* as one enormous ideogram," she says, "can help us recognize it as a critical study of history pervaded by Eleusinian values."[9] Eleusinian images of light and darkness and the figure of the initiate who endures both in order to achieve a final deliverance appear frequently in the *Cantos*.

While Pound had an accurate notion of the general function of the Eleusinian mysteries, he also accepted as fact many of the speculations about them that had appeared over the centuries, adding to them some of his own. The *Cantos* often seems to refer to the different and less secret ceremonies of the Alexandrian Eleusis, which are confused with the original ones in Greece, and to Orphic, Dionysiac, or other "mysteries" of the pagan world. Consequently, the facts known about the Eleusinian rite itself are far less relevant to his poem than the long tradition of bemused guesswork and speculation with which Pound was familiar.

It seems clear that a ritual had long been established at Eleusis, perhaps since the fifteenth century B.C., when the "Hymn to Demeter," which is dated between 650 and 550 B.C., was written to provide a rationale for the already ancient ceremony with its myth of Demeter and Persephone. The most recent authorities agree that the central portion of what became an elaborate eight-day ceremony was an agricultural rite in which the descent and return of Persephone was enacted as a parallel to the cycle of the seasons and a way of insuring the growth of the crops. Its supreme spiritual importance arose from the belief that the agricultural wealth it celebrated was the basis of civilization and from the promise made to its initiates that they would share the immortality of nature in a blissful Elysium.[10]

The participants were sworn to secrecy, and this injunction was so effective that most of the crucial facts about the Greater Mysteries, the climactic part of the rite, are still unknown. George E. Mylonas, the author of the most authoritative study of the Eleusinian rites, has said about them: "For years, since my early youth, I have tried to find out what the facts were. . . . A thick, impenetrable veil indeed still covers securely the rites of Demeter and protects them from the curious eyes of modern students . . . the ancient world has kept its secret well and the Mysteries of Eleusis remain unrevealed."[11]

It is known, however, that the ceremony honored Persephone and Demeter, the goddesses of seasonal renewal and grain, respectively. It is generally believed that at the climax of the celebration a secret and intensely moving drama took place, probably an enactment of Persephone's descent to the underworld and her resurrection. It seems to have featured a period of darkness spent in fear, grief, and anguish followed by a blaze of light and feelings of joy and ecstasy as the goddess reappeared, conferring some form of spiritual salvation. An important element of the ceremony was the display of "sacred objects" brought to the temple in special containers, but in spite of many fanciful speculations and dubious reports, these objects have never been positively identified. As we have seen, the meanings of rituals are not generally understood, and according to Mylonas, this is also true of the Eleusinian rite. At the end of his book-length study he admits that, while many of its details have been recovered, its ultimate meaning remains unknown.

Pound regarded the Eleusinian mystery as a vital part of the Western tradition that had been lost to the modern mind. Asking what has "gone out" of modern English verse, he suggests that it is the meaning of the ancient rite and that only a revolutionary reversion to the "wilds" of unconventional thinking can restore it: "The truth having been Eleusis? and a modern Eleusis being possible in the wilds of a man's mind only?" Poetry parallels the ritual because it can penetrate spiritual regions in a way which prose cannot. Beyond the limits of prose "are the mysteries. Eleusis. Things not to be spoken of save in secret."[12]

Pound's original source of information (and misinformation) about the influence of Eleusis, as Akiko Miyake has convincingly argued, was probably Gabriele Rossetti's *Il Mistero dell'Amor platonico*, but he knew other sources and formed his own ideas about it. He accepted the persistent tradition that the ritual included a sexual act which was regarded as a sacred counterpart of nature's fertility and he identified Kore or Persephone with the Egyptian Isis as an all-embracing nature deity. His "Terra Italica" quotes an Italian pamphlet that praises paganism for accepting "sexual phenomena" as an expression of divine vitality and laments the loss of this wisdom, "the light of Eleusis." (Mylonas, however, finds that there is no evidence for a sacred marriage and dismisses the idea that it could have formed part of the ceremony.)[13]

The persistent rumor that the ritual included sexual material also pointed to its climactic display, called the *epopteia*, which was said to arouse overwhelming emotions in the initiates. It seems clear that the *epopteia*, whatever it may have been, symbolized renewal of life, that the initiates who witnessed it were promised immortality and good fortune, and that it convinced them they had been lifted to a new level of spiritual awareness. It is sometimes reported to be the birth of a divine child, sometimes the display of "sacred objects" such as a phallus or a replication of the female pudenda, a millstone symbolizing grain, sacred cakes, sometimes the reappearance of Persephone. Pound once observed that "for certain people, the *pecten cteis* is the gate of wisdom." In using this term, he was accepting as factual the totally unsubstantiated speculation that one of the sacred objects was a replica of the female genitalia.[14]

I believe it can be shown that all of Pound's scattered ideas about culture, economics, history, social order, religion, and the function of poetry, as well as his thematic images and his enthusiasm for Fascism, can be traced to his ideas about the Eleusinian mystery and the rites he associated with it. Eleusis was originally a nature ceremony meant to promote the fertility of the soil; Pound translated this concept into mystic and religious terms. He accepted the parallel between the ritual's descent and renewal with spiritual regeneration, and he identified the goddesses of the rite with Aphrodite, Isis, and even Circe. Pound, to whom gods were eternal states of mind, could easily believe that these figures, secularized and idealized, became the beloved woman of chivalric and troubadour tradition. Eleusis, with its dramatic climax promising its initiates that they would share the immortality of the gods, is the prototype of the metamorphosis in which mortals "bust thru from the quotidien into 'divine or permanent world.' Gods, etc."[15]

Pound's unsystematic linking of the ceremonies of many cultures takes the Eleusinian mysteries as their archetype. The immortality promised by the ritual and its imagery of light as a symbol of knowledge and reason are echoed, Pound thought, in Egyptian, Chinese, and Christian religions. The *Cantos* reflects his belief that Eleusinian elements persisted in the early years of the Christian church and that traces of the worship reappeared in the *Divine Comedy*, among the Albigensians, and in the culture of the troubadours.

The phrase "KUNG and ELEUSIS" from Canto 52 announces a parallel in Confucian and Greek ceremonies that is developed in the following cantos. The odes of the *Shih-Ching* (Classic Anthology) collected by Confucius and

translated by Pound include songs that were apparently sung in temple ceremonies meant to encourage the fertility of the soil; Pound's versions suggest
their affinity with the Greek rite. Echoes and excerpts from his translations of
the odes are scattered through the later cantos and Kuanon, the Chinese
goddess of mercy, enters his pantheon as a counterpart of Isis, goddess of
nature. Figures from Egyptian history projecting abundance and compassion
appear in Canto 93; Pound connects one of them, Antef, with the grain rite of
Eleusis through the bread he distributed. In the later cantos, a ceremony of the
Na-khi people of southern Tibet is seen as a version of Eleusis because it is also
directed at encouraging crops.

Pound even associated the local Rapallo custom of floating lights on the
sea, a Christian celebration of the Madonna, with the fertility encouraged
by the pagan rites:

> Wheat shoots rise new by the altar,
>   flower from the swift seed.
>   (Canto 47)

The line "Begin thy plowing" in Canto 47 (in a passage paraphrased from
Hesiod's *Works and Days*), which is repeated or echoed three times, acquires
powerful ritual significance when we realize that the command has striking
parallels in Eleusinian and Chinese rites. The Eleusis ritual included plowing
at the sites where agriculture was thought to have begun, and ceremonial
plowing was also one of the obligations of the Chinese emperor. When one
emperor failed to perform it, famine followed. Canto 86 briefly recalls this
sacred act when it praises the reforming Emperor Joseph II of Austria by
saying simply that he "ploughed his furrow." Pound's repetitions insistently
point to the common origin of these rites in agriculture and attribute a
spiritual as well as a practical force to them.[16]

The light of the Eleusinian *epopteia* is one of a vast family of light symbols
that appears throughout the *Cantos*. With Pound, as with traditional symbolism, Milton's "Bright essence of bright effluence increate" is primarily the
visible representative of the ineffable and the divine and secondarily the
image of true knowledge and insight. It is never far from Pound's allusions to
ritual, where it is the mystical embodiment of the sacred, "the first light,
before ever dew was fallen" or "The light now, not of the sun." Light is treated
as a central icon in the many rituals and religions Pound embraces in the
Cantos, whether it is that of a sacrificial fire, the Chinese spirit called Lord of
the Fire, the light of Dante's *Paradiso*, the "sun's silk" of the *hsien* ideogram in
Canto 74, the "sunt lumina" of Erigena, the sun boat of Egyptian religion, or

the product of the sacred marriage ("Sacrum, sacrum in coitu inluminatio"). The ritual passage of Canto 39 climaxes its account of the conception of a god as the "bride" of the rite declares:

> Beaten from flesh into light
> Hath swallowed the fire- ball. . . .
> I have eaten the flame.

The light symbolism takes in the moon of Diana, the sun of Helios, and the sun worship of the Egyptians. The sacred marriage is sometimes regarded as a union of the sun and the moon, and one of Pound's favorite Chinese ideograms, *ming*, meaning "brightness," combines the radicals for the two. Pound noted that the garments of the women belonging to the Na-khi tribe, as seen in one of Joseph Rock's photographs, combined designs representing suns and moons, as the *ming* ideogram does.

When permanence is added to the other virtues of light, it becomes a solid brightness, the crystal, "the great acorn of light." Pound's associations appear in his prayer in the "Addendum for C":

> pure Light, we beseech thee
> Crystal, we beseech thee
> Clarity, we beseech thee. . . .

Uncorrupted and incorruptible, a hard form that receives and concentrates light, the crystal appears from time to time as a symbol of spiritual perfection. The names of some meritorious figures in Canto 91 are followed by "The GREAT CRYSTAL," and the image recurs in Canto 116, one of the last fragments of the poem.

"Eleusis," wrote Pound, "did not distort truth. . . . Only in the high air and the great clarity can there be a just estimation of values. . . . I assert that the Gods exist."[17] The truths ritual projects from its "high air" are universal ones: harmony with nature insuring the fertility of the land, human love, and the need for worship and respect for the divine if the order of the state is to be maintained. The *Cantos* extends this belief into the secular and historical sphere. Pound's historical heroes are those who recognize that ritual binds mankind and nature together and observe the rituals themselves. He condemns usury and economic systems based on it because the wealth they produce is spurious and not generated by the fertility celebrated in ritual. In Canto 52, says Rabaté, "Pound transforms his economic proselytism into a peaceful evocation of ritual. . . . one must respect the rhythms of Nature which alone creates riches." Anthony

Woodward has pointed out that Pound regarded usury as a "desecration" of sacred natural resources. In an illuminating insight, he says, "All the gritty economics that occur in *The Cantos* as well as their savage exemplification of economic corruption, look different when seen in the light of Pound's religious awe at the generative energies of the cosmos."[18] Pound's beliefs are supported by the general sense of a usable past, a tradition worth commemorating and renewing through ritual. And presiding over them is the ecstatic experience that ritual offers, a mystic sense of identification with the divine and the intuitive possession of transcendental truth.

While he was imprisoned in the United States Army's prison camp near Pisa, the Disciplinary Training Center known as the D. T. C., Pound wrote defiantly, "I surrender neither the empire nor the temples / plural." His belief in the pagan multiplicity of gods implied the need for sites dedicated to worshipping them. In his later years he said he would like to build a marble temple with columns near the castle of Brunnenburg where he was living, a plan that echoes Yeats's plan for Lough Key.[19] "Aram vult nemus"—"the grove desires an altar"—a theme that becomes prominent in the later cantos, appears earlier in Cantos 8 to 11, with their references to the church that Sigismundo Malatesta built or remodeled.

Pound considered the Tempio Malatestiana, as it is called (officially, however, the church of San Francesco) to be a forceful expression of two Eleusinian themes. He believed that its numerous sculptures and reliefs depicting gods and mythical figures constituted a revival of pagan worship and a challenge to prevailing religious beliefs. This idea was supported by the fact that the remains of Gemisthus Plethon, a defender of the pagan pantheon, were buried in the Tempio. But Pound also regarded the Tempio as a monument to Isotta degli Atti, Sigismundo's third wife, whose tomb is in one of its chapels. He believed that Sigismundo's extravagant love for her, celebrated by contemporary poets and recorded by the inscription on her tomb, continued the tradition of idealizing love that Pound identified with the worship of Persephone and Demeter and the poetry of the troubadours. Lawrence S. Rainey has argued that Pound interpreted the Tempio as an expression of secular love because he wished to replace the ritual of the past of Canto 1 with "another ritual" expressive of a "new paganism that would celebrate the vital powers of human sexuality and creativity."[20] These associations reverberate behind the simple "He, Sigismundo, *templum aedificavit*" of Canto 8 and the correspondence with builders and other allusions to the church in the following Malatesta Cantos.

Many of the repeated themes and images of the *Cantos*, including references to nature, grain, agriculture, love, economic justice, social order, rebirth, underworlds, and paradise, bear a ritualistic, and perhaps a specifically Eleusinian, subtext. In this way, ritual appears to be a center from which the various elements of Pound's world view radiate, forming an intelligible unity of impressive scope. His irrational certainties about politics and economics, such as his hatred of unearned interest (which he called "usura") and his faith in totalitarianism, have the covert metaphysical foundation of the sacred. For it must be added that while ritual is the center, it is, as we have seen, a dark center whose meaning is concealed, originating, as Eliot supposed, before the concept of meaning itself. Pound felt that the secrets of ritual should remain inviolate. "Eleusis. Things not to be spoken save in secret. The mysteries self-defended, the mysteries that cannot be revealed. Fools can only profane them."[21]

As we have seen, Pound's early essays recommend scientific experiment as a model for revolutionizing literature. This spirit moves through canto after canto, constantly differentiating them through new techniques. Pound brought to his major poem all of the innovations in poetic style he had pioneered in his Imagist and Vorticist doctrines and in *Mauberley*. But he also sought and transcended new horizons of expression, in keeping with his view that "without constant experiment literature dies." There is hardly a passage in the *Cantos* that does not make use of the *Mauberley* innovations, or of parody, paraphrase, metrical invention, asyntactic fragmentation, radical shifts of tone, foreign languages, and other radical departures from conventional poetic practice. In addition, the poem invents new ways of transcending its own language, as it introduces Chinese ideograms, pictographs, fragmentary quotations, and the musical score of Canto 75. There is a new dimension of experimentalism in the multivalence of these devices. Many of them force us to read at a new depth, making associations with other parts of the *Cantos,* exploring contexts and historical connections, and perceiving parallels and analogies only faintly suggested by Pound's elliptical presentation. A single effect may radiate so many multiple associations that the reader can never be sure that he or she has exhausted them; as a result, the poem as a whole remains open and indeterminate. The *Cantos,* in short, is experimental through and through, a prototype of modern experimentalism, advanced enough to satisfy at least some of the critical standards of the poststructuralist era. "Essentially," wrote M. L. Rosenthal in 1978, "most experimental method that interests us today . . . is fully anticipated in *The Cantos.*"[22] Ritual comes and goes, making frequent appearances, but the spirit of experiment is present in every line.

Christine Froula's study of the drafts of Canto 4 shows how Pound vigorously manipulated his materials during his revisions in order to try out his effects, shifting, omitting, combining, and reducing narrative insertions to unintelligible fragments of a word or phrase. "Pound's method of composition," she observes, " . . . was highly experimental." This experimentalism survives throughout the *Cantos*; there is no sense of finish or inevitable rightness of form; passages can easily be transposed without loss. The final *Cantos*, in fact, still has the aspect of a draft, an experimental stage of a text capable of further development.[23]

While there is not much overt science in the *Cantos*, surface indications of Pound's consciousness of science appear in his sense of fact, his poetic emphasis on the concrete, and his use of historical documentation. Froula points out that Pound did not employ his poetic imagination irresponsibly. When he dealt with history, "his vision always had to be tested in the world," a motive corresponding to scientific empiricism.[24] But there are more specific parallels: the consciousness behind the decentered, ambivalent, tonally inconsistent and ragged text of the *Cantos* is somehow linked with indeterminacy and the insight that the senses do not give an accurate report of physical reality.

A rationale for the apparently formless structure of the poem is suggested by a comment on the new physics from one of Alfred North Whitehead's 1925 Lowell lectures, delivered when Pound was putting together the disjointed materials of his first thirty cantos: "An event has to do with all that there is, and in particular with all other events. This interfusion of events is effected by the aspects of those eternal objects, such as colours, sounds, scents, geometrical characters, which are required for nature and are not emergent from it."[25]

Such "interfusions" are essential to the associative poetic of the *Cantos*. As Hugh Kenner was the first to observe, its structure, an accumulation of apparently unrelated units, has a scientific analogy in the concept of field theory, the idea that space is filled with energies inaccessible to the senses that enable physical particles to interact with each other indirectly.[26] In *The Cosmic Web*, N. Katherine Hayles explains that "a field view of reality pictures objects, events and observer as belonging inextricably to the same field; the disposition of each, in this view, is influenced—sometimes dramatically, sometimes subtly, but in every instance by the disposition of others." To clarify this, Hayles uses the metaphor of the kaleidoscope, an image applied directly to the *Cantos* by H. D., who wrote, after reading Canto 90 aloud, "I have been seeing or trying to see a whirling kaleidoscope." Hayles observes that the force-field view of reality is reflected in literary works where "the *self-referentiality* of language" appears. "Because everything, in the field view, is connected to everything else by means of the mediating field, the autonomy assigned to individual events by language is illusory. When the field is seen to be inseparable from language . . . every statement potentially refers to every other statement, including itself."[27]

Ian F. A. Bell has noted that Pound used this modern view of the cosmos to justify ancient philosophy; he found "ancient cosmology, in the form of pre-Socratic atomism, elucidated and made new by nineteenth-century field theory physics."[28] This premise, and many of its implications, are applicable to the apparently arbitrary juxtapositions of the *Cantos*, which can be seen as a reflection of the interdependence of matter envisioned by the science of Pound's time.

While Pound's materials may seem unrelated to each other, they interact when they can be seen as parts of a subtext, a "Great Bass" that corresponds to the forces enabling physical particles to influence each other. The occult or spiritual forces released by such practices as ritual corresponded, in Pound's thinking, to the invisible rays, waves, and energies modern science was discovering. As Ian F. A. Bell has put it, "energy in all its forms retained mystical properties for Pound; although quantifiable by science, it retained the signature of the 'gods,' and the energy of electrical waves was to be seen not as a displacement of that mysticism but as a union of shared perceptions."[29] Ordinary language, of course, distinguishes the two concepts of electricity and mysticism and separates the events and objects of the physical world from each other by giving them different names. Exploiting the particularizing power of language while using it also to convey the sense that all things are united by forces unavailable to direct perception was both a motivation of the *Cantos'* experimentalism and one of its problems.

Pound's "field" includes myth, history, old documents, memories, and his experiences of World War II. His sense of their interdependence, and of the reappearance of eternal truths in the form of passing events, transforms linear time into timelessness, creating a juncture between empiric experience and mysticism. As Anthony Woodward writes, the *Cantos* employs the memories of Pound's life to "attain in imagination a timeless condition akin to the recovery of sacred origins in traditional societies," an observation that brings us to Pound's effort to merge the novel insights given by experience or experiment with the timeless ones of ritual.[30]

Ritual emerges in the prevailingly experimental fabric of the *Cantos* with a variety of effects. Some passages blend the two commitments so thoroughly that it is hard to tell whether they are motivated by liturgical or experimental feelings. Passages of this kind seem to suggest that poetry is capable of formulating a union between mystical and rational views of reality. More often, however, ritual feeling and experimental techniques fail to merge fully, and the text seems to vibrate between two poles with an effect not of reconciliation but of tension.

Throughout the fifty-one cantos published between 1930 and 1937 as *A Draft of XXX Cantos, Eleven New Cantos,* and *The Fifth Decad of Cantos,* Pound's experimental poetics converge with three chief ritual themes: first, Odysseus's encounter with Circe and his descent to the underworld retold, in reverse chronological order, as a ritual with Eleusinian motifs; second, marriage or sexual union and its natural extensions into fertility and the idealization of women; and third, the paradisal state of transcendence.

The Homeric thread begins in Canto 1, where ritual and experiment are so successfully merged with each other that their union seems to be a triumphant production in a new genre. Pound regarded the *nékuia,* the part of Book 11 of the *Odyssey* which narrates Odysseus's descent to the underworld, as the oldest part of the Homeric epic. He put his translation of it at the opening of the *Cantos* because he wanted to begin his own poem by going back to origins. Guy Davenport has linked Canto 1 to the similar intent in David Jones's *Anathemata* by saying that the action of the canto takes place in the era of prehistory that Jones calls "rite and foretime."[31] Its innovation is, of course, the narration of the archetypal blood-sacrifice, with its invocation of Eleusinian deities in a poetic style that is completely foreign to Homer's epic but startlingly appropriate to its subject. While there is nothing overtly scientific about the experimentalism of the canto, the emulation of Old English poetry is derived from a philological tradition that applies scientific method to the study of language.

The use of a Latin translation to achieve a synthesis of the worlds of *Beowulf* and *The Seafarer* with that of Odysseus convincingly demonstrates the continuity of cultural transmission. With "Lie quiet Divus," Pound addresses the ghost of the Latin translator, a parallel to Odysseus's conversations with the spirits of the underworld, suggesting that his own translation is a ritual act of renewal. But the words about Divus's volume "In officina Wecheli, 1538, out of Homer" (in Wecheli's workshop) also rupture the ritual surface of the text in order to convey bibliographical information. It is a scrap of Reiss's "analytico-referential" discourse, contrasting with the "patterning" language of the narrative.

The enigmatic "So that:" at the end of the canto is borrowed from Browning's *Sordello,* where it signals a paradoxical hiatus. It can be taken to say that the poem which follows, in fact, the phenomenon of poetry itself, owes its existence to the ritual consciousness embodied in Odysseus's sacrifice. More specifically, the ceremony has shown its power both to revive the dead and to gain insight into the future, and Pound may well be claiming here that it enables him to accomplish something similar in the body of his poem.

But there is another link between the first two cantos that involves ritual. Though he is not mentioned, Tiresias is a background figure in Canto 2, for in the section of the *Metamorphoses* narrating the voyage of Dionysus, which is Pound's main source (and which he is, in effect, translating), Tiresias warns Pentheus that he must not continue in his contempt for the rites of Dionysus. Pentheus fails to heed these warnings and is torn to pieces as a consequence. In this way, both cantos can be seen as emphasizing the importance of the required rituals, a point made openly at the end of Ovid's tale which Pound leaves to inference.

Unless we accept the assumption that *all* the main personages and events of the cantos have parallels to the *Odyssey*, we can say that except for a brief passage in Canto 17, the Odyssean theme in its ritual form does not reappear until Canto 39. This canto opens with Odysseus's encounter with Circe, which can be seen as echoing, on a different level, the love poem of Canto 36, the translation of Cavalcanti's canzone. The earthly sexual acts in the first part of Canto 39 are continued and transformed into a sacred event that culminates in the ecstatic "Fac deum! Est factus." ("Make the god! He is made.") The ritual is not described, but it is undoubtedly a fertility rite in which sexual congress results in the conception of a god.

The extremely eclectic range of allusions and quotations in Canto 39 (from the *Odyssey* to the Nicene Creed) seems to center on the universality of nature worship. Circe's house offers physical satisfactions that parallel, on a lower plane, the transcendence that ritual achieves. Secular copulation and sacred marriage are linked as Circe tells Odysseus that he must go to the realm of Persephone and as the scenes of license at her house melt into a celebration of springtime growth generated, as the fragmentary Eleusinian ritual asserts, by the sympathetic magic of the sacred marriage. These characteristically clipped lines ("Thus made the spring, / Can see but their eyes in the dark") rise to a climax as they juxtapose the appearance of foliage with the transcendental light of Eleusis and the conception of a divine child. In the last lines of the canto, which seem to continue Persephone's acceptance of Odysseus in Canto 17—"For this hour, brother of Circe,"—the goddess is apparently declaring that Circe's sensual relation with Odysseus prepares her union with the divine fire:

> A girl's arms have nested the fire,
> Not I but the handmaid kindled,
>> Cantat sic nupta,
> I have eaten the flame.
>> (Canto 39)

The *Odyssey* narrative reappears in Canto 47, which repeats Circe's command to Odysseus; this time she tells him that he must seek "knowledge" in the ritual of the underworld. The chord of death is repeated ritualistically throughout the Canto as "*Kai* MOIRAI' ADONIN," the lament of Aphrodite blaming the fates for the death of her beloved Adonis, is repeatedly echoed, and we are reminded of our mortality—"So light is thy weight on Tellus." But numerous images of regeneration counterpoint this theme, as in "Adonis falleth. / Fruit cometh after," culminating in the ritual at the end of the Canto ("new shoots are brought to the altar"), which aligns the renewal of earth's fertility with the spiritual renewal to be found in the sacred marriage. Demetres P. Tryphonopoulos notes Pound's eclectism by observing that he "creates a composite rite which is, in fact, his own version of ancient cults. The various strands are brought together by the idea of the *hieros gamos* (sacred marriage)."[32] Daniel D. Pearlman, noting that Circe's command to Odysseus opens the canto, implies that his journey to the underworld is a fertility rite: "Odysseus is really searching for the secret of the rebirth of vegetation—and ultimately for the secret of cultural rebirth."[33]

Canto 47 is not only a ritual, however. Its liturgical elements are juxtaposed with the farming precepts of Hesiod and Pound's personal observations at Rapallo beginning "Here the mules are gabled with slate on the hill road." Similarly, Canto 49, the Seven Lakes canto, ends by repeating the line about Adonis's magical power over wild beasts just after a song about farming that recalls the passage from Hesiod, coupling it with "the dimension of stillness." In this way, Pound brings the practical cultivation of the land into relation with its metaphysical basis in ritual.

A passage that John Espey has termed "the very bedrock of the *Cantos*" incorporates a ritual cry in identifying human coition with the fertility of the earth.

> The light has entered the cave. Io! Io!
> The light has gone down into the cave,
> Splendour on splendour!
> By prong have I entered these hills:
> That the grass grow from my body. . . .
>   (Canto 47)

The line that concludes this passage, "By this door have I entered the hill," seems to mean that the speaker (usually taken to be Odysseus) has gained unity with nature, and perhaps power over it, by entering the *mons Veneris* in the ritual of the sacred marriage. In the Hesiod passage that is one of Pound's sources, the work day is "between a door and a door." These doors are ceremonies of renewal, and in the last lines of the canto fragmentary sentences referring to the ritual celebration of spring are intertwined, like ornamental wreaths, with the words of Aphrodite's lament.[34]

Pound's belief that the rites of Eleusis included a sacred marriage which celebrated sexual union as a path to transcendence emerges early in the *Cantos*. The marriage theme perhaps begins with "Venerandam" near the end of Canto 1, which comes from the Homeric hymn urging the worship of Aphrodite. It appears in a definite, if enigmatic, form in the second line of Canto 4, with the interjection "Aurunculeia!" the name of the bride in an epithalamion by Catullus, Carmen 61, which is echoed again later in the canto by the lines beginning "Hymenaeus Io," and by a brief glimpse of Catullus's marriage ceremony in Canto 5. Images supporting the theme of love and marriage, the black cock and the sea foam associated with the birth of Aphrodite, appear in the mythic landscape that follows the opening invocations of Canto 4. The pines taken to symbolize an old Japanese couple, the stories of Polhonac and Gyges, and the divine union of Danaë and Zeus all touch, in one way or another, on marriage.

But the lines "Vidal, or Ecbatan, upon the gilded tower in Ecbatan / Lay the god's bride, lay ever, waiting the golden rain" joins this theme with another ritual theme that has been running below the surface of Canto 4. Pound presents his paradisal city as the scene of the divine marriage, linking it with the religion of love through the name of one of the three men (two of them troubadours) who died for love. The idea of ritual sacrifice is not far distant here, and the elements of cannibalism in the Cabestan story and violent death in the Actaeon and Vidal stories support it. "Vidal, or Ecbatan": ritual sacrifice and sexual union with the divine are alternative concepts.

The concluding passage of Canto 4 offers a contrast between the valid and invalid worship of female figures. First the Danaë image, "the god's bride," is repeated, followed by a sharply contrasting allusion to a modern ceremony on the bank of the Garonne honoring the Virgin which Pound regarded as barbaric. This is juxtaposed with a swift move to another river, the Adige, on whose bank, in Verona, is a painting showing the Madonna among flowers, thereby suggesting her fertility. (Pound mistakenly thought Cavalcanti had referred to it in one of his sonnets.) "The Centaur's heel plants in the earth loam" seems to assert, obliquely enough, that fertile soil is productively seeded by pagan myth. The canto's last lines, "And we sit here . . . / there in the arena" may well be a fragmentary continuation of the love theme. It is a late addition and is said to refer to one of Pound's lovers, Bride Scratton, who was in Verona with him, where the two no doubt visited the remains of the Roman amphitheater.[35]

The image of the union of the god and mortal maiden at Ecbatan is accompanied, at the beginning of Canto 5, by a glimpse of the streets surrounding it and the country to the north occupied with secular concerns. But this is soon followed by divine fire accompanying a ritual of salvation—"the souls ascending"—and a wavering vision that becomes fixed as sharp details of Aurunculeia's wedding are seen. In Catullus's epithalamion, the cry "Da nuces" refers to the part of the Roman wedding ceremony in which the groom signifies his rejection of childish play by throwing walnuts to younger boys. This ritual of love is followed by love without ritual as Pound, working with Richard Aldington's translation, quotes Sappho's laments for an unfaithful lover. The barrenness of love leads to barrenness in nature, " . . . the vinestocks lie untended, new leaves come to the shoots, / North wind nips on the bough."

Canto 5 then abruptly turns to historical material that abounds in chaotic and violent sexual relations ("The air was full of women"). Most of the tales of treachery and murder center on corruption of the love ideal. This theme even embraces the murder of Alessandro de' Medici, who was lured to his death by an assignation with a woman and stabbed while he lay in bed waiting for her. The menacing "Caina attende," meaning that the first division of Dante's nine circles of Hell awaits the criminals, is from the speech of Francesca da Rimini in Canto 5 of the *Inferno*, who is speaking of the husband who murdered her and her lover, Paolo, an event she sums up as "Amor condusse noi ad una morte" ("Love led us to one death"). Benedetto Varchi, the historian who was Pound's source for most of these stories, expressed his inability to judge them by asking "Se pia? / O empia?"("Was it right? Or wrong?"), and Pound preserves his own indecision by quoting him twice.

The translation of Guido Cavalcanti's "Donna mi prega" in Canto 36 explains the nature of love in terms of the values Pound attributed to Eleusis. He had been occupied with Cavalcanti's poem for many years, had attempted an earlier translation, and had analyzed it in staggering detail. To judge from Pound's comments on it, he considered the canzone to be a perfect blending of ritual and experimental motivations. Akiko Miyake convincingly shows that an aspect of the canzone parallels the Eleusinian rite by seeing in its definition of human love a symbolic union of heaven and earth and "the transcendental with the empirical." The canzone's tone of worship, its acknowledgment of the cosmic power of love and the idea that love is a "counterweight" to death, the imagery of light, and above all, the line "Sacrum, sacrum, inluminatio coitu" reflect Pound's view of the Eleusinian message.[36]

But this strongly ritualistic element did not prevent Pound from noting the heretical tendency of the poem by saying that Cavalcanti "shows leanings toward not only the proof by reason, but toward the proof by experiment."

He took the view that it defined love as an expression of the freedom of personal feeling, a subtle challenge to medieval asceticism and authority. He thought that it reflected a heretical individualism, "dangerous thinking; *natural demonstration* and the proof by experience or (?) experiment" and that it spoke "for experiment . . . against the tyranny of the syllogism."[37]

The theme of heresy Pound emphasized in the canzone is carried into the conclusion of the canto, where Aquinas and Scotus Erigena appear as figures who diverged from received ideas. Finally, independence of mind is embodied in the actions of the warrior-troubadour Sordello, who is presented (mistakenly) as rejecting the rewards offered for his services. In this way, the canto presents the medieval religion of love, springing from the mystical roots of the Eleusinian ritual, as an assertion of personal freedom, a value new to medieval culture. Pound saw in the canzone an anticipation of his own poetic effort—the use of deep-lying atavistic emotions to assert vigorous new possibilities.

Ritual themes not directly connected with the Eleusinian values are treated in experimental fashion in many of the first fifty-one cantos through the appearance of the Olympian gods and the ideal landscapes they inhabit. Demetres P. Tryphonopoulos has shown that Canto 17 follows the structure of an initiatory ritual while withholding exact knowledge of the ceremony, in accordance with the secrecy of "mysteries." Ritual elements are, however, only one component of this canto, for they are interwoven with specific evocations of time and place. It begins with images of fertility, followed by a call to Dionysus or Zagreus, as Pound calls him. Its visions of gods and pastoral landscapes suggest the serenity of a transcendental realm, with their silence and "the light now, not of the sun."[38]

For Pound, however, a god is not a being distinct from humanity but rather "an eternal state of mind." Venice, too, embodied various precious states of mind for Pound, and the worlds of pagan myth and material reality begin to blend and alternate in the imagery of Canto 17 as we have a premonitory glimpse of Venice with "Marble trunks out of stillness." The voyager of the canto first sails from Venice into the realm of myth, the cave of the sea-nymphs called Nerea, and the paradisal landscape where he sees "Zagreus, feeding his panthers," accompanied by other gods. The traveller speaks of Venice as if it were another paradisal vision, and after being privileged to watch what is apparently a ritual dance from a secret hiding place (". . . supine in burrow, half over-arched bramble") and receiving encouragement from Persephone, he sees the Eleusinian light of deliverance, "Splendour, as the splendour of Hermes."

If the canto is taken as a narrative in which, as Tryphonopoulos says, the voyager undergoes conversion, the ritual dance changes his opinion of Venice, and he sees it as a place in which "Time is the evil," a place that destroyed its best citizens. In this view, the city undergoes a form of reverse transubstantiation as it is detached from the pastoral scene, turning from a spiritual world to a material one, from myth to history.

Canto 17 does not end with spiritual illumination but reverts, anticlimactically, to Venice and Sigismundo, matters of history rather than myth. Pound's vision blends the material city with the mythical natural scene, making it a "white forest of marble, bent bough over bough" with "stone trees." This identification may mean that Venice is akin to the pastoral paradise, as the speaker seems to be claiming. The fact that Borso and Carmagnola, historical heroes whom Pound considered to be defenders of Eleusinian values, were sacrificed there enhances its eucharistic role. Having flipped back and forth between the human and the divine, the canto ends with an image of time passing quickly, as experience of the actual world does, "Sunset like the grasshopper flying."

After brief visits to such historical sites as Renaissance Italy and Jefferson's America, Canto 21 embarks on a series of images recalling Italian settings Pound had visited. The sequence moves from dawn to night and then, with "Night of the golden tiger," opens on an obscure ritual scene. It is not a unitary scene, however, but a curious accumulation of fragmentary ritual elements whose purpose is explained by the interpolation "Confusion, source of renewals." The generative potential of ritual is emphasized as the flames of ritual fire are called "gonads in organdy," and a Greek phrase, *gignetei kalon*, announces that a thing of beauty is born. The leaves being swept by the old man resemble the sterile gold Midas created, in the absence of the vitality represented by Pan. Two instances of coupling are mentioned: the loving pines of Ise from Canto 4 and the sympathy of two rivers, the Nile and the Inopos, that were said to rise and fall in concert. A single line joins Apollo and a ritual epithet for the Virgin ("tower of ivory") as both figures are worshipped in rituals quite different from the Eleusinian rite. With the line "The hounds on the green slope by the hill," we glance briefly at the scene of sacrifice and metamorphosis depicted in Canto 4, the punishment of Actaeon. There follows an accumulation of divine presences: Athena holding her owl, the stag Actaeon became after his encounter with Artemis, the leopard associated with Dionysus, and the moon, symbolic of Artemis. Birds hover about a moonlit site, apparently an abandoned altar where the nymphs no longer dance and the sacrifice is no longer celebrated. The Eleusinian ceremony is not current; "Dis caught her up" tells us that Persephone has been carried off to the underworld.

While it is a mistake, as always, to seek a closure of meaning here, Pound seems to be sketching a decline in ritual observance that retraces the pattern seen earlier in the canto, where Jefferson's frugal request for a musical gardener is followed by Medicean profligacy. The closing image, "And the old man went on there / beating his mule with an asphodel," may well be taken as a reflection of indifference to the sacred, for the asphodel is the flower of Elysium.

The decline of ritual is also a theme of Canto 25, where the fussiness of the Venetian officials concerned with repairing the Doges' palace is contrasted with a generous pagan call to love that culminates in a transcendence achieved through ritual. After the Latin reassurances "pone metum" ("set aside fear") and "deus nec laedet amantes" ("nor does the god harm lovers"), we are momentarily plunged into a Dantescan underworld condemned to perdition by hollow religious ideas ("The dead concepts, never the blood rite"). Then we are lifted to a landscape alive with divinities, where wine, fire, and music evoke a ritual atmosphere that frees the imagination to rise to a concept of godhead as an eternal state of mind:

> Phaethusa
> There as she came among them,
> Wine in the smoke-faint throat,
> Fire gleam under smoke of the mountain,
> Even there by meadows of Phlegethon
> And against this the flute: pone metum.
> Fading, that they carried their guts before them,
> And thought then, the deathless,
> Form, forms and renewal, gods held in the air,
> Forms seen, and then clearness,
> Bright void, without image, Napishtim,
> Casting his gods back into the νοῦς.
> . . . and the mind there, before them, moving,
> so that notes needed not move.
>   (Canto 25)

By then reverting to a prosaic account of the painter Titian's negotiations with the Venetian Council about payment for his work, the canto effectively displays the contrast between the liberating effect of religion that ritually celebrates sex and sacrifice and the constrictions of the institutional Christianity that prevailed in sixteenth-century Venice.

While the American cantos (31-34 and 37) are not primarily concerned with religion, they nevertheless find in their heroes, Jefferson and John Adams, such merits as Confucian wisdom, detachment, and respect for nature. They employ the method first used in the Malatesta Cantos of assembling quotations from historical documents. With the picture of the pyramid at Ararat (a notion of Pound's not found in his source, John Quincy Adams's diary), Pound adds visual resources to his linguistic ones. Canto 34 ends with the first example of one of his most radical departures along this line: the inclusion of *hsin*, the Chinese ideogram for "integrity," in his text. This is the first of the many ideograms that appear in the *Cantos*, where they achieve a number of effects. They sometimes quote, and therefore recall, sources in Chinese literature; and they amount to graphic displays, forms that appeal directly to the Western eye as a substantial presence transcending the weak referentiality of alphabetic words. Ernest Fenollosa described Chinese writing as close to nature and thus shared the view of Leibniz and others, a view that Jacques Derrida characterizes as a belief that Chinese is potentially a universal language. With this in mind, we might feel that the ideogram represents the universality Pound sought in ritual and tradition. It has, says Michael André Bernstein, "a privileged, almost sacred value" to Pound and "like a religious icon, can induce calmness and meditation."[39]

Cantos 45 and 51 on usury, a topic carried over from the preceding cantos, are written in an incantatory meter and a pseudo-archaic dialect that inescapably resemble liturgy and endow Pound's condemnation of usury with a quasi-religious conviction. His economic views are linked to his belief in the efficacy of ritual, for his passionate beliefs about usury, Social Credit, and economic justice are based on the insight that wealth is the social form of the natural bounty dependent on ritual. He regarded agricultural production, the fruits of nature, as the ultimate source of wealth in contrast to interest, or "usury," which drains wealth off unproductively and is "CONTRA NATURAM." The Sienese bank of the Monte dei Paschi mentioned in Cantos 41 and 42, whose interest payments are based on grazing lands and "the abundance of nature," is contrasted with usurious institutions whose wealth comes "out of nothing." The attack on usury is an attack on spurious wealth that feeds off the cultivation of the soil celebrated in the union of human and divine powers enacted in the sacred marriage. The argument is driven home with the line "They have brought whores for Eleusis," which parallels the debasement of the economic system with the debasement of the sacred marriage.

Christine Brooke-Rose has observed that these passages are "like exorcisms" and the interjection of "*harpes et luz*" in Canto 45 introduces prayer, another kind of ritual. The phrase is a snatch of François Villon's "Ballade pour prier Nostre Dame," in which an old woman prays to the Virgin to be received in heaven, saying that the painted paradise in the church, with its harps and lutes, gives her joy. By accumulating sacred authority through its form, idiom, and allusions of this kind, the canto makes the point that economic justice depends on a spiritual awareness that only ritual can evoke.

Canto 51 closes out the first large section of the *Cantos* by reviewing some of its main themes in a liturgical rhythm. It begins with a forthright statement that attributes supremacy to "mind" and links it with the light of divinity, intelligence, and deliverance, all the elements of transcendence that are "more than the sun," yet symbolized by it, a light that is both Eleusinian and neo-Platonic. Napoleon's aphorism about mud, the element that basely contrasts with light, leads to a chant denouncing usury as the enemy of the true values embodied in art and aligning it with the debasement of ritual by repeating "Whores for Eleusis."

But the ritual mood is coupled with two sharply contrasting effects. Its rhythm disappears with the directions for making trout lures, an apparent digression into narrowly referential and objective discourse. This illustrates a clarity that contrasts with the imprecision of the work done under "usury" and is linked with the "mind of heaven," for those directions "have the light of the doer" and are godlike in their capacity to achieve definite form. The concluding ideogram, *cheng ming* (meaning "right name"), continues this theme, introduces the Chinese cantos, and is a second bold excursion into the new poetic territory opened by the *hsin* ideogram of Canto 34.

Pound's interest in China began with the poetic and linguistic topics of the Fenollosa papers, but as he pursued the subject, he discovered a civilization whose spiritual life rested on ritual. In China, the emperor was seen as an intermediary between heaven and his people, and the welfare of the state depended on his faithful performance of the enormous body of ritual commanded by ancient tradition.[40] The tradition exhibited astonishing longevity, for while its founding was attributed to the quasi-legendary emperors of the third millenium B.C., it became a part of Confucianism more than two thousand years later, lasting until modern times and the extinction of the imperial rule. While the emperor and the court were primarily responsible for performing the rites, surrogates were often used, and versions of the rites appeared in local ceremonies in connection with such purposes as sacrifice, the reception of visitors, military functions, appointments, and imperial announcements. The extraordinarily detailed rules underwent frequent modification throughout the centuries, and a good part of the state bureaucracy and enormous efforts of scholarship and interpretation were devoted to them.

The philosophic justification for the reverence accorded ritual in China has varied through the centuries, but it may be said to have had two fundamental aspects: it recognized the controlling power of the cosmos, and it promoted ethical values. The underlying concept was that of harmony. Ritual recognized the fact that nature and human society were interdependent, and it was thought that the performance of the ceremonies both promoted this harmony and was a form of participation in it. Prescribed actions were considered a defense against evil passions, and the comportment required for religious observances, each detail of which embodied some such virtue as humility or filial obedience, was also appropriate for daily life. Ritual also supported the authority of the state hierarchy and was thus an alternative to punitive methods of social control.

Séraphin Couvreur, the nineteenth-century French translator of the classic Chinese compilation, *Li Ki* or *Book of Rites*, a collection of sacred texts compiled in about the second century B.C. that was one of Pound's sources, defined the significance of Chinese ritual in this way:

> Le cérémonial résume l'esprit chinois tout entier. . . . Ses affections [de cette nation], si elle en a, sont satisfaites par le cérémonial; ses devoirs, elle les remplit au moyen du cérémonial; la vertu et le vice, elle les reconnaît au cérémonial; les rapports naturels des êtres de la création, elle les rattache essentiellement au cérémonial; en un mot, pour elle le cérémonial c'est l'homme, l'homme moral, l'homme politique, l'homme religieux, dans ses multiples rapports avec la famille, la société, l'état, la morale et la religion! [41]

The *Li Ki* covers both the rules of formal rites and rules about daily life, business, table manners, and the like. The conflation (or what the Western mind would regard as one) is natural, since the word for ritual, *li*, means both "ceremony" and "etiquette."

The long synoptic excursion into the history of China that occupies Cantos 52 to 61 affirms the central place of ritual in Chinese culture. In embracing Confucianism, the ritual-minded Pound willingly accepted such statements of the Master as: "Of all things by which the people live the rites are the greatest" (because they articulate the proper relationships between man and the spirits and among people themselves). The keynote of the Chinese cantos is the coupling "Between KUNG and ELEUSIS," which occurs for the first time in Canto 52 and is repeated, like the sounding of a gong, at the birth of Confucius in Canto 53. Critics differ widely about the meaning of this linkage. According to Daniel D. Pearlman, "Civilizations rise because of Eleusinian energy, but they are maintained in health and stability by Kung, the principle of order." Lillian Feder believes, on the other hand, that Confucianism and the Eleusinian rite are presented as parallel "symbols of productivity." Others, however, see the two as conflicting principles that Pound is trying to unify. Clark Emery has said that the *Cantos* as a whole is pervaded by "tensions" of "the effort to bring together the Eleusinian (or Dionysian) concept of natural fecundity and the Confucian concept of human ordering." Carroll F. Terrell declares that "the ethical system of Kung and the sacred mysteries represented by Eleusis" are the two major elements of the *Cantos*, and that "everything takes place between these poles." William Tay, noting Pound's identification of Confucius with other bearers of enlightenment, feels that in the *Cantos* "the divergent traditions of the Eleusinian energy, the Chinese rites and the Neoplatonic reason are merged and related to each other on the basis of Confucianism."[42]

However, as Akiko Miyake points out, what Confucianism and Eleusis have "between" them is an uncompromising emphasis on fertility ritual.[43] The ancestor worship of the Chinese ceremonials was intended to demonstrate a regard for the departed that would induce them to favor the growth of the crops. In both religions the ritual also had an effect of promoting spiritual regeneration and social harmony. Confucius emphasizes the importance of rituals in the *Analects* (translated by Pound) as an exercise of reverence for ancestors and a force for order and moderation in the state. Responsibility for performing them rested with leaders, especially the emperor, for "When men high up love the rites the people are easily governed."

When a disciple suggested that the sheep sacrificed in a ritual might have been spared, Confucius replied: "You, Ts'ze, love the sheep, I love the rite." The ceremony was of prime importance to Confucius: "Not to know the rites is to be without means to construct."[44] Interestingly, he seems to have realized that the significance of ritual could not be known. When asked for the meaning of the sacrifice, he answered, "I do not know. If one knew enough to tell that, one could govern the empire as easily as seeing the palm of one's hand." (He was more limited in this respect than Padre José Elizondo, who, Pound tells us in Canto 77, "learned what the Mass meant.") James Legge, the great nineteenth-century scholar of the Chinese classics, noting that Confucius's system lacked a metaphysical foundation, thought he was insincere because he accepted the practice of making sacrifices to the dead but did not connect it with any belief. In fact, the sage seems to have regarded the traditional rites as autonomous and nonreferential.

Pound, as we have seen, insisted on the mystery of ritual.[45] This enigmatic passage in Canto 53:

> Taught and the not taught. Kung and Eleusis
> > to catechumen alone.

refers to ritual, for a relevant entry from one of Pound's notebooks contains the words "The secretum . . . (revealed to the catechumen alone)."[46] This suggests quite clearly that the two traditions agree in concealing mysteries that are "not taught" but revealed only to initiates, a clear suggestion, in turn, of their dependence on arcane rituals.

The section of Canto 52 beginning "Know then" is based on the *Li Ki*, which details the innumerable ceremonies and forms of behavior developed in Confucianism, together with explanations of their rationale. Soon after, a passage very loosely based on the French translation of the chapter of the *Li Ki* called "Yueh Ling" gives a month-by-month account of the observances required of the emperor and his court. The original emphasizes the relation of the rituals to agriculture and other occupations, but Pound has transformed it into a lyric celebration of the natural cycle from summer to winter in sacramental language, with occasional allusions to the performance of rites ("To the hearth god, lungs of the victim"). The passage on usury that begins the canto and the allusions to Palmerston's accomplishments that end it suggest that the worlds of ritual and governance converge, a connection that the *Li Ki* itself makes, for it requires certain behavior from such groups as foresters, dyers, and soldiers in support of the rites, as well as from the emperor.

The agricultural origin of the Chinese ceremonies is continually emphasized, and is explained in Ode 245 as a response to the actions of the god, Hou Tsi.

> From him we have first-class seed, our classic grain
> blacks, doubles, reds and whites.
> To keep blacks, doubles, they be stacked a-field
> Red and white yield
> we bear a-back to barn
> or shoulder high,
> wherefore Hou made the rite yclept "return."
>
> What is our rite, become traditional?

The ode answers the question in the last line by an account of varied ceremonial actions, including cooking, augury, and sacrifice.[47]

With Canto 53, Pound begins his synopsis of Chinese history, based mainly on Joseph-Ann Marie Moyrac de Mailla's *Histoire Générale de la Chine* (1777-1783), an eighteenth-century translation in thirteen volumes of a Chinese work of the twelfth century, which was itself based on even older sources.[48] The ceremonial aspect of Chinese court life is interwoven with the annals of social, economic, and military affairs whose success, it was believed, depended on the rituals.

These Chinese cantos trace the long history of ritual observances. Thus, in Canto 53, the line "Chun to the spirit of Chang Ti" refers to De Mailla's report that the second of China's legendary emperors opened his reign properly in the third millenium B.C. with sacrificial rites. It is clear then that Confucius, whose birth is mentioned as coming over two thousand years later, was supporting practices that were already ancient. Later in Canto 53—and after another two thousand years—the emperor "Siuen" (in Pound's French Romanization) failed to perform the spring rite of plowing (also mentioned in the *Li Ki*); this omission was blamed for a drought and an ensuing famine. According to De Mailla, the empress fed silkworms as part of the fertility ceremony. These rituals were still followed many centuries later, for in a passage marked "a.d. 460" Pound says:

OU TI ploughed his festival furrow
　　his Empress did rite of the silk worms
　　　　　(Canto 54)

In Canto 58 we are offered a glimpse of the importance of ritual even after many changes of sovereignty and in the midst of warfare as a Manchu invader declares that in order to validate his promise to make peace,

　I sacrificed on this oath, a black bull to earth,
　a white horse to the Spirit of Heaven.

Canto 98 paraphrases a passage in the seventeenth-century *Sacred Edict*, a book of rules Pound uses as a source in Cantos 98 and 99, that enjoins the performance of the plowing and silkworm ceremonies. Finally, Canto 61, the last of the dynastic cantos, tells us that an eighteenth-century emperor revived the old plowing custom in a field in Beijing, following the prescriptions of the *Li Ki*.

The Chinese cantos are written in the cursory, elliptical style of a chronicle whose surface is varied with foreign phrases, quoted bits of conversation, dates, ideograms, and other unconventional devices. It is a new poetic style that presents history directly through bare facts and substantive language, a style that echoes the tone of such historical documents as the Anglo-Saxon Chronicle.[49] The allusions to ritual reflect Pound's belief that the teachings of Confucius could be made directly relevant to the historical situation surrounding World War II.

Jean-Michel Rabaté feels that Pound uses the unchallengeable authority of ritual in these cantos to assert the need for dictatorial political power. And in fact, one can detect the seeds of Pound's Fascism in his admiration of the Chinese emperors. Rabaté, more subtly, thinks Pound's repetitions here amount to "an increasing ritualization of history, which ends by the pure assertion of recurring order." He also finds that the application of Confucian doctrines "consecrates the ritual of history" in order to support imperial power and the order it imposes behind the mask of a religion of nature. The historical element is, to be sure, punctuated by the recurrences Rabaté has in mind, but it is too prominent to be, as Rabaté has it, "dissolved in returns and restorations."[50] His view ignores the linear, progressive impression the Chinese cantos make as they move through different historical periods, with the shifts in dynasties, the conquests of the Mongols and Manchus, and the changes in governance that Pound emphasizes. These cantos seem to embody a tension between Pound's two conceptions of history, the linear and the cyclical, between his beliefs that each period has its distinct character, and yet that "all ages are contemporaneous."[51]

In the *Pisan Cantos*, poetic ritual transforms the anguish Pound experienced as a prisoner in the D. T. C. into an encounter with transcendental reality. As is widely recognized, these cantos stand apart from the rest of the poem. In them, Pound frequently speaks directly about himself, in his own voice and on his own behalf, sometimes in a narrative mode, sometimes in a confessional one, moving between trivial daily experiences and grandiose thoughts about his relation to historical and legendary figures. The poetry here is more fragmentary, more miscellaneous, and more disjunctive than what has come before, but it is also more intense and more evocative, shot through with ritualization.

The many literary allusions are mingled with memories, the sights and sounds of the D. T. C., lectures on economics, brief expressions of personal emotion, and evocations of Olympian and other deities, often presented in an apparently random order and giving the impression of an uncontrolled interior monologue. Passages of concrete poetry appear as words and Chinese ideograms are spread over the page in graphic designs. These visual effects and the music manuscript in Canto 75 are added to the tonal shifts, repetitions, unexpected associations, subject rhymes, and intertextual references that appear in the earlier cantos to produce an extremely eccentric text. Pound employs this modernist poetic idiom to tell us, through much of the *Pisan Cantos*, that he feels himself to be living a ritual that opens into the world of ancient myth. As Anthony Woodward has put it, using some of Pound's language, "the chaotic self-consciousness of the modern, by some paradoxical feat, cultivates the rituals of permanence in the wilds of its own mind."[52]

Canto 74, the first in the *Pisan Cantos*, begins by associating the gruesome execution of Mussolini and his lover with the fate of the sage who founded Manicheanism and ends with passage over the river of forgetfulness, apparently to the Elysian fields. This pattern of sacrifice and redemption may well be seen in the *Pisan Cantos* as a whole. Pound accomplishes this transition and seeks refuge in his mythical world by attributing the redemptive significance of ritual actions to his experiences in the D. T. C. In Canto 74, he identifies a mountain near the prison camp with the holy mountain of Taishan where a Chinese emperor had made sacrifices, and he invokes the presence of Kuanon, the Chinese goddess of mercy. Passing from delight in what he sees from his cage in the prison camp to the sacred lore of several religions, he quotes the ninth-century philosopher John Scotus Erigena's declaration that "all things that are are lights." At some points these cantos rise to replications of actual ritual services. In this way, the beleaguered Pound worked his way toward a higher reality than the one that had mired him in the D. T. C., trying to "bust through from the quotidien into 'divine or permanent world. Gods, etc."[53] Rabaté aligns Pound's effort with that of David Jones, who said that he called his book *Anathemata* because it was about the redemption of what was condemned, about "Things set up, lifted up, or in whatever manner made over to the gods."[54]

In the *Pisan Cantos*, Chinese, Egyptian, African, Christian, heterodox, and even Hebraic materials join the dominant Greek deities to participate in Pound's ritualizations. A key phrase here is "each in the name of its god," a paraphrase of a line from the Book of Micah repeated several times with variations and in varied tones throughout Canto 74. The prophet uses this phrase to describe how people will worship in the future Zion, a land of peace and plenty corresponding to the sacred cities of Ecbatan and Wagadu that Pound invokes. (One of the few books Pound had in the D. T. C. was a Bible, and the *Pisan Cantos* has several allusions to the Old Testament, which Pound reviled elsewhere.) Like nearly everything else in the *Cantos*, the phrase radiates meaning in several directions. It, of course, supports the religious syncretism prominently displayed in the *Pisan Cantos* and defends Pound's right to believe what he chooses to believe. And since it is part of the famous Biblical passage predicting that the nations "shall beat their swords into plowshares, and their spears into pruning hooks" in order to live in peace, it can be seen as an expression of Pound's hope, in his desperate wartime situation, that nations will cease going to war.

Canto 74 frequently turns from its many other preoccupations to draw upon ritual imagery. The first ideogram in the canto, *hsien*, meaning "to manifest" or "mean clearly," which is quoted from one of "The Temple Odes of Chou" in the *Shih Ching* (the odes classic, known as the *Confucian Odes*), is placed in the margin of a passage naming many sacred things, including the ritual plowing of both Chinese and Eleusinian ceremonies. Pound thought that it was composed of pictographs for the sun, silk, and grain, for in his translation of the ode, he refers to the divine will by transposing the word into these images:

> Tensile is heaven's decree
> in light and grain without end.
> As the pure silk. . . .

The details Pound sees in *hsien*, according to Akiko Miyake, are all elements of Chinese fertility rites.[55] Indeed, "Est consummatum, ite," which follows two pages later, is the formula that closes the Mass, and seems to imply that what has gone before should be accepted as ritualization. But these are also the last words of Jesus on the cross, according to the Book of John, and their proximity to lines referring to the execution of the black soldier, Till ("black that die in captivity") also ritualizes Till's death as a ceremonial sacrifice.

As in the *Cantos* generally, the varied materials of the *Pisan Cantos* refer subliminally to a ritual center. Allusions to idealized women, deities, light, the Chinese classics, Sitalkas (a name given to Dionysus as a grain-god), and many other particulars circulating in the vortex of these cantos draw powerful meanings from their connections with Pound's ideas of ritual. But there is one passage, the most sustained passage of this part of the poem, that is openly ritualized: the lynx lyric of Canto 79.

Like others in the *Pisan Cantos*, Canto 79 begins with a mixture of memories and the sights of the D. T. C., interwoven with the perception that the birds perched on wires resemble musical notation. But these thoughts are gradually infiltrated with a plea to Athene for forgiveness and the rise of a sacramental consciousness. The lines

> 2 cups for three altars. Tellus *gea* feconda
>   "each one in the name of its god"

seem to suggest the preparation of an eclectic ritual celebrating both the fertility of earth and the beauty of Helen, whose breasts were said to have formed the mold for certain golden cups (a myth that Pound first mentioned in a dialogue called "Aux Étuves de Wiesbaden"). The ritual appears with the incantational "O Lynx, my love, my lovely lynx," a prayer addressed to one of the large cats associated with Dionysus and his power of fertility, asking protection for the speaker's wine and corn, fruits of the earth.

In this passage, Pound, at the nadir of his fortunes ("Old Ez folded his blankets"), makes the D. T. C. the scene of a prayer addressed to the Greek deities, especially Dionysus. He appears to be ritualizing some of his most personal and painful memories. H. D., in her memoir of Pound, reads the lynx lyric as a re-enactment of the time when she and Pound were surprised in making love. She adopts the language of the canto to address Pound as "Satyr" and "Lynx" and identifies the canto's "Maenad, bassarid" as herself, adding "God keep us from Canto LXXIX." [56] In her biography of H. D., Janice S. Robinson speculates that Pound, returning to the idealization of H. D. in the youthful verses he wrote for her in "Hilda's Book," is addressing her under the names of the goddesses he invokes in accordance with the religion of love.[57]

The long prayer or series of prayers punctuated by repetitions of the lynx invocation is addressed to deities associated with fertility, including Perse-phone, Aphrodite, Pomona, and, surprisingly, Manitou, the Algonquin deity who controls the forces of nature. A visionary landscape thronged with lynxes, gods, and their female attendants gradually materializes, interrupted by a miscellany of nonritual elements, including details of the D. T. C., anecdotes from Pound's past, and scraps of remembered conversation, some referring to degenerate modern forms of belief that contrast ironically with the fervor of the ongoing prayer. Before long, the divine power embodied in nature prevails:

> This fruit has a fire within it,
> > Pomona, Pomona,
> No glass is clearer than are the globes of this flame
> what sea is clearer than the pomegranate body
> > holding the flame?

and the speaker, praying that his fruit may be protected, is immersed in the divine presence. The significance of "Keep from Demeter's furrow" is clarified in Canto 80, where the line "Demeter has lain in my furrow" refers to the belief that at Eleusis ritual copulation took place in the fields as a way of magically insuring their fertility. The canto ends with a roll call of Eleusinian goddesses and an invocation to the puma, another Dionysian cat, associating the fruits mentioned earlier with these divinities.

Helen M. Dennis, who regards the *Pisan Cantos*, with its motifs of sacrifice and renewal, as a "modern cultural 'fertility rite'" that follows the pattern of the Eleusinian ceremony, puts the lynx lyric at the center of the group on the ground that the creative power of nature it celebrates is analogous to the poetic power.[58] It is only one of the many passages that revert to the world of pagan religion Pound shared with H. D. in his early years, but it also embodies Pound's colorful eclecticism, employing ritual language from other cultures. The Greek orthodox "Kyrie Eleison" (which Pound also used to title one of the hymns in his translation of the *Shih Ching*) and snatches of Biblical language also appear. The cry that greeted Dionysus at Eleusis, "Iacchos Io!" is said to have "root in the equities," a term favored by Pound that appears in a passage paraphrased from Mencius in Canto 83, where it means the righteousness that accompanies the processes of nature.

In this part of the canto, Pound spaced the words on the page with special care. Each invocation to the lynx is indented, as if to set it apart. The lines are often broken to isolate phrases for special emphasis or prominence. By interweaving his ritual with his memories and his environment, Pound sharply contrasts the grace and force of the ancient deities and the timelessness of the ritual world with the crassness of the events he ironically recalls and the sterility of the D. T. C.

Canto 81 begins with an enactment of the sacred marriage, "Zeus lies in Ceres' bosom," an image ritually connected with the priest's lament at the lack of true religion and with Dolores's invitation to "eat bread," whose ritual significance is underlined by Pound's declaration that "The religious man communes every time his teeth sink into a bread crust."[59]

Anthony Woodward interprets the "libretto" in Canto 81 as a ritualistic attempt to link poetry—even the relatively artificial Cavalier poetry of the seventeenth century—with a sense of the absolute. It is intended, he says, as "an affirmation that such poetry is an expression of religious mystery. . . . The lyric gracefully ritualises Pound's sense of himself as an artist. . . .it also hints at the religious mystery in which great art can participate." The fact that the libretto is a deliberate experiment in intertextuality is an appropriate expression of Pound's "spiritual tact," the reserve with which the modern mind treats religious feeling.[60]

These and other ritual intimations lead up to the visionary climax of the *Pisan Cantos*, the great penitential passage in Canto 81. "There came new subtlety of eyes into my tent / whether of spirit or hypostasis" records a meeting with a transcendental presence that is perhaps the answer to the prayers Pound has offered in previous cantos of the Pisan sequence. These eyes have often been anticipated, whether as the gray eyes (*caesia oculi*) of

Athena, the "suave eyes, quiet, not scornful" that seem to observe the building of Ecbatan in Canto 74, or the eyes of the lover in the medieval lyric of Canto 81. The vision emulates the structure of the Eleusinian rite:

> First came the seen, then thus the palpable
> > Elysium, though it were in the halls of hell. . . .

and opens the incantational confession, "Pull down thy vanity."

In Canto 82, another moment of communication with divinity occurs as Pound voices his desire to surrender to death in a prayer to the earth-mother, Gaia. He looks forward to the union with earth at his burial, riding into a mood of exaltation on the waves of ritualistic repetitions and rhythms. These are interrupted by recollections of Nicolo d'Este and Kipling that parallel the poet's thought (these figures also welcomed burial). But the mood descends into a fear of death and a return to the world Pound is unwilling to leave as he observes the birds on the wire fence of the prison camp.

The theme of return to earth appears in a more optimistic register in Canto 83, where Pound also links actuality with ritual. The wasp's descent to the ground, "to carry our news . . . to them that dwell under the earth," replicates Odysseus' descent in Canto 1 and affirms the continuity between the world of the war and the D. T. C. on the one hand and that of myth and ritual on the other. The allusions to the pagan goddesses of the underworld are followed by a naming of Christ in his aspect as Sun God, radiating the light of many religions. After recording the achievement of the wasp in joining upper and lower worlds, the poet is so deeply moved that "that day I wrote no further," an echo, perhaps, of what Francesca says in *Inferno*, V after she and Paolo were moved to make love by reading the romance of Lancelot and "quel giorno più non vi leggemo avante." The parallel suggests a feeling resembling love, but the emotions here are more complex. By following his pleased observation of the wasp with "There is fatigue deep as the grave," Pound tells us pessimistically that one need not wait for burial to die.

The devotional theme is still present in Canto 84, the last in the *Pisan Cantos*, where Pound presents particulars locating "our norm of spirit . . . whereto we may pay our homage." A reprise of the line from Micah reminds us that there are many valid gods, and a last line in Biblical idiom speaks of giving thanks for an end to suffering.

Pound's condition in the prison camp as he describes it in the *Pisan Cantos* resembles the liminal or intermediate phase of ritual defined by Arnold Van Gennep and Victor Turner. As we have seen, there is an aspect of liminality that confers temporary freedom and inventiveness, but while the participant is in this state he also suffers the afflictions of exclusion. Turner mentions the following among the characteristics of the liminal state: anonymity, absence of property, absence of status, nakedness or uniform clothing, absence of rank, humility, unselfishness, sacredness, continuous reference to mystical powers, foolishness, and acceptance of pain and suffering.[61] Pound mentions so many of these in recording the experiences of the D. T. C. that the *Pisan Cantos* seems to have an almost organic affinity with the liminal phase. This suggests that in spite of the passages describing transcendence, the group is only a prelude to the *Paradiso* Pound planned for the end of the poem, and the vision of the D. T. C. is the threshold of deliverance.

But if the spiritual achievement here is only partial, the poetic achievement is substantial. These cantos miraculously enfold the spirit of traditional devotion in the idiom of the modernist revolution. The effort, in Woodward's words, to "merge the novel insights given by experience or experiment with the timeless ones of ritual" is one of the triumphs of modern poetry. The swift movement between actuality and vision or myth puts the poet's history and his environment in a timeless context. Reality and ritual mold each other's meanings in a vital collaboration that extends to the language, whose ritual passages are infiltrated by the idiom and poetics of the revolutionary period, expressing transcendence in the fragmented lines, vivid imagery, shifting tones, and multivocal diction of an age that is beginning to know indeterminacy. Each of the two elements has its own voice and makes its own contribution. As a result, the *Pisan Cantos* offers a dialogue between two incommensurate heteroglossia whose rhetorical fabric reflects Pound's transitional spiritual state and that of his time.

The extravagantly unconventional *Rock-Drill* cantos (85-95), written in the mental hospital of St. Elizabeth's, are largely concerned with matters of law, economics, and governance, but in Canto 90 Pound returns to the spiritual deliverance of ritual and transcendental experience. The dominant theme of this ritual is the "amor" mentioned in the epigraph from Richard of St. Victor, the idea that the love of idealized women is an approach to spiritual salvation. The incantatory passage beginning "Sibylla . . . m'elevasti" addresses the prophetess of Delphi with words drawn from Dante's speech to the Creator in the first canto of *Paradiso*. After turning his eyes from the sun to Beatrice, Dante reports that the sight of his beloved has transformed him, adding "Passing beyond the human cannot be worded . . . it was Your light that raised me."[62] The passionate repetitions of "m'elevasti" carry deep personal conviction as Pound reports that he has been delivered from waste and sterility. An allusion to the fertility of nature—"semina motuum / to parched grass, now is rain"—and unfortunate references to Evita Peron and Hitler, who have their places in Pound's pantheon, introduce ritual themes. Female deities appropriately dominate the praise of "amor": Isis, the Egyptian goddess of nature; Kuanon, the Chinese goddess of compassion; and, through the reference to the ceremony of floating lamps at Rapallo, the Madonna. The "light perpendicular," Pound's familiar image of spiritual illumination, seems to link the passage with *Paradiso* 1, whose setting is pervaded by the light of God. "Grove hath its altar" is a reply to the "aram vult nemus" of earlier cantos, and the harmony of two Chinese rivers also signals deliverance.

At least one reader of Canto 90 has felt the duality of its mysticism expressed in the forms of modernist verse. H. D. reports that she read the ritual part of the canto to her analyst and in doing so experienced a conflict between two approaches to it:

> . . . the invocation, "m'elevasti" does invoke, does call one out from "under the rubble" of daily cares and terrors.
>
> My eye, following too rapidly the uneven lines of the difficult pages, was yet part of my intellectual equipment. I refused to be taken in. I must see clearly. I could not *see* clearly, but I could *hear* clearly, as I read "m'elevasti / out of Erebus," I could at least accept the intoxication of "Kuthera sempiterna" and the healing of "myrrh and olibanum on the altar stone" giving perfume.[63]

The personal hymn is followed by a metamorphosis that sets it in the context of a great ceremonial procession. The "rilievi" or reliefs carved on a mysterious stone, perhaps part of an altar, leap into life, becoming fauns, sirens, beasts, and birds in a woodland setting. Amid this profusion of pagan celebration, a triumphant ritual climax takes place:

> thick smoke, purple, rising
> bright flame now on the altar
> the crystal funnel of air
> out of Erebus, the delivered. . . .

The beneficiaries of the rite are mainly women of antiquity famous for "amor": Tyro, Alcmene, and Electra.

The ritual in this canto, should, I think, be read as a metaphor for a moment of transcendence Pound actually experienced, as if he felt that he was raised out of the hell of the asylum as he was once raised out of the hell of the D. T. C. The nature of these mystical experiences is explained in Canto 92, in conjunction with a prayer—"O Anubis, guard this portal"—to defend the values Pound regards as sacred from corruption. Massimo Bacigalupo has shown how this prayer, "a synthetic rite of purification through water and light with a fantastical collage of 'details,'" packs a wide variety of Pound's spiritual authorities together by means of fragmentary allusions and quotations. It might be a ritual of humanism, drawing upon Egypt, Dante, Homer on the birth of Venus, troubadour verse, and numerous other sources to piece together a suggestion of paradise ("in the great love, bewildered"). But great restraint is also present, for, as Bacigalupo observes, "The very nakedness of this verse . . . protects it from mawkishness," and we soon come to Pound's admission that the ritual moment does not last, and yields only temporary communion with a divinity that is everlasting:[64]

Le Paradis n'est pas artificiel
                              but is jagged,
For a flash,
            for an hour.
Then agony,
            then an hour,
                        then agony,
Hilary stumbles, but the Divine Mind is abundant
                  unceasing
                  improvisatore
Omniformis
            unstill. . . .

This insight is followed in Canto 92 by a passage contrasting survivals of the sacred tradition with contemporary influences that have denatured it, condemning, with many examples, "the degradation of the sacraments."

The intensely personal Canto 93 draws on motivations from both ritual and experiment to work out a poetic path to redemption. The conjunction of the rational and the intuitive is suggested early in the canto in the line "Agassiz with the fixed stars, Kung to the crystalline," where the scientist and the philosopher, with their different approaches to knowledge, are both assigned places of honor. In Canto 30, we heard Artemis's injunction against "pity," and in Canto 80 the chastened Pound's acknowledgment that he has been "hard as youth." In Canto 93 this remorse is embodied in an impassioned prayer that confesses his deficiency of "pitié" and asks it for his little daughter. The line "agitante calescimus" (being disturbed, we grow warm), from a passage in Ovid ("When he [the god in us] stirs, we are set on fire") establishes the poet's feeling that he is possessed by a divine presence.[65] Moved in this way, he addresses female figures in the prayer "Creatrix, / oro . . ." on behalf of his daughter. In invoking them, he approaches revelation—"the light there almost solid"—and sees the possibilities of "benevolence" and courage in the face of the unknown. This spiritual perception culminates in ideograms whose English translation has appeared in Canto 53 : "Tching prayed on the mountain and / wrote MAKE IT NEW / on his bath tub." The Chinese emperor performed a ritual while urging progress, and in Canto 93 Pound emulates him by joining his prayer with the Chinese motto he adopted as the motivation of his own poetic revolution.

It is possible to read Canto 97, from the section of the *Cantos* called *Thrones*, first published six months after Pound left St. Elizabeth's, as an argument that both economic life and language are kept vital by a consciousness of the values inherent in fertility ritual. The canto begins with allusions to economic abuses from Alexander Del Mar's *History of Monetary Systems* in a clipped poetry that Bacigalupo calls "an incongruous sequence of graphic experiments."[66] The ideogram that follows "New fronds / novelle piante" develops the idea of innovation, for it is from the "Make it new" motto. With the lines "The temple . . . is holy, / because it is not for sale," which is repeated twice later in the canto and accompanied by a pictograph of a classical temple, Pound emphatically divides money from art and religion. "Each sphere hath its lord," says a passage that ranges from the goddess Fortuna to the sculptor Brancusi's impatience with his work.

The canto ends with a grouping of elements (intermingled with many other significant scraps) in which devotional and linguistic virtues appear side by side, forming an argument for Pound's morality of language. The Chinese *cheng ming* ("the right word") formulates the doctrine of verbal economy, dating from Pound's Imagist days. It introduces a passage where a somewhat fussy debate over Greek usage is followed by the assertion that the spirits of the dead gods, including Pomona, the deity of fruitfulness, are still at large. The statement in one of Pound's sources that words are "mortua" and "sepulta" ("dead" and "buried"), is denied by the listing of three plants that are sources of renewal. In the margin, the Chinese words for "old horse god" allude to rites in which victorious race-horses are sacrificed. They are followed by a quotation from the *Analects*, where Confucius addresses the words "do not tire" to his disciples. The canto ends, therefore, with the idea that rituals can restore life and meaning both to religion and to language that is considered dead.

Canto 97 provides an opportunity to turn to two matters of ritual that run through much of the *Cantos*. We are perhaps surprised that Pound should admire a long period of antiquity because there was "no blood on the altar stone," for in Canto 21 deities are praised as "Strong as with blood-drink," and in Canto 25, beings languishing in a Dantescan underworld lament "the dead concepts, never the solid, the blood rite," as if sacrifice were essential to the validity of ritual. This view is changed in Canto 94, where the phrase "Was no blood on the Cyprian's altars" expresses a preference for the fertility ritual of Aphrodite over sacrificial ritual, and the passage on virtuous figures in Canto 97 includes "no blood in that TEMENOS." Robert Casillo, as we have seen, attributes Pound's aversion to the ritual shedding of blood to his anti-Semitism and to his association of blood sacrifice with the Talmud and the Old Testament.[67] Carroll F. Terrell, however, observes that Pound regarded the rejection of sacrifice as an advance in civilization. Perhaps one of the major movements of the *Cantos* is the one that begins with the bloody sacrificial ritual of Odysseus in the underworld and ends with the benign and nature-centered rites of the Na-khi (which did, however, involve animal sacrifice).

The conjunction of "Luigi, *gobbo*" (hunchback) and the ideogram, *tan* ("morning"), are links in Pound's complex chain of light images, showing how ritual can embody the experimental value of innovation. "Luigi, *gobbo*, makes his communion with wheat grain / in the hill paths / at sunrise" refers to a crippled peasant Pound knew who, according to Canto 104, "chews wheat at sunrise." Pound assures us in Canto 103 that "This is grain rite / Luigi in hill path / this is grain rite / near Enna, at Nyssa," linking Luigi's ritual with the site of Persephone's abduction and seeing it as a survival of the Eleusinian agricultural rite.

Luigi's morning ritual is also linked through *tan* to morning light, a familiar image of occult revelation. (Yeats, we recall, belonged to the Order of the Golden Dawn.) Both the ideogram and the ode in the *Shi-Ching* from which Pound quotes it speak of renewal. The line in which *tan* appears, "In the sunrise I am alone," occurs in a poem whose translation Pound entitled "Alba" (Old Provençal for "dawn"), which laments a death but declares that after a hundred years, in Pound's translation, "we come to one house together." The core image is no doubt the light of Eleusis, and *tan* itself is given a ritual role in Canto 91: "They who are skilled in fire / shall read tan, the dawn. / Waiving no jot of the arcanum." In employing this traditional symbol, found in the rituals from many cultures, Pound emphasized its capacity for promoting renewal, a value it shares with the experimental spirit.

Cantos 98 and 99 consist mainly of a reprise of a work called *The Sacred Edict* (*Sheng Yu*), which was based on a set of sixteen Confucian rules of behavior written by the emperor K'ang Hsi. Pound's source included an extended commentary, the *Wen li*, written by the emperor's son and published in 1724, and a colloquial version by the author Pound calls the "Salt Commissioner," together with an English translation.[68] This sequence of sober ethical principles enjoining such virtues as filial duty, learning, and hard work is entirely different in tone from the religious mysticism with which it is joined in these cantos.

In the two cantos enigmatic excerpts from the Chinese documents are intermingled with such varied materials as Homeric quotations in Greek letters, imagistic allusions to personal memories, parallels from European history, and a quotation from a fellow patient at St. Elizabeth's. The level of discourse shifts frequently as the poet turns aside to identify his sources, to evaluate the merit of translation, or to make some such comment as "Sixteen bitched by an (%) interest rate."

The two cantos employ this experimental idiom in showing that ritual extends into daily life. Canto 98 begins with instances of the infusion of the spirit of the divine into human affairs. Ritualistic images of fire and incense follow, seeming to affirm that the presence of the divine endures. Its metamorphic nature is illustrated in the allusion to the maiden Leucothoe (not to be confused with the similarly named goddess), who was buried alive by her father because she had loved the sun-god, Apollo, and who emerged from below in the form of a bush bearing frankincense, the scent identified with worship. This leads to the reminder that sacrifices are still offered to the goddess Leucothea, the daughter of Cadmus, and to a restatement of the theme, "est deus in nobis" (there is a god in us). While a divine presence lurks in human activities, it must not be corrupted by them, for Canto 97's "The temple . . . is holy, / because it is not for sale" is repeated insistently here.

Canto 98 emphasizes the elements of light and agricultural fertility seen in the Eleusinian rites. The divine presence can be perceived only with the aid of light, symbolic of "awareness," for as the canto says, "there is no sight without fire." The opening survey joins the sacred Eleusinian light with sun-deities and the ritualistic "fanned flame" that responds to the movements of the gods and then, after a long excursion into the Chinese text, it surfaces again in an allusion to Dante: "Paradiso, XIV: this light does not disunify." It is in Dante's Canto XIII, however, that St. Thomas, positioned in one of the flames that circles the poet, speaks of a light, the Son, that illuminates the world without being separated from its divine source, the Father, or from love. His speech begins with an image from agriculture, where he speaks of his discourse as stalks of grain that are being threshed. In this way, light, love, and fertility, all elements of the Eleusinian complex, are brought together in the canto's ritual celebration.

Pound employs the banal injunctions of the *Sacred Edict* to lead up to a passage where light and Nature, Dante and a Chinese emperor come together in a climactic expression of spiritual illumination. The fertility theme begins with the ideograms i[4] and shen[1] (meaning, respectively, "righteousness" and "profound") and is continued with an echo of the fourth section of the *Edict*, "Without grain you will not eat." The *Edict* speaks of clothing and the need for cultivating the silkworm as well as sowing seed, familiar activities replicated in the traditional rites.

Massimo Bacigalupo characterizes a series of allusions in Canto 98 as the transformation of the source into ritual.[69] The canto achieves this by drawing on the rituals of many religions. When he interrupts the summary of the *Edict* to write "Without ²muan ¹bpo . . ." Pound is referring to the ritual of still another religion, that of the Na-khi people of southwest China, a ritual which he regarded as truly efficacious and introduced in later cantos. The *Edict* enjoins work on the soil, and Pound is sufficiently moved by its definition of the virtuous life to use it as part of the basis for the paratactic litany near the end of the canto.

This climactic passage, beginning "Deliberate converse," identifies the eighteenth-century emperor "Ion Cheng" (Yung Cheng), who glossed the *Edict* and who is mentioned in Cantos 60 and 61, as one who followed Confucian doctrines and performed the ritual plowing. The *hsien ming* ideograms ("manifest light") proclaim that the light of the doctrines is shining and are followed by an intricately punning praise of illumination.

> hsien
> ming
> by the silk cords of the sunlight,
> Chords of the sunlight (*Pitagora*)

Here Pound asserts the underlying harmony of the cosmos by weaving his association of *hsien* with threads of silk and the sun radical of *ming* into a bilingual knot that identifies the rays of the sun with the mathematical order of musical notes discovered by Pythagoras. The date and title of the *Sacred Edict* conclude what Bacigalupo calls a "ritualistic score," an invocation of the sacred virtues Pound has located in both the *Paradiso* and the Chinese text. The canto ends with a final affirmation of the importance of ritual from the speech of the emperor himself, who ordains "There are six rites for the festival / and that all should converge!"[70]

Canto 99 continues this emphasis on the rites, and on the pieties they inculcate, baldly declaring their importance:

> The State is corporate
> > as with pulse in its body
> & with Chou rite at the root of it
> The root is through all of it,
> > a tone in all public teaching. . . .

The canto has already declared that "food is the root," and the need for the fruits of nature is firmly linked with the ritual principle through the ceremonial responsibilities of the imperial couple:

> From of old the sovereign likes plowing
> & the Empress tends the trees with reverence. . . .
> The plan is in nature
> > rooted
> Coming from earth. . . .

Social behavior itself is conceived as a part of the harmony of man and nature. Service to the state and care of the soil require the same attentiveness: "Keep mind on the root / Ability as grain in the wheat-ear." The concept that etiquette, like ritual, is rooted in nature appears in Canto 99, where the "sages of Han" are quoted as saying:

> Manners are from earth and from water
> They arise out of the hills and streams. . . .
> Kung said: are classic of heaven,
> They bind thru the earth
> > and flow
> With recurrence,
> > action, humanitas, equity. . . .

Pound uses "equity," a word from his translation of the *Shih Ching*, to express the Confucian ethical ideal, a virtue shared by nature and man, and to argue that the rituals and practices of various cultures all spring from nature: "Different each, different customs / but one root in the equities. . . ."

Occasional references to interest and prices in these cantos make the point that the absence of the Confucian spirit and the ritual it enjoins is the cause of contemporary economic difficulties. In this way, the mundane problems of subsistence are seen to depend for their solution on the lofty spiritual belief of "est deus in nobis."

When Pound came across the work of Joseph F. Rock in the course of his Chinese studies, he discovered an entirely new ritual culture. Rock, an indomitable botanist-explorer of Austrian origin and American nationality, who spent many years in southwest China working for the Department of Agriculture and the National Geographic Society, among other employers, had become absorbed in the study of the Na-khi, an aboriginal tribe of the region. A crusty and impatient perfectionist, Rock despised the Chinese but devoted much of his small capacity for affection to the Na-khi, hiring them as servants and assistants and producing enormously detailed scholarly monographs about them, their language, their land, and their culture.

Rock had completed a four-volume study of the Na-khi religion and had made an extensive collection of documents and photographs by 1941. Dodging the Japanese attacks in that part of the world, he had this material sent by sea from Calcutta, but the ship was torpedoed, and Rock's work was lost. "Mr. Rock still hopes to climb at Mt. Kinabalu," says Canto 110, "his fragments sunk (20 years)." With characteristic persistence, Rock returned to the Na-khi country after the war to repeat his research, and wrote the studies that Pound used as sources in the later cantos.

Pound was attracted to Rock's material on the elaborate rituals of the Na-khi, the ²muan ¹bpo, or "Sacrifice to Heaven," and the ²Har-²la-¹llü ³k'ö, or "wind sway perform," as Rock translates it.[71] The first was a ceremony of lustration and thanksgiving for the gifts of nature involving prayers that narrate cosmological myths, an analogue of the Eleusinian rite found at the other end of the world. And the second, which concerned the suicide of frustrated lovers, had a theme somewhat resembling *amour courtois*. According to Rock, the ²muan ¹bpo ceremony went back to a time when the aboriginal Na-khi were still free of Chinese domination and led a nomadic existence.

In Canto 113, Pound pays tribute to "Rock's world that he saved us for memory / a thin trace in high air." Rock's book, *The Ancient Na-khi Kingdom of Southwest China*, like another of Pound's sources, the *Odyssey*, is an account of a journey, but it is distinctly factual and unpoetic in tone. As a botanist, Rock had much to say about the plants and geology of the mountainous area, and many of his photographs show the landscape, but for Pound its significance rested on the fact that it was a setting for ritual. As John Peck has put it, in Pound's hands, "Rite becomes the consummation of landscape, landscape the expression of rite."[72]

The allusions to trees, a rope bridge, taxes paid in buckwheat, and other enigmatic phrases in Canto 101 come from Rock's *Ancient Na-khi Kingdom*. Ritual appears after the Na-khi name for the "Lion Mountain," with "To him we burn pine with white smoke, / morning and evening."[73] There is little about the ²muan ¹bpo ceremony in this book, but a photograph showing its altar and a priest appears facing page 140, and Pound made use of this by alluding to the altar in Canto 110. In Canto 101 he describes the priest in the photograph by saying "the ²dto-¹mba's face (exorcist's) / muy simpático."

The Na-khi scene returns in Cantos 102 and 104, where, among numerous echoes of Pound's classical world, there are further glimpses of Rock's landscape and two reversions to the pine-branch fire of Canto 101. With "the pine needles glow as red wire" in Canto 104, Pound provides some ritual exegesis. The Greek "KAI ALOGA " and "APHANASTON" tell us that the rite is "unspoken" and "inscrutable," and Pound's apparently deliberate misquotation of a Homeric line, "they want to burst out of the universe," expresses the transcendental aspiration he ascribes to the ritual.

Canto 104 announces ritual as one of its themes by first repeating the ideogram *ling* ("sensibility"), that stands like a banner at the opening of the *Rock-Drill* cantos and then repeating the lower part of it, which is the separate word for ritual, *wu*. After discussions of corruption in the modern world, the burning pine needles of the Na-khi ritual are seen again, and then, carefully spaced for emphasis, the statement

Without ²muan   ¹bpo
      no reality

echoes a sentence from Rock's translation of a Na-khi text: "If ²*Muan* ¹*bpo* is not performed all that which we accomplished is not real."[74] The "calescimus" that follows, we recall, refers to the warmth felt in the presence of the divine. A prophetess and the ritualizing Luigi emerge briefly from the memories that occupy much of the canto, and those who lack intuitive perception are condemned. On the other hand, "Webster, Voltaire, and Leibnitz," figures who set things in order, did so "by phyllotaxis / in leaf-grain." The Greek borrowing, meaning the orderly arrangement of leaves on the stem of a plant, accomplishes a telling effect. It demonstrates the compatibility of scientific heteroglossia with the religion of nature, and, through its context, offers natural order as an analogue for legal and social justice.

Canto 104 concludes its contrastive alternating of the sacred and the profane by a return, through an allusion to a passage in the *Chou King*, one of Pound's Chinese historical sources, to a pastoral and ceremonial environment.

A Latin sentence tells us that "he cares to reflect on permanent things" and words from the Chinese history book are an invitation to "come and dance ceremoniously." Other details from Chinese history—varnish, silk, and the system of weights established by an emperor—illustrate achievements made possible by ritual.

In Canto 106, Pound pursues his vision of paradise by turning from the Na-khi country and reverting to the Greek and Eleusinian themes of earlier cantos. The Chinese sources now take a back seat. In fact, the canto opens by setting a Chinese text that emphasizes agriculture lower than the Greek tradition, which rises to the levels of love and transcendence—symbolized by the cup modeled on Helen's breasts—that are permanent values, "not in memory, / in eternity." Allusions to media of exchange that, as we have seen, are far from irrelevant to Pound's religious views, lead to the introduction of a ritual passage. "That the goddess turn crystal within her / This is grain rite" announces the role of Persephone in the Eleusinian ceremony. In this way the earthly dependence on grain at the root of the ritual is linked, through the sacred marriage, to the crystal that, as the solidification of light, represents the condition of spiritual perfection.

There follows a prayer that brings the idealization of women into relation with this aspiration, for it is addressed to a conflation of female deities: Circe, Athene, and Artemis. The regular rhythm and broken syntax of this passage combine to achieve an effect that is powerfully, if not obviously, emotional. Pound summons a rich repertory of images to convey a sense of devotion to the belief that paradise is entered through physical experience. The prayer adopts a rhythm of tripartite lines (which Massimo Bacigalupo calls a "ritual chant") that ranges over images combining the sacredness of Eleusinian elements with sheer visual beauty. With "That great acorn of light bulging outward," the crystal of spiritual perfection is embodied in a metaphor that links it to the plants mentioned in the prayer. The sequence of landscape, royal and mythical figures, all female, all potential objects of idealization, terminating in the image of temple dancers, "White feet as Carrara's whiteness," rises to an ecstatic experience of identification with the divine: "God's eye art 'ou."[75]

The last three cantos Pound completed, 107-109, are mainly concerned with legal tradition, but allusions to the religious themes of the poem maintain a spiritual perspective. Canto 107 ends with a long excursion back to paradisal images. After quoting from the legal authority, Coke, Pound continues "this light / as a river" by listing some of the favorites of his own tradition, Kung, Ocellus, Agassiz, and Gaudier. The decline of justice is lamented through a parallel that recalls a grain ritual: "Wheat was bread in the old days . . . Alan Upward's seal showed Sitalkas," an allusion to the depiction of the Greek grain-god on a ring owned by Upward. Finally, in Canto 109, after a series of fragmentary quotations citing just and proper legal and economic provisions recorded in English history, further allusions to Pound's pantheon occur, including Helios, god of the sun, and Ino, who was transformed into the sea-goddess Leucothea and generously lent her veil to Odysseus. Three Roman churches are also mentioned, surprisingly, perhaps, in this admiring context. The telling word of the passage is the isolated "phyllotaxis," nature's orderliness, repeated from Canto 104.

Canto 109, and the completed part of the whole vast poem ends, significantly no doubt, with a phrase from Dante's warning to unbelievers at the beginning of Canto 2 of *Paradiso* (repeated by Pound on several earlier occasions) not to attempt to follow him on his voyage.

Ritual is especially prominent in the uncompleted "Drafts and Fragments" because Pound depended heavily on his Na-khi material in them. With Canto 110, he turns to another elaborate set of these ceremonies, the ²Har-²la-¹llü ³kö (or, rather, to Rock's account of the narratives connected with them). These ceremonies are intended to propitiate or commemorate the spirits of lovers who committed suicide to avoid forced marriage, an occurrence so frequent among the Na-khi that it became the subject of an extensive literature and generated a family of rituals. According to Rock's introduction, the process of suicide itself approached ceremony, as the lovers went to an isolated mountain spot, spent a few days playing music, and then put an end to themselves, usually by hanging themselves from a tree. The custom is romanticized as a way of entering a new life in the embrace of nature, and the scenes where such suicides have occurred are given poetic names reflecting their wind-swept and wooded character.

Canto 110 alternates between ritual-mythic imagery and episodes from a contemporary world occupied mainly with war and concludes with a call to prayer.[76] The brief glimpses of nature in its first two pages refer to the scenes from Rock's account of the suicide-myth that is the basis of the ²Har-²la-¹llü ³kö ritual and to the imagery the lovers use in their speeches. The line of Italian with which these fragments are introduced, "che paion' si al vent" has a double relation to the Na-khi stories: it is a variant of Dante's request to speak to the lovers Paolo and Francesca (*Inferno*, Canto V), and by speaking of them as carried lightly on the wind, it establishes a parallel with the Na-khi belief that the souls of those who die alone are taken by seven demons of the wind and must be recovered through the ²Har-²la-¹llü ³kö ceremony.

The canto soon turns to the different though related *²muan ¹bpo* ceremony, with a typographical replication of the arrangement of the plants on its altar:

heaven   earth
     in the center
        is
      juniper

Pound had seen the photograph of this arrangement in *The Ancient Na-khi Kingdom* and had read, in Rock's account of the ceremony, that the altar space contained two small oaks, representing heaven and earth, on either side of a juniper, representing the emperor. Rock's Latin name for one of the plants used in the rite of purification recalls the name Artemis, and leads to a sharp modulation as Pound now turns to (mainly) Greek myths. The prevailingly mournful texture of the canto is punctuated by ideograms from Pound's vocabulary of ideals, and attains a final ritual note of hopefulness:

ching[4]
pray   pray
    There is power
Awoi or Komachi,
   the oval moon. . . .

It is a conclusion that recommends the ritual dancing of a Noh character under the moon as a way of resisting evil and echoes the allusion to Artemis, goddess of the moon as well as woodlands.

Canto 112 consists nearly entirely of excerpts from the prayers of the *²muan ¹bpo* ceremony. The idea that the blessings of the soil are attributed to divine power—"rice grows and the land is invisible"—is entirely in the spirit of the ritual. The striking circular graphic at the end of the canto is copied from Rock's text, where it appears as a Na-khi pictograph showing a winnowing tray. Although Rock says that the sign has only a phonetic value, Pound exploits its winnowing function to make it stand for fate. He "translates" it into "luna," a Western symbol of "Fortuna," adds his own pictograph of a half-moon, and throws in the melodious "Arundinaria," the name Rock gives for the bamboo of which the tray is made.

The subject of Canto 113 is a meditation on the co-existence of such contraries as good and evil in the world. A passage that recalls Canto 3, written more than forty years earlier ("Gods float in the azure air") encapsulates the dialogic nature of this canto, and the *Cantos* in general:

The Gods have not returned. "They have never left us."
They have not returned.

However, the canto seeks affirmation in spite of obstacles: "Sea, over roofs, but still the sea and the headland." And it seeks this affirmation through a ritual form, the culminating prayer addressed to Artemis and Helios that speaks of life after death.

In Canto 116 and the other final fragmentary cantos, the aged and tormented Pound appears to be evaluating his poem and its effect as if he were a priest offering a ritual:

I have brought the great ball of crystal
                    who can lift it?
Can you enter the acorn of light?

If the statement "These concepts the human mind has attained" borders on complacency, the poet also acknowledges his failure in scattered phrases appearing toward the end of Canto 116:

And I am not a demigod,
I cannot make it cohere. . . .
i.e. it coheres all right
                    even if my notes do not cohere. . . .
A little light, like a rushlight
to lead back to splendour.

Here two significant words echo the language of the dying Heracles in Pound's translation of Sophocles's *Women of Trachis*. In Pound's version, Heracles, while writhing in the flames of the shirt daubed with the blood of the centaur he has killed, acknowledges the justice of his punishment and the fulfillment of prophecy by exclaiming:

SPLENDOUR,
                    IT ALL COHERES. . . .

Pound added a footnote to say that this was the "key phrase" of the play. In the *Cantos* there is an earlier echo of Sophocles, when, in Canto 100, Pound uses the Greek for "coheres"—"SUMBAINAI"—in bold capitals to insist on a characteristic subject rhyme: that the fate of Marie de' Medici, who died in exile, and that of an English banker buried in a Venetian church are related.

"Splendour," which appears several times in earlier cantos, is associated with the Eleusinian light and divine presence; "coherence" is the unity and justice of the creation that Pound apparently felt intuitively but found that he could not shape into a poem. The personal confession of Canto 116 uses the two key words to express a final failure of confidence in his way of structuring his poem and his universe. Pound, a poetic Heracles writhing in the agony of his consciousness of failure, affirms an intuitive faith in cosmic unity, but can only hope for a rushlight glimmer of the Eleusinian light that might reveal it.

The *Cantos* was begun as an expression of early-century modernism, but it supports many of the principles favored by the critical climate that arrived as the last cantos were being written. On the one hand, it is an obvious candidate for deconstructive analysis; on the other, it preempts the postmodern critic by employing such effects as contradictions, aporias, writerliness, deferral, dispersion, and dissolution of the subject. An example of postmodern criticism that seems to point directly to the *Cantos* comes up in the course of Jacques Derrida's argument that writing must not surrender to the restricting influence of science, for it is in the process of overcoming "linearity" and regaining the "pluridimensionality" it has had through most of its history. A realization that the age of linear writing is past, says Derrida, leads to a rereading of the texts of the past as well as to a pluridimensional discourse. The *Cantos'* poetic idiom of multiple meanings and intertextual techniques might well be the sort of writing Derrida has in mind.

Derrida specifies as fields that have undergone revolutions challenging linearity those of philosophy, science and literature. According to Pound's original intentions, these three sources of revolution were to be among the axes on which the vortices of the *Cantos* were to revolve in generating their many dimensions of meaning. In addition, other centers of productive disturbance—"confusion, source of renewals"—appeared over the sixty-year period of composition. The escape from linear writing, Derrida points out, entails a different sense of history, a result perfectly illustrated by the treatment of historical texts in the *Cantos*. Derrida predicts that the end of linearity will bring about the end of the epic and the book itself. "What is thought today," he says, "cannot be written according to the line and the book."[77] Pound's poem may be taken as a dramatic validation of Derrida's point, for his intention of achieving some final unity in the *Cantos*, an ambition perhaps viable in the period before World War II, seems to have become impossible of fulfillment as times changed.

The ritualizing aspect of the poem contributes to this frustration, supplying ample evidence to support Catherine Bell's argument that the ritual process itself falls prey to the disabilities pointed out by deconstruction.

This orchestrated deferral of signification never yields a definitive answer, a final meaning, or a single act, [but only] the sense of a loosely knit and loosely coherent totality, the full potential of which is never fully grasped and thus never fully subject to challenge or denial. One is never confronted with "the meaning" to accept or reject; one is always led into a redundant, circular, and rhetorical universe of values and terms whose significance keeps flowing into other values and terms.[78]

This description inescapably recalls the *Cantos* as it moves from canto to canto and from section to section, its themes becoming enriched and diversified as Ulysses, Dionysus, Sigismundo, Baldy Bacon, and Confucius follow each other, while many other signifiers come and go, only intermittently producing the click of correspondence, contrast, or some other definable relationship. The sense of "deferral" in Derrida's analysis of language was always present in Pound's mind, for he acknowledged the incoherence of his poem as it progressed but said that its significance would become clear when its final parts were put in place. However, the *Cantos*, by its own admission, remains incomplete and unexplained. It can easily be seen as a performance that corresponds both with the deconstructionist characterization of language and with Catherine Bell's account of the effect of ritual.

None of Pound's critics has written so well on the ritual aspect of the *Cantos* as Anthony Woodward. Woodward is fully appreciative of the conflicting sensibilities that impeded Pound's struggle toward his vision of cosmic unity. He regards what he calls "rituals of the self" in the *Pisan Cantos* as the efforts of a modern mind to fulfill the requirements of sacred devotion but finds that Pound was kept from fully surrendering to belief by esthetic purposes and modern skepticism. Divine presence is always qualified, as in Canto 81:

nor was place for the full Eiδωs
interpass, penetrate
    casting but shade beyond the other lights.

By describing the religious emotions of the *Cantos* as "something exploratory, oblique," accompanied by Pound's "twentieth-century feeling for the flux of experience," Woodward touches on their experimental character. He envisions Pound "inventing . . . certain rituals for the articulation of his religious need" but feels that the ritual repetitions and incantations of the text are no more than "a self-conscious imaginative participation in primitive religiosity." Pound's concern with the timeless world of myth and ritual, he feels, is no more than "the aspiration of a rootless epigone of genius shoring fragments of eternity against the ruins of the present."[79] It should be added that the transmutation of visionary experience into poetry must involve some withdrawal if it is to avoid incoherence and banality. In the *Cantos* this withdrawal becomes more conspicuous as Pound employs ritual in ways that avoid mere atavism, compel the reader to transcend habitual limits, and attempt to get off the dead parts of the reader's mind, as Pound put it.

Woodward attributes the "distance" felt in the poem's religious passages to the "eclectic" quality of Pound's thought without specifying that contemporary science was an important element of that eclecticism. The effects of science and the indeterminacy noted by Catherine Bell can be attributed to experimental influences that anticipated poststructuralism by at least a generation. The staccato, paratactic quality of the verse, its typographical eccentricities, and its reckless indifference to chronology have their roots in the defiance of conventional language voiced by the Italian Futurists before World War I. Futurism, the first of the modern literary movements, aimed to adapt language to the consciousness of a culture dominated by science and technology, and Pound's Vorticism, which arose as a kind of answer to the Italian movement, had similar motivations. Richard Sieburth finds that the *Cantos* avoids final meaning through the use of techniques derived from Dadaism, a movement nearly contemporaneous with Futurism, which advocated incoherence as a criticism of traditional ideas of order. In the *Cantos* the use of signifiers to refer to other signifiers initiates an eternal regression leading to a terrain where specifiable meaning disappears, and it is precisely this experimental effect that imparts a "ritual dimension" of mystery to the poem. Sieburth feels that the deconstructive methods of the *Cantos* question the possibility of meaning, a "metasemiotic" quality, that, as we have seen, is also one of the characteristics of religious ritual.[80]

Since the poem's Dada ironies are contradicted by the religious feeling embodied in the ritual passages, the question arises as to how we are to respond to this skepticism. Octavio Paz has offered a way in which this characteristically modern indecision may be regarded as a kind of decision. In describing the opposition between art and life so often scrutinized by modern works he says:

> The game of opposites dissolves, without resolving, the opposition between seeing and desiring, eroticism and contemplation, art and life. . . . the moment of the poem is the intersection between absolute and relative, an instantaneous reply which undoes itself ceaselessly. The opposition is always reappearing, now as the negation of the absolute by contingency, now as the dissolution of

contingency in an absolute which, in turn, fades away ... the non-solution which is a solution, is not a solution.

Paz connects Pound's poem with this general feature of modernism by observing that in the *Cantos*, "analogy is continuously torn apart by criticism, by ironic consciousness."[81] The interplay between ritual and experimental elements is, of course, one prominent aspect of this conflict.

A case for the unity of the ritual and secular passages might be made by employing Catherine Bell's point that the agencies generated by the ritual process envelope the secular world and control its meaning. Ritual, she says, generates "redemption" by imposing "coherence" on the world.[82] "Coherence," as we have seen, is a key word in the lexicon of the *Cantos*, connoting not only the intelligibility but also the justice of the cosmos, and it is possible that Pound intended the ritualized elements of his poem to confer "redemption" on the secular elements. But scientific or rational cognition does not often come under the ritualizing control to which Catherine Bell refers. Pound was forced to acknowledge in the "Drafts and Fragments" that "coherence" is precisely what escaped him, and what he accomplished is no doubt less than redemptive.

The conjunction of ritual and experiment differs from canto to canto, sometimes achieving harmony, sometimes contrast or discord, as the poem strains to establish relationships between types of sensibility lying far apart on the spectrum of human consciousness. That effort is the source of much of its poetry, a confirmation of Yeats's observation that poetry emerges from our differences with ourselves. Woodward does not ignore the value of Pound's ambiguity and wisely sets aside the question of belief. "All that counts," he says decisively, "is poetic effectiveness."[83]

Pound seems to have felt that the ritualizing and experimental elements of his poem would achieve some sort of closure because the ultimate meanings of both escape final definition. Ritual, following Catherine Bell's characterization, can be seen as the enigmatic, unmeaning center of Pound's system. The results of experiment are contingent, open to varied interpretation, subject to the changing consensualism of the community. As they operate in the *Cantos*, however, their indeterminacy has the effect of denying that the text has any final transcendental dimension, thus contributing to the unfinished, disunified quality of the poem as a whole.

If the metaphysics of ritual and experiment fail to achieve unity in the *Cantos*, each of the procedures exhibits virtues that probably account for the powerful attraction the poem has had for its readers. Its use of ritual conveys a sense of transport, brings significant mythical realities into presence, demolishes barriers among the faiths, and confers the aura of tradition on ordinary experience. In its experimentation, it displays a courage that confronts intractable problems of expression, conveys the pleasure of discovery and invention, and praises the discipline of objectivity. These values need not be considered incompatible with each other, and it is on their level that the integrity of the *Cantos* as a single work may be found.

8
—
H. D.

what is Greece if you draw back
from the terror
and cold splendour of song
and its bleak sacrifice?

—H. D., "The Islands"[1]

Nearly every line of Hilda Doolittle's poetry seems to be spoken in reverential tones as part of a pagan rite. Yet her poetic forms exemplify the economy and precision that were the stylistic aspirations of modern poetic experiment, and her mystic visions of reality sometimes correspond with the discoveries of modern science.

Feminist critics have differentiated H. D.'s work from the general body of modern poetry on the grounds that it embodies rebellion against the patriarchal attitude of other modern poets and achieves a specifically feminine poetic discourse. Her position on the issue of gender has been interpreted in a variety of ways. Some find that a long personal struggle led her to reject masculine values in favor of distinctly feminine ones, but some feel that her effort resulted in a spiritual androgyny that merged the two, in a parallel to her own bisexuality. Gender, however, is only one of the many polarities that occupied H. D.; ritualization and experiment is another. Susan Stanford Friedman, who has emphasized the feminist aspects of H. D.'s work, nevertheless observes that, in spite of her troubled relations with the early modernists, ". . . the shape of her poetic oeuvre—from innovative image to cosmic epic—tracks that of her male peers" and that her poetry is "naturalizable within many of the traditional categories of (male) modernism."[2] While her emphasis on feminine themes is by no means irrelevant to H. D.'s use of myth and her invocation of ritual values, the analysis of ritual and experiment in her poetry is best followed on lines appropriate to modernism generally.

At various times in her life, H. D. was open to both rational and intuitional influences, although she was increasingly dominated by the latter. On the one hand there was the influence of her mother, who gave lessons in music and painting and raised H. D. in the Moravian tradition of her family. As an adult the poet displayed much interest in the rituals of this mystical, pietistic sect, and its influence appears in her poetry. On the other hand, her father, a professor of astronomy and an active scientific researcher, hoped she would become a scientist and sometimes took her with him to the meetings of learned societies. Her long friendship with Ezra Pound, her marriage to Richard Aldington, and her association with the writers connected with the *Egoist* in London during World War I opened her to the possibilities of literary experiment. Friendships with Havelock Ellis and D. H. Lawrence encouraged her to accept the validity of personal feelings, so that while the psychoanalytic treatment she went through with Freud and other analysts brought her into contact with one aspect of modern science, she still trusted intuitions that told her that her therapists were not always right. Freud, of course, regarded her visions and dreams as psychological manifestations, but she believed that they demonstrated psychic gifts, and she willingly followed them into the world of the occult.

H. D. accepted scientific facts but characteristically endowed them with mystical values. Her father's astronomy led her to astrology, and Freud's philosophy, as she wrote in *Tribute to Freud*, gave a negative value to the influence of both parents, putting her in the shadow cast by the light of her father's science and her mother's art. Occasional crumbs of scientific vocabulary appear in her poems, and in "The Flowering of the Rod," the Mage, Kaspar, has a mystical vision of time that corresponds to Einsteinian theories of what would happen if it were possible to exceed the speed of light.

In later life, H. D. immersed herself in the study of the pagan mystery religions, hermeticism, numerology, astrology, and Tarot cards, fashioning a kind of religion out of these esoteric disciplines. This was a region of thought that Yeats inhabited, and one in which the early Pound had lingered, but H. D. entered it independently, on the basis of her own occult experiences. The "mythic system" of her later poems, observes Susan Stanford Friedman, "is more religious than Williams or Pound, more esoteric than Eliot, and more syncretist than Yeats."[3] It is also innovative and experimental; H. D. recognized that her psychoanalysis involved the convergence of two different ways of thinking, wondered whether she ought to continue "this experiment," and realized that she and Freud "sometimes translated our thoughts into different languages or mediums."[4] The small figures of Greek and Egyptian deities on Freud's table, which he had collected as mere artifacts, seemed to H. D. "like the high altar in the Holy of Holies . . . each the carved symbol of an idea or a deathless dream." She valued them more than Freud's teaching, for they "were symbols of Eternity and contained him then, as Eternity contains him now." Her intuitions both anticipated and challenged the Professor's ideas, and she felt that beyond his doctrines "there is another region of cause and effect, another region of question and answer."[5]

She extended this feeling to the discoveries of modern science in general, writing in a letter to a friend that psychoanalysis was a "true Aquarian science, along with X-ray and television and those things—science plus something uncanny or supernatural, not science in the old sense of the word."[6] Her experimentalism has only the slightest of scientific tones, but it does contribute to her work a strong interest in innovation, especially innovation in the occult. In this region existed archetypal relationships that H. D. sometimes called "patterns," a word that, as we have seen, signals prerational discourse, and the ritual sensibility.[7] At a stage where analysis seemed unable to explain her feelings, she wrote: "There is a formula for Time that has not yet been computed."[8] After Freud had helped her to analyze a dream, she wondered, "Do I wish myself, in the deepest unconscious or subconscious layers of my being, to be the founder of a new religion?"[9]

Thus, while in her early years, she might have felt, like the autobiographical character of her novel, *HERmione*, that "I am swing-swing between worlds, people, things exist in opposite dimension," her powerful poetic imagination later obliterated the line between fact and intuition, so that she could write, "There are no frontiers of the spirit."[10]

In *Tribute to Freud*, H. D. observed that the tripod she had seen in one of her visions was a ceremonial object, the traditional seat of the priestess of Delphi. But she also regarded it as a symbol of the integration of thought and feeling. "Religion, art, and medicine," she wrote, "through the latter ages, became separated; they grow further apart from day to day. These three working together, to form a new vehicle of expression or a new form of thinking or of living, might be symbolized by the tripod."[11] H. D.'s poetry might be regarded as an effort to create that vehicle, a poetic art in which the religious and the scientific forms of cognition might coexist in a spiritually therapeutic unity.

Most of the early lyrics of *Sea Garden* (1916) are ritualistic invocations addressed to an element of nature or a Greek deity. In them, H. D. speaks as if she were intoxicated by the anthropomorphism and polytheism of Greek religion. Yet her verse is strictly controlled. It has the immaculate Bauhaus-like trim of modernism in appearance, brief lines, without capitals, the white spaces of the page isolating individual phrases or words as though they were on an altar. This style of typography was to be her hallmark throughout her career, and, of course, was to influence many younger poets.

H. D.'s modernism and inventiveness go beyond appearance, however. Cyrena N. Pondrom has argued convincingly that the clear, nondiscursive imagery of H. D.'s first poems, which led Pound to identify her as "Imagiste" in the famous scene in the British Museum tea-room, showed Pound what Imagist poems should be.[12] They achieved the ideal of cold, hard, enduring form recommended by T. E. Hulme. The poetry H. D. produced in this style sweeps rhetoric and overt emotionalism aside and generates intense feeling through simple, sharp images, using the familiar diction and free verse that were aspects of the modernist rebellion.

H. D.'s early work undertakes the dangerous project of employing the ancient religions as vehicles of personal feeling. Like Pound, she identified the gods with states of mind, and her early lyrics, like his, are invocational, often actual supplications, that both express a feeling and address the deity who embodies it. Eileen Gregory has suggested that the poems of *Sea Garden* are the utterances of a woman undergoing a rite of initiation who addresses a vague composite deity. Consequently, the reader must "grasp the ritual intent of the whole volume . . . enter the sea garden, a world ritually set apart, as an initiate in its mysteries."[13]

The religion that presides over these poems and the sequence called *The God*, however, is not Greek polytheism, but the worship of love and "beauty." H. D.'s early love-lyrics project an intensity that is related to the insatiable passion analyzed in Denis de Rougemont's *Love in the Western World*, one of her favorite books. Their language is like the language of prayer, in accordance with the theory held both by De Rougemont and Pound that the love poems of the troubadours were encoded expressions of religious devotion. Like the early Pound, H. D. believed in "beauty" as a Platonic essence that distinguished works of art. In her novel, *Bid Me to Live*, the autobiographical character, Julia, shows that she regards beauty as a mystical goal by asking herself: "Did the past and the future blend (or would they) in one eternal circle of the absolute, find beauty?" H. D.'s early poems offer "beauty" as their highest value, though her conception of it includes hardship and discipline. In "Sheltered Garden," for example, she proposes "to find a new beauty / in some terrible / wind-tortured place." "The Islands" insists that "beauty is set apart" and that one must face it, though it is "terrible, torturous, isolated" and seen in rocks, shipwrecks and the wind (*CP*, 21, 126-27). "The Tribute," after surveying the evils of modern urban civilization, devotes a long final passage to the assertion that "beauty" is immortal and survives commercialism and violence.

The poems of *Sea Garden* look out on a rocky littoral landscape where growth is twisted and deformed by the forces of wind and sea. They recall "The Forsaken Garden" by Swinburne, a poet whose work H. D. read with Pound in her youth:

> In a coign of the cliff between lowland and highland
>> At the sea-down's edge between windward and lee,
> Walled round with rocks as an inland island,
>> The ghost of a garden fronts the sea.

The gods of H. D.'s landscape are both destructive and fulfilling, and this is also a Swinburnian theme, applied to Persephone, the deity of Eleusis, in the "Hymn to Proserpine" through a parallel with another god:

> Yea, is not even Apollo, with hair and harpstring of gold,
> A bitter God to follow, a beautiful God to behold?

By embedding such themes in clipped, irreducible lines of free verse, H. D. showed that one did not need Swinburne's incantational meters to address the gods or to speak about them.

In *Sea Garden* we encounter a feature that pervades all of H. D.'s poetry: a purposeful interweaving of external reality and subjective impression so that the object cannot be detached from the impression it makes. Flowers, cliffs, and sea are both sharply sketched and enigmatically symbolic. Janice S. Robinson's observation that in H. D.'s poetry, "the perfect fusion of physical and metaphysical reality in the single image creates a mystery," suggests how close her effects are to those of the Eucharist and other rituals. But, as Robinson also observes, the poetry H. D. and Pound were writing at this time was "conceptually consistent" with the ideas of Einstein and Freud; in Pound's theories, she writes, "the line between subject and object has all but disappeared."[14] This phenomenological terrain is H. D.'s poetic environment; it corresponds to the erosion of Cartesian dualism that was to characterize both the art and the scientific philosophy of the later twentieth century.

I have mentioned Peter Bürger's observation that as the modernists regarded art itself as sacred, their individual works became secular rituals that replaced religion.[15] This insight applies perfectly to H. D.'s poetry. The atmosphere and symbolism of ritual are always present, even in the absence of actual ceremonies. While they characteristically take place away from the inner shrine, the reason may be that her world is itself a place of ritual, and formal performance would be redundant. "The Shrine" and "The Cliff Temple" describe places of worship that promise beauty and salvation, but the speaker is cut off from them because they are in forbidding surroundings, and she can feel their influence only at a distance. A climactic section of "The Walls Do Not Fall" describes the path to the temple as a wasteland and takes us only to the gate, with a final agonized question. Ritualism without ritual is characteristic of the *Sea Garden* poems. Eileen Gregory explains it as an instance of liminality, the threshold phase of ritual, which, as we have seen, involves independence, flexibility, and experimentation.

The brief drama, *Hymen,* is perhaps an exception to H. D.'s avoidance of actual ritual performance. It was written between 1916 and 1921, at a time when H. D. was translating Greek drama, and is an imitation of the form. It enacts a marriage with choruses and music, specifying exact details of the costumes and coiffures of the actors. The stage directions describe the movements of the groups, as if they were dancers, achieving an intensely stylized and, in fact, ritualized form. After the bride is praised with much luscious flower imagery, the male figure of Love is called "the plunderer," as if the metaphor of "deflowering" a virgin is being called into play. If it is regarded as a ritual, *Hymen* can be seen both as a re-enactment of some definitive primordial event and as a comment on the ambiguity of sexual initiation.

The heroine of *HERmione* often feels that her life is a continuity of the Greek tradition. She imagines that the cook is motivated by "things out of Hesiod," sees her mother as "Eleusinian," and identifies her feelings with Olympian figures ("like the shafts of a Pythian goddess, I will slay and kill"). The significance of this habit becomes clear when she says: "Dealing with terms of antiquity became a sort of ritual. It was all out of reality. . . . The very centre of spark of the divinity was in a Greek boy praying," a reference to a small figure she has seen at a friend's house.[16]

Though she is apparently excluded from places of worship, H. D. constructs her own rituals. The speaker of "The Gift" dismisses the "initiates" who claim to have had communion with a superior race, asserting that her experiences as a lover surpass their moments of transcendence:

I have lived as they
in their inmost rites—
they endure the tense nerves

through the moment of ritual
I endure from moment to moment—
days pass all alike
tortured, intense. (*CP*, 17)

H. D. seems to regard the Eleusinian rite with skepticism, while acknowledging its influence. Her *Notes on Thought and Vision*, written in 1919, offer a rather personal interpretation of the rite; she declares that patterns corresponding to its three spiritual stages of animal feeling, intellect, and final revelation exist in the contemporary world. In the closing entries of this notebook, she recognizes the Greek mystery as a celebration of earth, and blends its doctrines and symbols with those of Christianity, emphasizing the difference that Eleusis was centered on a mother figure, while the God of Christianity is a father.

But she treats Eleusis together with all formal observances less favorably elsewhere, while reserving admiration for its presiding deity, the mother figure Demeter, whom she seems able to separate from the ritual itself. In the dramatic monologue, "Demeter," the goddess includes the paraphernalia of ceremony in a long inventory of vanities that are "useless" and insists that she, as a figure of human suffering, should be kept in mind. Men may seek oblivion by worshipping other gods, but Demeter declares that she remains conscious of the darker aspects of life, the hardships Dionysus underwent as a child, and the rape of her daughter, Persephone. (*CP*, 111-15). Another poem, "At Eleusis," deals with an ineffective episode of the ritual, as the participant is unable to examine his past honestly. The rite fails because "what they did / they did for Dionysos', / for ecstasy's sake," instead of sincerely seeking a spiritual goal, and the priest fears the consequences of taking the place of the goddess. (*CP*, 179-80).

There is a similar theme in "The Mysteries," which opens with reactions of despair to natural disasters and war. Then a voice speaks, claiming to sanctify nature and uplift and resurrect it to counteract the destructions of man. It claims also to sanctify "all ancient mysteries," but the climax of the poem reveals that the mysteries mentioned are those of the seasons that promote the fertility of nature. The voice declares that it lends its power to two of the Eleusinian deities, Demeter and Iacchus (or Dionysus), and closes by declaring that it is embodied in their sacramental foods of bread and wine, in the listener as well, and ultimately in all beings. H. D. has apparently given this speaker authority over the gods of abundance (while making it difficult to identify him or her with any known deity, though Gaia, the earth mother, is a possible candidate) in order to transfer the magical power of fertility from the symbolism of ritual to the actuality of the living and growing world. In spite of these reservations about the value of the Eleusinian ritual's forms, imagery found throughout H. D.'s poetry, such as sacrificial fires, sacred potions, bursts of light, and especially her responsiveness to the figure of Demeter, suggest that she had it in mind as the prototype of ritual.

Most of *Trilogy* was written about twenty years after H. D.'s early poems. At the time she was living in wartime London, sharing the terror and hardships of the Blitz. Like "East Coker" and the *Pisan Cantos, Trilogy* is an effort to justify the value of visionary poetry in the face of the horrors of World War II. It corresponds in many respects to "the modern poetic sequence" described by M. L. Rosenthal and Sally M. Gall. Neither a narrative nor a coherent discourse, it presents itself, in their language, as "a progression of specific qualities and intensities of emotionally and sensuously charged awareness" whose structure consists of "felt relationships" among "centers of intensity" that interact with each other to achieve an impression of organic unity. The sequence exhibits both the "pressures" and the movement toward balance and resolution mentioned by Rosenthal and Gall.[17]

Trilogy can be read as an expression of personal feeling, a critique of contemporary civilization and war, and a defense of mysticism. It is also a dialogue of many voices that pits opinion against opinion, meets assertions with skepticism, and answers puzzlement with affirmation. The text moves freely from one topic to another without transitions and contains a miscellany of genres, including speculation, interrogation, narrative, prayer, lyrics, and many others. Among its intertextual foundations are psychoanalysis, the lore H. D. had assimilated from her studies of the occult, Christian symbolism, and the Bible, especially Revelation. On the one hand, the poem expresses unmistakably personal feelings and insights with extraordinary poetic effect; yet the speaker indicated by "us" and "I" remains indefinite, and the conflicting emotions and tones defeat any attempt to see this subject as a unity.

One of the experimental aspects of *Trilogy* is its form, an anomalous mixture of freedom and control. Each of its three parts—"The Walls Do Not Fall," "Tribute to the Angels" and "The Flowering of the Rod"—consists of exactly forty-three sections, mostly in free-verse couplets. While there is no rhyme scheme, the lines are often interlaced with subtle phonetic echoes in the form of assonance, alliteration, or even outright rhyme, a feature seen in H. D.'s poetry at least as early as 1916. As the following example from "The

Walls Do Not Fall" shows, this is an original device, and may claim to be one
of H. D.'s innovations (emphasis has been added):

Evil was active in the *land,*
Good was impoverished and *sad;*

Ill promised adventure,
Good was smug and *fat.*

Dev-*ill* was after us,
tricked up like Jehovah:

Good was the tasteless *pod,*
stripped from the manna-beans, pulse, lent*ils:*

they were *angry* when we were so *hungry*
For the nourishment, *God;* (*CP,* 511)

Alicia Ostriker has appropriately titled the essay in which she discusses this
prosodic method "No Rules of Procedure," for it is without any exact
precedent; it is a flexible, generally unobtrusive technique that operates
subliminally, corresponding, as Ostriker says, to "the receptive psychic states
of dream and vision" that are important elements of the poem.[18]

The most profoundly experimental aspect of *Trilogy* is its effort to "Make
it new," to adapt occult traditions to the demands of the modern mind. An
exchange that begins with the irony of section 30 of "The Walls Do Not
Fall" warns against the uncontrolled mysticism that "spews forth / too many
incongruent monsters" and leads to "*reversion of old values / oneness lost, madness.*"
(*CP,* 534) H. D. differentiates this from the esotericism of her own "initiates"
by claiming that they perceived order in apparent chaos—"we found the
angle of incidence / equals the angle of reflection" (*CP,* 535)—and calling
for a more pragmatic spirituality. The difference between the two is that the
first arises from the chaotic subconscious, while the second is consciously
guided.

In a later section of the poem, "The Flowering of the Rod," the poet claims
rationality by saying that her predictions are not the "madness" of a "frozen
Priestess" but rather "simple reckoning, algebraic, / it is geometry on the
wing." Her kind of spirituality, she continues in "The Walls Do Not Fall,"
will be morally responsible:

. . . let us not teach
what we have learned badly

. . . nor invent

new colours
for blind eyes. (CP, 536)

This spirituality will follow an imperative that sounds very much like a
rational approach to esoteric material,

Let us substitute
enchantment for sentiment

re-dedicate our gifts
to spiritual realism . . . (CP, 537)

This will mean carrying on artistic work in the Hermetic tradition of "the
eternal verity," in a time that calls for "initiates" "to re-value / our secret hoard
/ in the light of both past and future" (CP, 538).

This emphasis on reinterpretation is a persistent theme of *Trilogy*. Its first
section begins with a parallel between blitzed London, where H. D. was
living, and the Egyptian temples at Luxor, which she had seen about twenty
years earlier. Her reciprocal metaphors here establish continuity between the
Egyptian hieroglyphs, which project their meanings out of ruins, and "we,
the people or artists of London, who preserve the secrets of ancient wisdom
amid the ruins left by German bombs. The inventions of the ancient gods of
writing are "magic, indelibly stamped / on the atmosphere somewhere
forever," (CP, 519) but the recuperation of that wisdom is pursued, paradoxically, in an innovative spirit.

This spirit emerges in the first section of "Tribute to the Angels," where
H. D. praises one of her favorite gods, "Hermes Trismegistus . . . inventive
artful, curious," who is urged to gather what has been destroyed by the
"new-church" and to "melt down and integrate, re-invoke, re-create / opal
onyx, obsidian, / now scattered in the shards / men tread upon" (CP, 547-48)
And the Lady who appears later in this section as an integration of all the
female deities into a single goddess is not "hieratic" or "frozen"; the book she
carries "is not / the tome of ancient wisdom, / the pages, I imagine are blank
pages / of the unwritten volume of the new" (CP, 570).

Further possibilities for experimental innovation are inherent in H. D.'s point that each mind sees "the eternal realities" in its own way.[19] Her way—or one of her ways—is through the perception that spiritual secrets are concealed in words. As she writes in "The Walls Do Not Fall":

> I know, I feel
> the meaning that words hide;
>
> they are anagrams, cryptograms,
> little boxes, conditioned
>
> to hatch butterflies. . . . (*CP*, 540)

H. D. frequently demonstrates her method in *Trilogy* by extrapolating a word's meaning through etymology, puns, or associations, displaying an experimental sense of language very like that seen in *Finnegans Wake*. Early in the sequence she declares that writing is justified in wartime because "Word" is prior to "Sword." The example given in "The Walls Do Not Fall" is the identification of "Osiris" with "O-Sire-is" and "Sirius" which, according to H. D., "relates resurrection myth / and resurrection reality / through the ages." She offers this example to show that her thought, although "not too well equipped" can remedy the errors of philosophy, "correlate faith with faith" and discover the one divinity who is the true Creator (*CP*, 540-41).

Similar verbal experimentation is seen in section 8 of "Tribute to the Angels," where the poet, claiming to perform a kind of alchemy, puts the Hebrew *marah*, meaning "bitter," through various transmutations, until it yields

> mer, mere, mère, mater, Maia, Mary,
>
> Star of the Sea,
> Mother. (*CP*, 552)

H. D. performs a similar linguistic feat in defending two goddesses. The root of "Venus" suggests lasciviousness to many, but H. D. repudiates this with another punning association by relating the name to "venerate, / venerator." In the same passage, she exploits the name of the Syrian sea-goddess, Astarte, by saying that ships have been wrecked because they "lost your star" (*CP*, 554).

The first part of *Trilogy* closes with the hope that experimental innovation will lead to spiritual salvation. The bombed ruins left by the Blitz make it necessary to get about London in new ways. H. D. cleverly parallels this with the need for following new methods in pursuing the spiritual quest, and the pun of the section's last lines shows how the routes to deliverance can be found in language:

> *we know no rule*
> *of procedure*
>
> *we are voyagers, discoverers*
> *of the not-known*
>
> *the unrecorded:*
> *we have no map;*
>
> *possibly we will reach haven,*
> *heaven.* (*CP*, 543)

While *Trilogy* does not enact ceremonies, the language of prayer, supplication, and vision play a prominent part in it. An actual ritual is called for in "The Walls Do Not Fall," where the "world-father," whom H. D. calls "Amen" (her spelling of the Egyptian Amun-Ra), appears. The moment of regeneration is to be marked with a fire ceremony and chants to the sun, an invitation to what is clearly a rite; but the fire will be a "new fire," and the chant will consist of "new paeans." It is clear, then, that ritual must have a modern justification and a modern validity. The tension between old and new is still unresolved however, as the poem declares that the image of Christ, who is freely identified with Amen and other male deities, must be disengaged "from its art-craft junk-shop / paint-and-plaster medieval jumble" (*CP*, 525).

The prominence of Egyptian deities and Egyptian themes in *Trilogy* exhibits an extension of H. D.'s syncretism, a result of her visit to the temples of Luxor and the Valley of the Kings with Bryher in 1923. In the poem "Egypt," apparently written during this visit, she reproaches Egypt for the "poison" of its preoccupation with death. But by a "perverse fate" the "poison" has brought benign things with it, "belief enhanced, / ritual returned and magic." This was achieved, according to the last stanza, by "wisdom," whose grey eyes suggest Athena, and by a fire in Egypt's desert that brought light and produced "Hellas, re-born from death," by the modifications of Greek religion (*CP*, 141).

H. D.'s knowledge of Egyptian mystical doctrines and their relation to Greek religion gave a new spaciousness to her esotericism. In section 33 of "Tribute to the Angels," she perceives that Hermes was descended from the Egyptian god of writing, Thoth, and that the "T-cross," the Egyptian ankh, evolved into the caduceus. The Egyptian visit also confirmed her belief in ritual, for, as Barbara Guest has observed, H. D. found among the "ritualistic Egyptians" a congenial mysticism missing from Greek religion that led her deeper into the occult.[20] As she perceived the continuity between Egyptian magical lore and that of Greece, Egypt and its ritual symbols became a vital element of her poetry. In *Trilogy*, it is also a source of the inspiration she feels amid the horrors of war, for, as we have seen, the poem opens by aligning the ruins of bombed London with the ruins of Egypt on the ground that both display the survival of spiritual tradition after material destruction. Among the ruins "the Luxor bee, chick and hare / pursue unalterable purpose" and "eternity endures" (*CP*, 509).

H. D.'s term for those who share her views, "initiates," suggests that they have gone through some rite. In observing that ritual sheds a sacred aura on its implements so that in declaring that "grape, knife, cup, wheat / are symbols in eternity" (*CP*, 523), she chooses images from fertility rites, as L. S. Dembo has noted.[21] Those who attribute a timeless value to these common objects carry out the bonding effect of ritual; they are "companions of the flame . . . keepers of the secret, / the carriers, the spinners / of the rare intangible thread / that binds all humanity" (*CP*, 521-22).

The sense that the modern world is a ritual site still fit for the worship of the ancient deities is strong even in bombed-out London, for the seventh section of "Tribute to the Angels" declares that a "levelled wall / is purple as with purple spread / upon an altar" (*CP*, 551) and presents the ruined city as a scene of resurrection. This part of the poem declares that the Londoners of World War II are unconscious worshippers of the fires they have watched and that they possess the power of flame, which is also seen in candles and the stars. Thus, the flames of the Blitz, like all shining things, tend to share the sacredness of a ceremonial fire. The universality of the image is continued as the gleam of rainwater in a furrow and the shining of a spear are associated with Hesperus (or Venus), the star that shines steadily at both evening and morning. Finally the poet, as if fearful that Venus will lose her true significance with the end of some fire-centered ritual, urges, "O swiftly, relight the flame / before the substance cool . . . / Swiftly re-light the flame, Aphrodite, holy name" (*CP*, 553-54).

Adalaide Morris has shown that alchemical transmutation serves as a metaphor of spiritual transformation both in the detailed imagery of *Trilogy* and in the general structure of the poem.[22] Further, the parallel between the quasi-alchemical process of spiritual illumination and religious rituals of transubstantiation is often suggested and is made overt in at least one instance. In "Tribute to the Angels," when the poet comes across a half-burnt tree that nevertheless stands flowering among ruins (an incident no doubt based on an actual experience), she feels a "new sensation" of religious afflatus. This encounter forces her to say, "we admit the transubstantiation, / not God merely in bread / but God in the other-half of the tree," and she feels that she has been redeemed through "the flowering of the rood," identifying the tree with the cross. The place becomes sacred, a "high-altar," and the poet realizes that "from the visible / there is no escape" (*CP,* 560-61). The insight offered by a chance personal experience is linked to Christian ritual, and the conviction that the path to the transcendental lies through the material world is affirmed.

The tale of Mary Magdalen, Kaspar the Mage, and the Nativity that occupies the last two-thirds of "The Flowering of the Rod" reflects H. D.'s reservations about traditional ritual. The scene enacted by the other Magi in receiving the Christ child is called "this ritual," but H. D.'s hero, Kaspar, stands aside from it "and placed his gift / a little apart from the first" (*CP,* 611). His gift is a symbol of skepticism. It is a jar of myrrh, a substance used in pagan rituals, but it is one of two identical jars containing myrrh of unequal quality, and Kaspar is not sure he has brought the best one. The Virgin thanks him for its fragrance. But he knows that it is still sealed; the fragrance rises from "the bundle of myrrh / she held in her arms" (*CP,* 612), the Christ-child, the real, rather than the ritualized source of spiritual deliverance.

Traditional and innovative motivations are thoroughly blended in H. D.'s notion of ritual. The Lady who appears as a universal symbol in "Tribute to the Angels" is emphatically distanced from the usual values associated with female figures; her book will exhibit "the same attributes, / different yet the same as before" (*CP,* 571). Hence, when the prayer addressed to "Amen-Ra" declares that the messages of the stars are to be released by "prayer, spell, / litany, incantation," we can be sure that these sacred formulae, though addressed to one of the most ancient gods, will not be simply repetitions of old ones.

H. D.'s feats of linguistic transmutation and other deviations may be said to combine experiment with esotericism, to use innovative faculties for the purpose of reviving moribund traditions. But there is also a tension between the two. The mystic in H. D. never forgets that language has its limitations in the face of visionary experience. When she complains that she cannot find a name for the color of a jewel seen in a vision, her mentor commands, "invent it," but the poet answers that she cannot. The mystic refuses to encapsulate the jewel's occult qualities in language. The ritual consciousness, we might say, maintains its independence of the experimental one, but as many passages of *Trilogy* insist, it must express itself in ways that meet modern and personal needs. The ritual planned in section 17 of "The Walls Do Not Fall" will reject "empty / old thought, old convention"; its celebrants will "chant new paeans to the new Sun" (*CP*, 524). In another passage, H. D. values the childhood Dream of the Holy Ghost because it "explains symbols of the past / in today's imagery," merging "distant future" and "distant antiquity" (*CP*, 526).

H. D.'s last ambitious work, *Helen in Egypt*, exhibits the same urge to renew and subvert tradition that we see in *Trilogy*, but it is directed toward myth rather than ritual. In this poem, H. D. follows the idea of the Greek poet Stesichorus and Euripides' tragedy, *Helen*, that Helen herself was transported to Egypt, while the figure in Troy was a mere double or simulacrum, so that "The Greeks and Trojans alike fought for an illusion."[23] This setting enabled H. D. to base her references to divinity on the syncretism that linked Egypt with the classical world, so that, as she says in this first speech, Amen is another name for Zeus. She does not, however, follow the ancient deviations from Homer but rather develops her story in original ways and opens new spiritual and psychological depths in it. In *End to Torment* she refers to her Helen as "my creative reconstruction." As Joseph Riddel has observed, reconstruction is not separable from deconstruction.[24]

Her poem embraces numerous themes, including love, death, war, and the nature of women, so that it is especially resistant to summary. A series of lyrics spoken by various characters, each prefaced by a prose gloss, it does not conform to any recognized genre but is, in its major dimension, a meditative search on Helen's part for her true identity, her place in the myth of Troy.[25] There is an obscure narrative line, partly based on various secondary legends connected with the Homeric story, partly invented by H. D. Achilles after his death joins Helen at the temple of Amun-Ra at Luxor, and Helen recalls that he was one of her lovers. At a meeting on a "desolate beach," he tries to strangle her, but Helen saves herself by invoking the name of his mother, Thetis. Trying to forget the events of the Trojan war for which she has been held responsible, Helen feels that she herself has become the pattern they form, but a divine voice proclaims her independence of them.

In the second of the poem's three parts, Helen finds herself on the island of Leuké, where the ghost of Paris comes to remind her of his suffering at the fall of Troy, to say that he will not forget her, and to deny that Achilles loved her. Then another former lover, Theseus, counsels her to forget her division of mind and to seek some transcendent deliverance. When she suggests that she is still devoted to Achilles, Theseus reminds her of the many women he has betrayed, but Helen, becoming her heroic self, replies that none of this matters in comparison with the momentous events of the Trojan War that called forth their deepest passions and united them with each other.

She begins to find peace by moving to a visionary level where she can merge the identities of the figures around her in a dialectic blending of the oppositions that have claimed her. But before yielding to the Absolute, she asks for time to remember and to "encompass the infinite" in actual time. In the final section, a Helen who is in contact with actuality succeeds in understanding that such opposites as love and death are identical when seen from the perspective of eternity, and in seeing the events she has lived through as aspects of infinite time. By achieving this mystical vision, she resolves the problem of her identity.

Helen in Egypt has some of the aspects of a spiritual autobiography. H. D.'s treatment of Helen illustrates Lord Henry's reflection in *The Picture of Dorian Gray*: "When we thought we were experimenting on others we were really experimenting on ourselves." With the *Pisan Cantos* in mind, H. D. readily accepted the view that in writing it, "I completed my own *cantos*."[26] But it is also a reply to the traditional Helen represented in the *Cantos*. H. D. attempts both to correct tradition by redeeming Helen, the figure in her earlier poem who is hated by "all Greece" as the cause of the Trojan War (*CP*, 154-55), and to recapitulate her own spiritual development through her version of the myths. Helen, says the earlier poem, would be loved if she were dead, and in *Helen in Egypt*, all the characters have, in fact, passed the gate of death, for "Egypt" is an obscure afterworld where they come together to discuss the parts they have played in life.

The problem of Helen's identity is created partly by the appearance of her phantom self in Troy and partly by the differing views offered by her three lovers. It is not a question of her physical existence, but of her character as a myth or a legend, for her career is deftly intertwined with legendary archetypes: as one who searches for a loved one, she resembles Isis, Demeter, and Aphrodite; as one bent on a quest, she is like Demeter and Theseus in search of the Golden Fleece; as a woman who has been forcefully abducted, she is like Persephone; as the lover and protector of Achilles, she is like his mother, Thetis. [27] In fact, Theseus tells her, in one of the most incantational lyrics of the poem, that she embodies opposites and that they are reconciled within her.

Helen acknowledges that she exists as what is written—and, it should be added, as what is thought. At one point, she decides to study the "indecipherable" hieroglyphics carved on the walls and pillars of the Luxor temple, no doubt because she thinks they record insights into the transcendental. Knowledge of the inscriptions is unnecessary, the gloss tells us, because "she herself is the writing." And later, she seeks answers to her problems through physical contact by *touching* the incised carvings. But the fact that the hieroglyphics are representational—H. D. repeatedly mentions chick, bee, and hare—suggests that nature itself is a sacred writing, that "the timeless, hieratic symbols can be parallelled with symbols in-time." (107)[28]

Because she exists as a concept expressed in writing, Helen ultimately decides that the Trojan War, whatever its destructive effects, has united her forever with Achilles, that "the dart of Love / is the dart of Death," and that the "finite moment" of their union has become a myth that will withstand the pressure of infinity. This commitment to a vision that sees earthly events as part of a greater, unaltering pattern is beautifully expressed in the triad that concludes the penultimate lyric:

the seasons revolve around
a pause in the infinite rhythm
of the heart and of heaven. (304)

Helen in Egypt moves fluidly among the speeches of the characters and that of an authorial voice, merging the past with the present, dream with waking, memory with meditation, and the illusionary with the actual. This loose structure is nearly without precedent, though that of Tennyson's *Maud* resembles it. In an even more serious digression from convention, by telling its story in the prose introductions to each lyric, as well as in poetry, H. D. puts "analytico-referential" language side by side with a "patterning" language that deals with the affairs of legendary figures and pagan divinities. The prose exposition or analysis speaks from a point of vantage outside the mythical context, sometimes speculating and correcting itself; but the characters speak from within their emotional situations in verse that is headlong and passionate, even when it forms questions, tacitly accepting a mythic universe whose subtleties are unknown to the prose world.

This freely shifting content, however, is contained in a rigid form consisting of a general plan based on numbers. The poem is divided into three sections, each consisting of seven books, except for the last, which has only six. Each "book" has eight numbered parts consisting of a lyric or narrative poem prefaced by a prose gloss. The poems are consistently cast in triplets, but they exhibit varying meters, and the phonetic correspondences characteristic of H. D.'s work sometimes appear and sometimes are dropped.

While myth is the chief source and narrative idiom of *Helen in Egypt*, themes connected specifically with ritual form a minor but important thread in it. Achilles, finding Helen preoccupied with the hieroglyphics in the Luxor temple, perceives that she is interested in restoring the "ancient Mysteries" of Egypt and bringing them to Greece. She has, in fact, found satisfaction in these rites and has told Paris of their healing quality. She says,

> No, I will not challenge
> the ancient Mystery,
> the Oracle . . . (64)

and she apparently does what H. D. herself did on her visit to Luxor: she explores the temple and walks along the Nile.

Many of the lyrics take the form of prayers to the gods. In one of them, Helen prays that Achilles may be spiritually redeemed, and in the first lyric of "Eidolon," Achilles acknowledges the authority of "the High Priest of love-rites" by saying that he and Helen are reliving the story of Persephone and Hades: "in Egypt / we are in Eleusis." He adds that the Luxor temple, where they are now, embraces the creeds of Greece as well as those of Egypt (208-209).

Ritual rhythms appear among the many tones the poem adopts. The first lyric of Book Six of "Leuké," for example, begins with an incantational chant: "Cypris, Cypria, Amor, / say the words over and over." And lyric 7 of this book, where Theseus asserts that Helen herself encompasses the meeting of opposites found in the Absolute, has the enigmatic repetitiveness of a litany:

> Thus, thus, thus
> as day, night,
> as wrong, right,
>
> as dark, light,
> as water, fire,
> as earth, air. . . . (190)

Toward the end of her musing, Helen confirms Theseus's lesson by formulating the mystic insight of the ritual moment: opposites such as time and timelessness no longer exist; "there is no before and no after, / there is one finite moment / that no infinite joy can disperse" (309). What she has gained through this reconciliation is "a rhythm as yet unheard."

Helen is well aware, however, that rituals do not yield their meaning, a principle, we recall, that T. S. Eliot insisted on in his paper for the Harvard seminar. In "Pallinode," she acknowledges that

> . . . you may penetrate
> every shrine, an initiate,
> and remain unenlightened at last. (79)

and again,

> you may work or steal your way
> into the innermost shrine
> and the secret escape you. . . . (83)

As she moves toward the final vision of time within timelessness, H. D. does, in fact, challenge the traditional rites while preserving the principle of ritual itself. The most ancient foundations of the Mystery endure, while its forms and the places of worship can change. H. D. insists on this flexibility by reinterpreting ritual episodes from the myths in ways that amount to radical subversion. For example, the prose gloss to lyric 6, Book 5 of "Pallinode" (74) tells us that Helen identifies herself with her sister's daughter, Iphigenia, who was lured to death as a sacrifice but spared at the last moment. H. D., recalling that Iphigenia was brought to Aulis by the promise that she would wed Achilles, transforms the sacrificial ritual into a kind of bridal ceremony, in which both mother and daughter invoke their divine ancestry "before the altar" and defy the military clique that would have sacrificed her.

The traditions of ritual sacrifice are threatened again when Achilles says he is ready to substitute Helen for Iphigenia as a sacrifice (243-44). Helen experiences the transcendence of a ritual experience as she feels (or imagines) Achilles's touch on her throat and stops him by speaking the name of Thetis, who dwells in "the caves of the Mysteries." Achilles, like Helen herself, undergoes a spiritual conversion and serves the high priest of love, making it possible for this event to "weld him to her" and to be the beginning "of the ever-recurring 'eternal moment'" in which the union of the two represents transcendental unity. As the poem approaches its conclusion, Helen swings back and forth between "trance" and waking, between painful recollections of the Trojan War and a mystical insight. Ultimately, the memories are replaced by

> ... thoughts too deep to remember,

> that break through the legend,
> the fame of Achilles,
> the beauty of Helen,

> like fire
> through the broken pictures
> on a marble-floor. (258-59)

In this way, Thetis brings about Helen's version of the Freudian dialectic, the union of love and death that at last becomes *her* myth of the Trojan War.

And, in fact, "the Mysteries" she has consulted become one of the elements of the past that are to be forgotten as "too deep to remember" in her final awakening. The darkness at the core of ritual reappears in the gloss of the penultimate lyric, for while the poem formulates the final assertion that the moment of union and the pattern of eternity coexist, the gloss warns that "perhaps we do not wholly understand the significance of the Message" (303).

In adopting a variant form of the Helen myth and extending it into a tale that involves the metamorphosis and spiritual resurrection of both Helen and Achilles, *Helen in Egypt* continues the theme of renewal seen in *Trilogy*. That poem called for "new imagery" and "new paeans" suitable to the modern age. Springing from personal motives, it nevertheless implies a general power to reinterpret and renew the intellectual heritage of the past, and *Helen in Egypt* demonstrates that power.[29]

In these late poems the conjunction of religious emotion and new poetic techniques produced a more unified, more plausible merging of the ritual and experimental spirits in poetry than that achieved by any of H. D.'s contemporaries. The success of this merger is suggested by the fact that critics can attribute her violations of spatial and temporal limits both to mythic conventions and to the distant influence of modern physics.

This is not to say that H. D. has achieved the synthesis of faith and reason anticipated by some of the nineteenth-century thinkers. What she accomplished in her later work is well reflected in some comments from *End to Torment* written in 1958. Reflecting on Edmund Wilson's observation that the artist was "a kind of prison from which the works of art escaped," she observed hat there is nevertheless "an intermediate place or *plane*" in which the artist can work:

> Let go . . . the grandiose, let go ambition; scribble and write, that is your
> inheritance, no grim compulsion.
>   Make no mistake. Poles apart, two poles made communication possible.
> Establish the poles. Others may use our invention, extension, communication.
> We don't care any more. Only, watching, a purely instinctive gesture impels us.

The late poems follow this program. They do not seek a grand reconciliation between the two metaphysics identified with ritual and experiment but rather recognize the values of both and seek only to express the intuition that they can coexist, leaving the consequences of this insight to others. The sentence that follows reverts to one of the implications of this view: the need for the subversion of ritual, especially the sacrificial ritual that is a theme both in *Trilogy* and in *Helen in Egypt*. When H. D. enjoins:

> We would reach out, snatch a victim from the altar. *Aztec.*
> *Aztlan.* What can we do about it?[30]

she has in mind such reforms as the one embodied in her Iphigenia and Helen stories, where the "spiritual realism" of the modern consciousness intervenes to modify the barbarism of sacrifice.

As we have seen, H. D. declared that poetry might become an instrument of spiritual deliverance through the experimental resources she brought to it. Those resources are intensively centered on the expressive potentialities of language itself. Unlike the other poets in this study, she did not use a religious or political system as an armature to support her body of poetry but spoke directly from personal conviction, depending on the power of words alone to articulate her insights. Unlike the early Pound, the early H. D. does not resort to established poetic forms; on the contrary, she strips her words bare of rhetorical structure. Her short lines and asyntactical passages focus on isolated words or phrases sometimes in order to exploit their full effect, sometimes to introduce subtle subversions. Similar displacements occur with the gods and holy places of Greece that appear so prominently in her poetry: they lose some of their traditional character and become semiotic devices that participate in the deviation that H. D.'s poetry as a whole pursues.

The defiantly revisionist spirit that appears in such reworkings of myth and ritual is an identifying characteristic of all of H. D.'s poetry. As her feminist critics have abundantly shown, her position as a woman writer led her to reinterpret traditional themes in radically subversive ways. Her challenges to authority appear also in her original prosody, her revaluations of legendary figures, her linguistic explorations, and her use of Freud's teachings as materials for poetry. H. D. maintains that ordinary minds have not looked deeply enough into ordinary experience and shows that love entails agony, that beauty is difficult, and that death is desirable. Her justification for revealing such unwelcome truths is grounded neither in religion nor science; while she accepts neither supernatural dogmas nor quasi-scientific common sense without skepticism, she makes use of both, as she said, to prepare a way for the future of poetry.

9

David Jones

composite, experimental
—*The Anathemata* on the Ram

David Jones participated more fully in the modern revolution of the word led by James Joyce and the American expatriates than any other British poet. Both ritual and technical experiment are integral elements of his works and are perhaps more essential to them than to those of the other modernists. Jones was a remarkable figure, a graphic artist and poet of great originality, who closely resembled William Blake in his achievements. His major literary works, *In Parenthesis* (1937) and *The Anathemata* (1952) won ample recognition, especially from other poets, but he has escaped until recently the torrent of critical attention that descended on the major modernists. W. H. Auden, reviewing *The Anathemata* in 1954, declared that it was one of the most significant poems of the time and asked, "But where are the bells? Where are the cannon?"[1]

Jones responded to contemporary and historical influences with exceptional sensitivity, confirming Pound's view that artists are the antennae of the race. The preface to *The Anathemata* names fifty or more contemporary authors as a partial list of those to whom Jones acknowledges indebtedness. Pound is not one of them, however, and though *The Anathemata* closely resembles the *Cantos*, Jones did not read it until his own poem had been published. All of the poets I have discussed were personally influenced, to some extent, by Pound; Jones, who never knew him, is the exception.

Although Jones was born in England, he was nevertheless inspired by his Welsh father's heredity to devote himself to Welsh traditions. His studies at art schools just before and after World War I introduced him to book illustration and to the work of such figures as Blake and the Pre-Raphaelites. Through his service in World War I he came to believe that war was an integral and significant aspect of the human experience, agreeing with other veterans he met that World War I embedded itself in one's character in a fundamental way. The war is the scene of *In Parenthesis* and military analogies and examples continued to appear in Jones's writing years after he had left the army. The war also led him, indirectly, to become a Roman Catholic convert in 1921.

Jones spent some years in the Ditchling Common community of Eric Gill, where he learned engraving and improved his skills as an artist in a monastic atmosphere that demanded a strong Catholic commitment. After leaving Ditchling in 1924, he felt the influence of some of the most advanced modern artists on the English scene and also that of a circle of friends who joined a devotion to Catholicism with an interest in politics and in contemporary art and writing. At about this time, he had the first of his mental breakdowns, underwent psychoanalytic therapy, and became familiar with Freudian theories. On a visit to the Near East in 1934, he spent some time in Palestine, where the presence of the British soldiers serving under the British mandate recalled his war experiences, impressing him as strongly as the Biblical sites. Jones, who thought of himself as a graphic artist, did no writing until he began *In Parenthesis* in 1928. After its publication in 1937 with an introduction by T. S. Eliot, he wrote prolifically, producing many shorter poems and essays as well as *The Anathemata.*

Everything that Jones wrote—and much of his artwork—was thoroughly infiltrated by allusions to his reading. His unusual method, following Eliot's *Waste Land* example, of appending notes to his poems, exhibits a wide-ranging and somewhat pedantic knowledge of classical and secondary works centering on religion and the history and literature of the Greco-Roman and Celtic civilizations but also venturing into many other fields, including geology and anthropology.

As a deeply religious artist trapped in a secular age, Jones developed a philosophy of art rooted in two basic beliefs: form must follow content; and all craftsmanship, even the most humble, is sacramental. The first of these principles led him to experimentalism; the second, to ritual. His ideas appear in the essays, introductions, speeches, and the like collected in two volumes, *Epoch and Artist* (1959) and *The Dying Gaul* (1978).

Jones's work, like the other experimental works I have discussed, is so thoroughly unconventional that it is difficult to assign it to specific genres. *In Parenthesis* is generally regarded as a poetic work, but one critic unhesitatingly discusses it as a novel, others call it an epic, and the bookstore where I bought the paperback edition shelved it under "biography." Jones acknowledged that his roots lay in the modern period and that the innovations in his work resembled those of the other experimentalists. Observing that "modern painting tends, among other things, to be idiosyncratic and personal in expression and experimental in technique," he asserts that the modern painter nevertheless works within a tradition that lacks formulation: "It is rather a tradition of feeling-toward, it is one of exploration and specialization. Here I suppose the artist shares something with the contemporary physicist."[2] According to Jones, the modern artist cannot ignore the technological atmosphere of his time. We recognize motivations found among other experimentalists when he says that if the modern artist's work is to be "valid," it must have "now-ness," a "sense of the contemporary." In the preface to *The Anathemata* he writes: "The artist deals wholly in signs. His signs must be valid, that is valid for him and, normally, for the culture that has made him."[3] His effort to express his conviction, through "valid" poetic forms, that the events commemorated in the Eucharist were central to all history launched much of the experimentalism we see in *The Anathemata*.

Jones's sensitive reactions to the scientific tone of the cultural environment justify us in relating his style to the technology-inspired Futurist and Vorticist language of the verbal revolution. There was probably no conscious association here, but in the violation of ordinary linguistic norms, the clashing juxtapositions of tone, the technical terms, and the fragmented language we find clear echoes of the experimentalism initiated by Filippo Marinetti, Pound, and Wyndham Lewis. Jones's view that the content of his work exists primarily to support a "shape in words" parallels the earlier period's experiments with depersonalization and abstraction. Neil Corcoran, after suggesting that Jones's emphasis on contemporaneity resembles Pound's "Make it new" in spirit, adds: "Jones is nowhere more thoroughgoing a modernist than in his rigorous insistence on the necessity of formal and structural experimentation."[4]

Jones concedes that technology has a powerful and ambiguous influence, demanding "a new and strange direction of the mind, a new sensitivity certainly, but at considerable cost."[5] For while he admits that science opens new possibilities to the imagination, he deplores the spiritual effects of what he called "technocracy" and wonders how new inventions can fit into the framework of tradition. He fears that the dominance of science and technology will deprive man of the sacramental and artistic sense that is latent in all his endeavors. He admits that he has no solution for the "dilemma" created by the split between the two and attributes the nervous breakdowns he suffered to his effort to reconcile the traditions he valued with the dominance of technology.[6]

This effort is an essential aspect of Jones's poetry. His extraordinary recollection of the details of his war days and his firm grasp of particulars reflects a mind of pronounced empirical tendencies. After a brush with geology, he writes, "Incredibly 'romantic' these exact scientific things are, and the more factual so much the more moving." He cannot understand why Darwin's scientific work made him unable to enjoy poetry and thinks it should have had the opposite effect. Poetry, he writes, is capable of making particulars "radiant . . . so that they become intimations of immortality, or . . . intimations of some otherness of some sort." The preface to *In Parenthesis* observes that while war makes it hard to praise "the action proper to chemicals" (xiv), it is nevertheless full of beauty. He once wrote that he was thrilled to learn the scientific fact that water was "the womb of all life,"and added, "no wonder baptism is by water."[7] In a poem about "Domine Deus," he writes:

> I have felt for His Wounds
> > in nozzles and containers.
> I have wondered for the automatic devices. . . .
> I have been on my guard
> > not to condemn the unfamiliar.
> For it is easy to miss Him
> > at the turn of a civilisation. (9)

The preface to *The Anathemata* goes right to a point of crucial importance to artists. Scientific formulations of reality cut away emotional and traditional associations, says Jones, yet these associations are vital parts of the culture to which the artist (and, it might be added, his audience) belongs. He feels that modern artists or "sign-makers" suffer from a historical situation that has stripped signs of all but the barest meaning.

According to Jones, the emphasis on form was the modern artists' way of responding to this situation. Deprived by science of the symbolic and metonymic powers formerly found in content, they turned to abstract "shape," an increasingly significant word in Jones's critical vocabulary. He defines a work of art as an object that signifies "something other" than itself. But he discounts mere mimesis, preferring to emphasize the modernist principle that abstract qualities are what make a sign an autonomous work of art. In a letter defending abstraction written as late as 1950, Jones declares that the factor common to all the arts is "a certain juxtaposing of forms," a statement that echoes Pound's view that art consists of "planes in relation."

Jones observes that the products of technology cannot avoid exhibiting the "intransitivity" or nonreferentiality of art works if they are made in some deliberate shape or form. He divides form sharply from content or purpose when he perceives beauty in war planes and bombs, a view that corresponds to the attitudes of the Italian Futurists and echoes the sculptor Henri Gaudier-Brzeska's praise of the wooden stock of a rifle. Gaudier-Brzeska's reaction to World War I supports Jones's view that the evil effects of technology paradoxically encourage the artist to leap from representation to abstraction. Revolted by what he was seeing at the front, Gaudier-Brzeska wrote, in blazing capital letters, that henceforth, "I SHALL DERIVE MY EMOTIONS SOLELY FROM THE *ARRANGEMENT OF SURFACES.*"[8]

Jones read a translation of Jacques Maritain's *Art and Scholasticism* about 1923 and found in it confirmations of some of his own convictions. In his essay "Art and Sacrament," Jones maintains, as Maritain does, that human beings are inherently motivated to create, following the example of the Creator of the universe. Further, they are impelled to make works of art because these are, using Maritain's term, "gratuitous" as distinguished from things that are functional or "utile." This is a vital distinction for Jones. The "gratuitous" or "intransitive" is the identifying characteristic of art, an expression of the free will and rationality that distinguishes man from the other animals, while the "utile" is merely the result of need. "It is the intransitivity and gratuitousness in man's art that is the sign of man's uniqueness"; gratuitous acts are "this creature's hall-mark and sign-manual." They are also counterparts of the work of God. "I understand the theologians to say that God's creation of the cosmos was a gratuitous act; it is interesting therefore that it is the very quality of gratuitousness which we recognize in the creative works of man. A kind of worship is implicit in the works of man-the-artist." Jones's "intransitivity" corresponds to the autonomy modernists favored; their views, coming from different sources, converged in insisting on the independence of the artifact, and the esthetic characteristics that implied. [9]

Jones argues that even the most primitive art works were attempts at "anamnesis," at calling something beyond the work itself to the mind of an observer; since they had meaning and implied permanence, suggesting "that anthropos has some part in a without-endness," they amounted to signs, or, as Jones prefers to put it, *signa.* "A sign must be significant of something, hence of some 'reality', so of something 'good', so of something that is 'sacred'. That is why I think the notion of the sign implies the sacred."[10] The artist, he said, believes in "transubstantiations of some sort. The sign must *be* the thing signified under forms of his particular art,"[11] a demand that recalls Ernst Cassirer's description of ritual events: ". . . they do not merely copy or represent, but are absolutely *real.*"[12]

It follows then, that "the activity called art is, at bottom and inescapably a 'religious' activity, for it deals with realities, and the real is sacred and religious." In this way, Jones justifies his contention, in the teeth of a secularized period, "that man is unavoidably a sacramentalist and that his works are sacramental in character."[13] As a result of this conviction, Jones can regard nearly every creative activity as a ritual.

Two dominant themes of David Jones's work, the violence of World War I and the crucial importance of ritual, are exactly the same as the two pillars of Girard's theory, for in *In Parenthesis* he writes of war as if it were a sacrificial ritual. The supreme work of art, for Jones, is the Eucharist, an opinion that corresponds with Mallarmé's, but is based on an entirely different rationale. According to Jones, the Mass, like the Last Supper, which it replicates, is an art work because it employs material means to create certain forms that are signs of "something other." It is supreme because God, taking advantage of man's natural sacramental bent, has commanded him to embody the Christian belief in this particular form, using the "quasi-artefacts" of bread and wine. These convictions are deeply embedded in *The Anathemata*. "For David Jones," says Neil Corcoran, "the Roman mass, in all its transforming metamorphoses, incarnates, and makes again operatively present, in an objective form, the final purpose of human life and the final meaning of human history. *The Anathemata*, as a result, both celebrates this religious art form and uses its nature as a great ritualistic drama of incorporation, as a model and principle of metamorphic form."[14]

Jones perceives a parallel between the theological doctrine of real presence embodied in transubstantiation and the esthetic principle that the work of art is an autonomous entity. He told an interviewer that the idea that a work of art was a sign of some reality "had quite a lot to do with my seeing the Sacraments of the Church as fitting in perfectly with all human *poesis*— nothing could be more 'post-impressionist' in *that sense* than what the Church predicated of the Mass, where 'sign' and 'thing signified' are said to be one."[15] His identification of art with religious ritual is clearly reflected in such statements as "What the artist lifts up must have a kind of transubstantiated actual-ness." Jones used the same theological term in complaining of the artist's difficulty in capturing the physical: ". . . the bugger of it is how to 'transubstantiate' these qualities into whatever medium one is using."[16]

But while the Mass may be the prototype, Jones argues that all actions that produce "signs" projecting meaning, even the most unpretentious, such as making a birthday cake or wearing a rose in a buttonhole, have the nature of rituals. Since sacraments have a spiritual dimension, only human beings are capable of celebrating them, and they are, indeed, fated to perform them day in and day out in pursuing their ordinary activities. "It is a predicament of being human. . . . Man: sacrament at every turn and all levels of the 'profane' and 'sacred,' in the trivial and in the profound, no escape from sacrament."[17]

One of the elements of ritual that attracted Jones and formed a bridge that enabled him to assimilate it to experiment in poetry was its specificity of form. He often includes "the shape of a liturgy" or "the liturgical act" among his examples of works of art whose value is determined by their abstract quality. But in spite of his repeated emphasis on the importance of pure form, Jones acknowledged—it was a part of his general theory—that the abstract was not free of substantive connotations. Among his earliest convictions was the belief that a successful painting formed a "precarious balance" between the "interstresses" of abstraction and representation. In the preface to *The Anathemata* he observes that poetic forms cannot avoid reflecting the poet's cultural situation. Thus, while the creation of a form may be a new autonomous reality, it is also a "sign" that projects meaning.

This congruity of form and content seems to be the motivation behind Jones's experimentalism. M. L. Rosenthal and Sally M. Gall in *The Modern Poetic Sequence* find *The Anathemata* too complacent to be really revolutionary, but it is remarkable, considering Jones's limited exposure to modern poetry, that the form of his long works should correspond to so many of their specifications for the modern poetic sequence and to the methods of Eliot and Pound. Elizabeth Ward observes that while Jones may not have been directly influenced by any specific poem except for *The Waste Land*, it is clear that he drew much from the general atmosphere of modernism.[18]

Like other modern poems, Jones's works are paratactic in structure, juxtaposing texts that interact by contrasting sharply in tone and style, veering from prose to free verse without transitions. In addition, *The Anathemata* includes "illustrations"—some of them Latin inscriptions designed by Jones—as part of its text, and Jones reported that he had planned graphics for *In Parenthesis* as well. He depends heavily on the dramatic monologue, but the speaking voice is often unidentified, and unprepared shifts in the point of view often occur, a feature that anticipates the postmodern theme of the subverted subject. Jones considered historical periods to be counterparts of each other, a view that resembles Yeats's cyclical one. By treating real events and personages as replications of archetypes in myth and history, he achieves an effect resembling that of Pound's "subject rhymes," slipping from one context to another without warning.

Jones began *In Parenthesis* in an experimental mood. He says that he wrote its opening sentences "in 1927 or '28," while occupied in painting. "I had no idea what I was letting myself in for. However: we proceed from the known to the unknown."[19]

In its seven sections, *In Parenthesis* narrates the movement of an infantry company from its embarkation for France through its life in the trenches to a disastrous attack some months later. It often follows the thoughts and movements of Private John Ball, a character closely modeled on the author, who is wounded at the end of the story, as Jones himself was during the war. The events follow the history of Jones's battalion, the 15th Royal Welch Fusiliers, so closely that they might, in some respects, be taken as documentary reports. Even minor events, such as the spreading of a particular rumor and an officer's report of a successful attack, can be verified from outside sources. The place names given are accurate, and many of the characters can be identified with members of Jones's unit. In spite of all this verisimilitude, however, *In Parenthesis* is far from realistic. The events, characters, and settings are presented in sketchy, impressionistic fashion, sometimes in verse, sometimes in prose, sometimes aligned with metaphoric or mythic parallels, but with little attempt at completeness or narrative coherence.

While it begins as a prose narrative, with Private John Ball's late arrival at formation, *In Parenthesis* quickly exhibits its experimental nature by rejecting the premises that govern ordinary narratives. The action is not continuous; the angle of observation changes frequently. On the one hand, the text presents fine details that create a powerful impression of realism; on the other, it often veers off into fanciful parallels from Arthurian and Welsh legend. The prose text, itself widely variant in style, often deviates into free verse. The voices and thoughts of the soldiers mingle with a narrative voice, so that the reader is unable to place himself in a fixed position with regard to the scene. In addition, the varying tones, dialects, ranges of allusion, and recollections of previous experience completely demolish the concept of a single authoritative narrator.

Jones declared that he aimed only to create "a shape in words," with the experiences and feelings of war as "data," but *In Parenthesis* straddles the line between external reference and self-referentiality in a particularly intractable way. It moves from reporting the squalid facts of daily life at the front to such lyrical passages as this description of the destructive artillery:

> Brast, break, bough-break the backs of them,
> every bone of the white wounded who wait patiently—
> looking toward that hope:
> for the feet of the carrier long coming
> bringing palanquins
> to spread worshipful beds for heroes. (178)

The notes carry this dichotomy further, supporting the text with factual information and even with undisguised personal observations.

Jones often exhibits indifference to the usual notions of linguistic decorum and consistency. Numbers and abbreviations rupture the text with their sharp and often enigmatic functionalism. In one example officer ranks are expressed in Signaller's Alphabet:

> Do you suppose
> that rows of Field-Marshals
> Don Ac Ac Gees,
> G Esses O, 1, 2 and 3 and
> Ac Ac Q Emma Gees will
> fall on their dress swords. (142)

The text is rich in parodic effects and allusions drawn from sources as remote from each other as the medieval *Y Goddodin* and the coster's cry one soldier recalls from civilian life. Its variety of voices and tones veers from the colloquial to the Biblical, many of them jarringly incongruous. For example, a sharp irony is achieved as the problem of rescuing the wounded is discussed, momentarily, in the voice of a society matron: "Nothing is impossible nowadays my dear if only we can get the poor bleeder through the barrage and they take just as much trouble with the ordinary soldiers you know and essential-service academicians can match the natural hue and everything extraordinarily well" (176). Intertextuality ranges widely. The image of the soldiers wandering through the woods, "men from walking trees and branchy moving like a Birnam copse" effortlessly combines the Bible and *Macbeth*.

Snatches of song and signs seen on the battlefield punctuate the text. A colloquial context may contain a thoroughly incongruous literary allusion, and a lyrical passage may be violated by some technical military term. The chronicle of war contains allusions to Lewis Carroll's Alice books, and the most harrowing section, where many of the soldiers are killed or wounded, draws its title from Carroll's frivolous ballad "The Hunting of the Snark." When confronted with the need for especially expressive language, Jones resorts to neologisms, archaisms, and other verbal excesses. The word "rownsepykèd," used to describe trees maimed by gunfire is certainly not standard but may be obsolete or dialect. When someone asks, "Does he watch the dixie-rim," he refers, in army slang derived from the Indian service, to a cooking pot. An iron post protruding from the earth is brilliantly called a "dark excalibur." Men posted at intervals are said to be "transilient," a word normally used for the gaps in geologic formations, no doubt because their work is "systemed."

The resemblance of the poem's idiom to other modernist styles confirms Jones's view that similar conditions produce "convergences" among artists. For example, the following description of the landing of an artillery shell, with its inadvertent clue, "vortex," recalls the explosive excess of Vorticist and Futurist language:

> Out of the vortex, rifling the air it came—bright, brass-shod, Pandoran; with all-filling screaming the howling crescendo's up-piling snapt. The universal world, breath held, one half second, a bludgeoned stillness. Then the pent violence released a consummation of all burstings out; all sudden up-rendings and rivings-through—all taking-out of vents—all barrier-breaking—all unmaking, Pernitric begetting—the dissolving and splitting of solid things. (24)[20]

Jones denied having read *Ulysses*, but numerous passages of *In Parenthesis* correspond in style to passages from Joyce's novel. Both works make extensive use of interior monologue, and many passages of *In Parenthesis* recall the ruminative style of Leopold Bloom. A conversation among fellow soldiers (139) resembles the rambling conversation between Stephen Dedalus and Bloom in the "Ithaca" chapter. A period of boredom gives rise to a vacant, flowing, cliché-ridden conversational style corresponding to that of the "Eumaeus" chapter (144). Unassigned scraps of talk create a text like the hubbub near the end of the "Oxen of the Sun" chapter:

> Yess I hav always, yes, never touch the stuff, no.
> Always 'ad fags corporal, always 'av' of.
> Seen you with a pipe, Crower.
> Not me corporal.
> Who are these pipe smokers—'35 Float, you're a pipe man.
> Somehows right off it corporal, since they brought us into this place.
> 'Struth—very well—one packet of *Trumpeter* all round—you whoresons must we fetch you immaculate *Abdullas* out of this earth. (72)

Joyce was recapitulating the development of prose by a steady progression of contrasting styles in his "Oxen of the Sun" chapter, but Jones's aim in slipping in and out of various dialects and forms of speech was to replicate the collective voice of the soldiery.

Readers of *In Parenthesis* are usually dismayed to find that Jones regards war not only as a normal historical event but also as a ritual with sacred significance. While fully recognizing the excruciating moral dilemmas warfare poses, Jones maintains that its prominence in artistic and cultural history cannot be ignored and, further, that it shares some of the qualities of art and therefore of religion. It is one of Jones's fundamental convictions that "man as artist hungers and thirsts after form," and he maintained that "the art of war is capable, at all events, of a form-creating quality."[21] In "Art and Sacrament" he carried this further, arguing that since military strategy shares some of the qualities of art, it also participates in religion. It moves shapes about to form a patterned whole, it renders vacant space "radiant with form"; like other arts, it is "a sign of the form-making activities universally predicated in the Logos," that "causes man's art to be bound to God."[22] These statements reflect Jones's conviction that man is compelled to act sacramentally, no matter what he does. But they also sever the sacred process of form-creation sharply from questions of morality.

Accordingly, *In Parenthesis*, while assimilating the realities of army life into an experimental text responsive to contemporary needs, also presents war as a ritualized activity. Jones feels that its monasticism, repetitiveness, and communality made army life a religious analogue, and he develops this parallel with quiet assurance. Thomas Dilworth finds that the narrative as a whole, from the embarkation in England to the battle at Mametz Wood at the end, has the form of an initiation rite corresponding to the Eleusinian ceremony, and that smaller units of the poem exhibit the same form.[23] The irony implicit in this analogy between the sacred and the destructive is not lost on Jones, but it emerges as only a minor theme.

Jones regards the rhythmic repetitions of army talk, such as marching chants, relayed orders, and conversational tags, as ritualistic. In his preface, while explaining that he has omitted the indecencies common in soldier's language, Jones says that repetition made them seem "liturgical" and that emotional expletives heard in the army might have the force of religious imprecations. Cockney is to the army, he says, as Latin is to the Church. Thus, the "left-right" and other orders of an officer marching his troops are called "the liturgy of a regiment departing" (4). Jones's view that military commands put into effect what they signify makes them the speech-acts of a specialized system of order, a ritual language.

The narrator often declares openly that the soldiers who go to the waste land of the battlefields and huddle in its trenches are participating in a ritual. For example, the soldiers' march is called "the ritual of their parading," the sergeant's commands are "ritual words," and we are told that John Ball finds in the march "a kind of blessedness" because it seems to "transubstantiate" his recent unpleasant experiences. More subtly, the words at the opening of part 3, the orders for a night march, "Proceed . . . without lights . . . prostrate before it" (27), are taken from the priest's directions for the unobtrusive recital of the Good Friday service, so that a parallel is established between the service and the maneuver. Not only is military action analogous to sacrament, but both share an esthetic value, for "the liturgy of their going-up assumed a primitive creativeness, an apostolic actuality, a correspondence with the object, a flexibility" (28).

As Thomas Dilworth has observed, the ritual allusions in *In Parenthesis* are drawn from Hebrew and pagan as well as Christian sources. Although Jones believed that the earlier worships were assimilated into the Christian sacrament, his eclecticism here, as in *The Anathemata*, suggests that, like Pound, he valued the idea of ritual they embodied. A letter written late in Jones's life recalls his early, instinctive attraction to Catholic ritual. Especially crucial was his "first sight of a Mass," which occurred during the war, close to the front. Jones explained that while searching for firewood he peeped into a partially wrecked outhouse and saw a priest saying Mass for some members of his battalion. He declared that he sensed an authentic relation between the priest and the hardened soldiers that he had never seen in Protestant services. "It made a big impression on me," writes Jones, whose conversion to Catholicism soon followed.[24]

Overt allusions to ritual are not continuous throughout *In Parenthesis*, but, as David Blamires has observed, "what is perhaps most remarkable is the way in which the seemingly casual word or reference keeps alive throughout the whole of the work an atmosphere of latent transubstantiation. At almost any point the trivial act or tawdry object may be transmuted into a thing of numinous significance."[25] What he has in mind are such phrases as "hierarchic words," "catechumen feet," and "helmets of salvation." Dilworth points out that a ritual subtext accompanies many of the wartime activities, even when no liturgical clues appear. The meals, the allusions to changing seasons, the soldiers' chant demanding that the Kaiser be hanged, and even the artillery duels form part of the poem's ritual texture.

Following this principle, Dilworth suggests that the ritual allusions imply a "correspondence" between the climactic battle of Mametz Wood narrated in part 7 and the Canon of the Mass. Jones's notes to this section identify numerous borrowings from church services. The sacred aspect of the attack is established at the opening of part 7 with Latin phrases from the Psalms and the Good Friday service and the report that the soldiers waiting to advance sing some of the Psalms. Biblical themes dominate the nervous outpouring of allusive and parodic language that marks this time of intense apprehension. The battlefield is a new Golgotha—"the place of the skull." After the soldiers have had the warning that their time of trial is only two minutes away, the words "Responde mihi" (answer me) appear; Jones's note identifies this as a part of a Dominican service for the dead, but it is also Job's demand that he be given a reason for his suffering. It is soon followed by uncontrolled pleasurable images, the secular fragments enclosing an echo of the Song of Songs. The story of the Agony in the Garden, says the narrator, is read many times:

> you can't believe the Cup wont pass from
> or they wont make a better show
> in the Garden. (158)

While Jones denied that the soldiers are to be identified with Christ, the implication that the battle is a reenactment of the Passion is irresistible. When the murderous enemy barrage is over, the silent forest where the dead soldiers lie is transformed into a chapel:

> Down in the under-croft in the crypt of the wood, clammy
> drippings percolate—. . .
>   Aisle-ways bunged-up between these columns rising,
> these long strangers,
> under this vaulting stare upward,
> for recumbent princes of his people. (182)

In spite of the strong Christian tone, the principle of ritual that dominates is nonsectarian, for allusions to other rites emerge as parallels to the battle. In addition, the passage seems to have as a subtext the Girardian principle that the slaughter represents the redemptive violence of pre-Christian ritual. Dilworth points out that Eleusinian elements and imagery suggestive of pagan fertility rites form a prelude to the battle. When the troops encounter gunfire, says Dilworth: "Ritual promenade gives way to ritual sacrifice. . . . Infantrymen . . . come to resemble personators of Attis, who are castrated by the goddess Cybele during midsummer nuptials."[26]

The climactic episode of the section is a ritual invented by Jones that also has pagan rather than Christian affinities. As the wounded John Ball struggles to drag his rifle with him, the Queen of the Woods appears to award symbolic floral gifts to the dead soldiers, German as well as English. Dilworth offers a thorough discussion of the prototypes and analogues that Jones may have had in mind in creating this figure, ranging from Persephone and Demeter to Joyce's Anna Livia Plurabelle. He attributes overwhelming importance to the fact that this idealized figure, embodying all the healing powers that women offer in their many roles, as lovers, wives, mothers, and deities, comes at the end of the poem as a resolving force: "She is the feminine principle nullifying the masculine malice of battle. . . . In her nature and grace are one."[27] The healing and consoling power of this archetype appears earlier, at the beginning of part 7, in the Latin quotation from a Holy Week service lamenting the death of Christ which is based on a Biblical passage in the Book of Lamentations. It foretells the feelings of the dying as they ask for the sacramental foods: "Matribus suis dixerunt: ubi est triticum et vinum? Cum deficerent quasi vulnerati . . . cum exhalarent animas suas in sinu matrum suarum." ("They say to their mothers: where are the wheat and wine? While they fail as if wounded . . . while breathing out their souls in the bosom of their mothers" [153]). The appearance of the Queen of the Woods expresses Jones's hope that the spiritual dilemmas of war will somehow be resolved by ritual. After the ceremony, Ball decides to abandon his rifle: "Let it lie for the dews to rust it." (186).

The fusion of ritualizing and experimental literary resources seen in part 7, but characteristic of *In Parenthesis* as a whole, places the war scenes within a mythic context, connecting them with the resonances of the past. It implies that the modern state of mind, conveyed both by the freedom and creativity of its rhetoric and by the horror of war, is not beyond the saving power of the ritual consciousness. The reportorial treatment of war does not contradict this power, for, to quote Jones again, "the activity called art is, at bottom and inescapably a 'religious' activity, for it deals with realities, and the real is sacred and religious."

In his preface to *The Anathemata*, Jones says that he is not concerned with the long debate about "the radical incompatibility between the world of the 'myths' and the world of the 'formulae,'" but rather with the effect of "such unresolved elements" on contemporary art. By boldly juxtaposing colloquial, scientific, and specialized idioms with snatches of prayer, Jones's text suggests that language has the power to cancel the absolute division between different kinds of discourse, and the irreconcilable ways of thought they represent.

Jeremy Hooker has argued that the mythic and realistic elements of *In Parenthesis* are unified by the pattern of initiation.[28] This is a pattern Jones finds in all experience, as the mind passes from one state or reality to another. Since rituals and experiments are both initiations, the two can be seen as uniting in *In Parenthesis* to embody a process of spiritual discovery. The unconventional language and rhetorical effects open the mind to new horizons of meaning, and the sacred performances embedded in this unfamiliar context gain a cogency they have not had before. The experimental rhetoric shapes new forms adapted to content; the ritual language and effects express traditional faith in divinity. The joining of the two suggests that they have the same purpose, in accordance with Jones's idea that the creation of form is analogous to the divine creation of the world. Because they work so well together, it is hard to resist the conviction that Jones has been more successful here than either Eliot or Pound in assimilating ritual and experimental elements into a poetic text.

Like *In Parenthesis*, *The Anathemata* was begun as an experiment. Jones says in the preface that it began in "experiments made from time to time between 1938 and 1945," and while it was extensively rewritten, it has not lost this character. Jones's account of his procedure sounds like Lévi-Strauss's *bricolage*. He says that his task was to work "from such sources as have by accident been available to me and to make a work out of those mixed data." Like its title, a word which Jones took to mean both blessed things that are cursed and profane things that are redeemed, but which are in any case, "lifted up . . . made over to the gods," the poem weaves together modes of feeling that are generally considered irreconcilable.[29]

The eight sections of *The Anathemata* are written in the mixed verse and prose of *In Parenthesis* and make use of nearly all the modernist devices of the earlier poem, with some unconventional additions. Graphics are inserted, not as supplements, but as integral parts of the text. Some of the illustrations are pictures, but the others are inscriptions, one in Old English, the others in Latin, written in Jones's handsome calligraphy. Notes, even more copious than those of *In Parenthesis* (and, it might be added, more necessary) appear on or near the same page as the text so that they participate in what the poem says. The reader is required to shift constantly from the imaginative and esthetic plane of the text to the discursive, referential one of the prose notes. [30]

Jones cultivates a tone of tentativeness by relying on obliquities and putting much of his material in the form of questions. These elaborate interrogative constructions and the poem's frequent asyntactical fragments invest the information they contain with a provisional, speculative quality. In addition, such riddling eccentricities as:

> Yan, tyan, tethere, methera, pimp
> sethera, lethera, hovera, dovera dick

and

> *et gentium, cenhedloedd, und Völker* (A, 77, 241)

create a linguistic environment that recognizes no limitations, even when they are explained in the notes.

When W. H. Auden asked whether *The Anathemata* had been modeled after the *Cantos,* Jones replied that he had not read Pound's poem until after he had completed his own, and said: ". . . all sorts of similarities—sometimes quite astonishing similarities—are arrived at by different artists by diverse routes. After all, the same thing happens in the field of scientific experiment, and it is not difficult to see why."[31] While it seems fair to say that both poets employ linguistic deviations because their visions transcend the ordinary, this does not explain why the deviations are so similar. Two reasons may be given: We see from the last quotation that Jones, like Pound, aligned his innovative efforts with scientific experiment; and the major poems of both combine science-related forms and idioms with a ritual consciousness.

The eight sections of *The Anathemata* are so different from each other that they might be considered separate poems. They begin with prehistory, and proceed by touching on successive periods of European history, with many digressions and cross-references. However, a single topic runs through these varied parts, like Pound's image of the string that runs through the holes of Chinese coins: the Eucharist, which Jones sees replicated in events occurring both before and after the time of Christ. Jones wrote in a letter to a friend: "The action of the Mass was meant to be the central theme of the work for as you once said to me The Mass *makes sense* of everything."[32] *The Anathemata,* says Neil Corcoran ". . . implies that the centre of meaning in history is to be found where all perspectives recede to a point, the once-and-always of the eucharistic action."[33] It was Jones's view, derived from his reading of an English translation of *The Mystery of Faith and Human Opinion Contrasted and Defined,* by the French theologian Maurice de la Taille, that the Mass signifies both the Last Supper, where Christ offered himself as a symbolic sacrifice, and the Crucifixion, where the sacrifice was actually performed. According to De la Taille, both events are parts of the same sacrifice, the first being figurative and ritualistic, where Christ has the function of a priest, the second, "real, bloody, all-sufficient immolation," where he is the sacrificial victim.

Jones admitted that the knowledge he used in conjunction with this theme was subject to change as new knowledge emerged and that ". . . the poet, of whatever century, is concerned only with how he can use a current notion to express a permanent mythus"(*A,* 82,n.). Jones's poem might be seen as being controlled by the interplay between two of his favorite concepts, which represent the "permanent" and the "current" respectively: anamnesis, the recollection of the "deposits" of the past through ritual, and metamorphosis, the experimental transformation of these enduring essences into material contemporary forms.

While the ritual theme is often submerged, it is nevertheless an ever-present subtext. In his preface, Jones says that *The Anathemata* consists of the sort of ideas that go through his own mind while attending Mass. Following this suggestion, Dilworth convincingly maintains that the poem as a whole consists of a communicant's freely associated meditations during the short interval between the prayer of Consecration at the beginning of the poem and the actual consecration of the chalice at the end of it.[34] Jones's premise means that the text is at once instantaneous and developmental, interior monologue and devotion, and history contained within ritual, consisting of associations that are both free and thematic.

Jones confronts the issue of science and poetry in the preface by asking whether "H_2O" can be employed for poetic effect. While it has been possible, at some points in the past, for poets to reconcile ideas from different fields of thought with each other, the present time, he says, is characterized by a disparity between "the world of 'myths' and the world of the 'formulae'" that amounts to a "lesion" (*A*, 17-18). Jones does not pretend that he can heal this wound. Instead he asks "when times turned?" from prehistoric sacramentalism to technology and ironically answers that the change can be traced to primitive inventions (*A*, 60-61).

He is concerned with the difficulty of finding material for poetry at a time when traditional symbols are losing their resonance. While the artist seeks permanent values, he must also respond to those of his own time, for his works, "unless they are of 'now' and of 'this place' can have no 'for ever.'" In "Rite and Fore-Time," the first section of the poem, Jones follows this principle by using scientific concepts and diction side by side with sacramental and poetic language, openly risking the possibility of discord. He links the modernist deviations of his verse to the technology he feared but felt to be unavoidable by boldly building geological and anthropological information and language into his poetic framework. Hence,

> Before the microgranites and the clay-bonded erratics
> wrenched from the diorites of Aldasa, or off the Goat Height in
> the firth-way. . . .
>   As though the sea itself were sea-borne
> and under weigh
>   as if the whole Ivernian *mare*
> directed from hyperboreal control-points by strategi of the
> axis were one complex of formations in depth. . . . (*A*, 72-73)

Jonathan Miles has defended these specialized terms with arguments that Jones himself might have used: ". . . the thinking man of this century lives in the shadows of the specialists; any interest or exploration can hardly help but become enmeshed in webs of jargon. Man's vision of himself has become complex and scientific."[35]

It is the theme of "Rite and Fore-Time" that the sacrament defined by the Last Supper was anticipated not only by the practices of prehistoric man, but in prehuman times by the formation of the earth's geology. Jones uses information gathered from scientific sources to present prehistory as a majestic ritual. As Neil Corcoran has put it, "Geologic process is viewed both as making possible, and itself dramatising or enacting, liturgical process."[36] Jones's imagery frequently refers to this "enactment" in the imagery of drama. Of the changes that took place during the glaciation of the Pleistocene period, he says, "There's where the world's a stage / for transformed scenes / with metamorphosed properties / for each shifted set" (A, 62). Prehistory successively becomes a "Vorzeit-masque," a Mass, an indeterminate ritual, and a fertility rite, before "the proto-historic transmogrification of the land-face" leads to the recorded history that forms the next act of the play, as "they rigged the half-lit stage for dim-eyed Clio"(A, 68).

The fanciful, eclectic text, with its unstable tones, verbal ingenuities, far-ranging allusions, and mystical ritualism is supported by a solid framework of the geologic and anthropological knowledge available at the time.[37] These resources implement Jones's master metaphor, the identification of prehistoric events with the Mass.

The metaphor is employed in the description of the Ice Age, which blends the beneficial effect of glaciation on the earth with the priest's division of the wafer as he breaks it in half. This image of the Titan, Cronos, coupled with a Christian context and terms that disclose Jones's familiarity with psychoanalysis characteristically bring different ages and forms of consciousness together in a bold convergence.

> Across the watersphere
> over the atmosphere, preventing the crystal formations
> ambient grew the wondrous New Cold:
> > trauma and thauma, both.
> This is how Cronos reads the rubric, *frangit per medium,* when
> he breaks his ice, like morsels, for the therapy and fertility
> of the land-masses. (A, 69)

"Rite and Fore-Time" begins with a priest performing Mass in a modern church whose details of construction reflect the sterility of modern spiritual life. This is followed by a passage describing the preparations made for the prototype of all Masses, the Last Supper itself. Next comes a parenthetical insertion identifying the hill of Jerusalem with other notable heights. By calling it the "unabiding rock" (A, 55), Jones is relating Jerusalem to what he later calls "this unabiding Omphalos / this other laughless rock" (A, 58), meaning the Agelastos Petra or "laughless rock" in the temple at Eleusis where Demeter is supposed to have rested. The section framed in a series of questions, beginning with "Who" or "What" asking about the creation of the earth, identifies the events of pre-Christian and prehistoric epochs as proleptic counterparts of the Last Supper.

The answer to these questions turns to liturgical language and Latin phrases to ask peace for those who perform ritual or make artefacts. It invokes the power of "uteral marks" and "penile ivory," prehistoric art works symbolic of fertility that Jones unashamedly links to the sacraments that will develop from them. The main body of the answer is phrased in a long sequence of clauses beginning "Before . . ." that survey prehistoric events anticipating the Eucharist. It culminates in a declaration that all history and prehistory, going back to the earth's creation, was a ritual of salvation performed by the Maker.

> From before all time
> > the New Light beams for them
> and with eternal clarities
> > *infulsit* and athwart
> the fore-times:
> > era, period, epoch, hemera.
> Through all orogeny:
> > group, system, series, zone.
> Brighting at the five life-layers
> species, species, genera, families, order. (A, 73-74)

In this way, Jones envisions creation itself as an example of his *signa*, a sign that qualifies as a work of art because it is gratuitous and signifies "something other," that is, the archetypal ritual, the Eucharist.

Infulsit brings both ritual and one of Jones's graphics into the text. It means "shone forth," and is quoted from the preface provided for the Mass at Christmas; Jones reproduces a passage from this service in his distinctive calligraphic style (the page facing page 77).[38] The inscription contains an indication that Jones regards pagan worship as a valid anticipation of the one true ritual, for in the left margin of the inscription expressing Christian doctrine he has placed the words "Minerva Jovis," and in the right margin "capite orta" ("risen from the head"), an epithet for Athena, who sprang from the forehead of Jove. The pagan deities are included, no doubt because their presence can be evoked by rites comparable to the one celebrated in the quotation from the Christian service.

Jones's lines employ light, a common figure throughout the Eucharistic texts, as a symbol of spiritual deliverance, and through "orogeny," or the formation of mountains, allude to the sacred and legendary hills that have been mentioned, especially to the hill of Calvary. The terms borrowed from anthropology and geology infiltrate the religious comment on raised places by a scientific consciousness that would seem to be alien to it. In the context of Jones's eclectically mixed diction, however, the scientific terms simply take part in the intricate dialogue being conducted by the various heteroglossia.[39]

The ritual pattern of salvation is continued when early humans appear, and the idea that all productive actions replicate the sacrament is lightly touched in some of the passages about them. The long series of questions concludes by asking whether the earliest people performed rituals that were also works of art:

> Did the fathers of those
>   who forefathered them
> (if by genital or ideate begetting)
>   set apart, make other, oblate? (A, 64)

The affirmative answer will come several pages later with "From before all time / the New Light beams for them" (A, 73).

A series of questions beginning "How else . . . " offers justifications for regarding all creation as sacred. The message is that the acts and objects of human civilization—all artifacts, in Jones's generous definition—could not have come into being without the Christian mystery of the Incarnation. The poet asks, "How else her iconography?" referring to the Virgin, and "How other his liturgy?" referring to Christ, closing the section with an echo of Job's demand, an imperious "Answer me!" (A, 75). All should be remembered when Christ is remembered "daily, at the Stone"; that is, the sense of divine presence in the archetypal work of art, the Mass, should be extended to all creative activities.

The first of a long series of questions connects the sculptor who fashioned the prehistoric Venus of Willendorf, "the form-making proto-maker," with the artists of the Lascaux caves who "do, within, in an unbloody manner, under the forms of brown haematite and black manganese on the graved lime-face what is done, without / far on the windy tundra / at the kill" (A, 60). Jones sees the same metamorphic relation between the cave painting and the hunt it apparently commemorates as the one in Catholic doctrine that regards the Last Supper and the ritual based on it as "unbloody" counterparts of the Crucifixion.[40] The section closes by suggesting the origin of ritual in agricultural ceremonies, asking, "How else" the primeval earth could produce the grain belonging to Him who said, "I am your Bread."

In "Middle-Sea and Lear-Sea" Jones moves forward from prehistory to antiquity. Continuing the experimental style of the first section, he aligns the events of the pre-Christian period with the Biblical events that are the prototypes of Christian sacraments. Its rationale is given in a note observing the parallels between Roman and Christian religions: "We Europeans have participated in both traditions—of the one by right of cultural and racial inheritance, of the other by 'adoption and grace'" (*A,* 85n.).

The chronology of "Middle-Sea and Lear-Sea" ignores the linear conception of history. It begins with Troy, but soon moves to the Roman period, which Jones values as the scene of the Christian drama, then reverts to Greece, which he values for its art, the embodiment of the sacramental. Allusions to Greek statuary lead to a parallel with Christianity and to Kore (or Persephone), who is identified with Helen of Troy, Eleanor of Aquitaine, and Guinevere. The connection of Persephone with the Eleusinian rite introduces an ironic contrast between the Laughless Rock of Eleusis and those other stones, the smiling female figures of archaic sculpture:

> Agelastos Petra . . .
> > and yet you smile from your stone. (*A,* 92)

In Jones's view, Eleusis and its Laughless Rock, like other pre-Christian rites, were merged with Christianity. In his description of a voyage from the "Middle Sea" of the Mediterranean to the "Lear-Sea" of British waters, a ritual is performed aboard the ship, and the sailors' prayer to a goddess of the sea contains the ejaculation "Agelastos Petra / cleft for us! "(*A,* 104), bringing together the sacred pagan stone and an echo of Christianity. Eleusis and Christianity also converge when we are asked these questions about the ship's skipper:

> Is it the Iacchos
> > in his duffle jacket
> Ischyros with his sea-boots on? (*A,* 97)

where he is called both by the name given to Dionysus at the Eleusinian mysteries and by the Greek "strong" from a liturgical formula used to denote Christ. Through its mingling of pagan and Christian motifs, this section anticipates the continuity of religion that is to result from the meeting of north and south.

"Middle-Sea and Lear-Sea" ends by asking whether the voyage ended safely, and the next section, "Angle-Land," by opening with similar questions, seems to continue the strangely interrogative narration. Actually, however, this is a different and later voyage by Germanic invaders of the fifth century along the coasts and rivers of southern Britain. This section, like the next, "Redriff," has little to do with religion but rather focuses on verbal experiment. In asking whether the travellers touched at various points in "Angle-Land," Jones mingles terms from the languages used historically in Britain into a multilingual idiom. The abrupt shifts in the level of discourse are exceptionally sharp. "What's the cephalic index of the *môrforymion* . . ." (*A,* 113) employs both a term from modern anthropology and the Welsh word for water-maidens, bringing together not only two languages, but two entirely different ways of seeing the world.

"Redriff" consists mainly of a dramatic monologue in which Eb Bradshaw, a naval carpenter (and Jones's grandfather) refuses a proposal to hurry his work for extra payment. Eb mingles the speech of London streets with terms of his trade, as in "We'll spokeshave those deadeyes for him as smooth as a *peach* of a cheek" in a tirade that heaps contempt on the proposal made to him. His ultimate claim to integrity is his closing assertion that even if he were assigned to make the Cross, he would do the work with care.

"The Lady of the Pool" continues the method of "Redriff," consisting mostly of a dramatic monologue spoken by a lavender seller in London of what is apparently the sixteenth century, who gives her name as Elen Monica. This figure, a hearty, full-blooded woman often compared with the Wife of Bath, Molly Bloom, and Anna Livia Plurabelle, begins her speech in a Cockney dialect but soon reverts to an unstable idiom full of allusions and constructions that would not appear in the language of a person of her class—or, for that matter, of any person of any class. In expressing contempt for university students, a class to which a former lover belonged, she employs numerous terms from the medieval curriculum as she asks:

> Is their chilly curia a very thalamos: is Lady Verity with Poesy now wed, and at that bed, by Prudentia curtained close, does the Trivium curtsy and does each take hand to the Quadrivium call: Music for a saraband?
>
> And does serene Astronomy carry the tonic *Ave* to the created spheres, does old Averroes show a leg?—for what's the song b'Seine and Isis determines toons in caelian consistories—or so this cock-clerk once said. (*A,* 129)

Elen Monica employs specialized nautical terms as well as learned neologisms and verbal distortions. Her effusive sentences can be immensely long and periodic in construction, piling up parallel clauses breathlessly as they defer conclusions, sometimes for pages, so that they give the impression of mere inventories before they arrive at closure. There are also actual inventories, and the language is often crammed full of colorful particulars. Her monologue resembles the headlong, multileveled idiom of *Finnegans Wake*, and there are even some convergences as when, for example, she calls the Julian calendar "pontiff Juliuses 'versal colander,'" quotes one lover as saying "Sanfairyann" and echoes ALP with "here's all alluvial."[41]

Although they are overshadowed by vivid characterization and linguistic experimentalism, there are significant ritual elements in "The Lady of the Pool." Jones has conceived his promiscuous streetwoman as one who is sensitive to religion and who has a scholarly knowledge of it. She calls her song an "introit" and the surveys of London churches she gives both before and after her stories of lovers and voyages show that she knows that many were built on the sites of pagan worship. Hence, "Delphi in sub-crypt" and "At Paul's / and faiths under Paul / where / so Iuppiter me succour!" (*A*, 127)

In Elen Monica's account, the troubled voyage of the *Mary*, a ship captained by one of her former lovers, is overlaid with religious and sacramental significance.[42] An allegory of the Annunciation is subtly implied, for the ship, we are told, was "overdue a nine month" and at its arrival, "Gabriel already has said *Ave!*" During a storm the ship's superstructure is "veronica'd" with foam, an allusion to the handkerchief of St. Veronica with which the saint wiped Christ's brow while he was bearing the Cross and which is supposed to retain an impression of his face. The attribution of sacredness to the ship reaches its climax when, during the storm,

> All her sheer
> the entire trembling keel-length of her vessel of burden
>   silvered of
> driven rain
>   gilted of
> bends of paly light
> white as the Housel of spume.
>   The tilted heavers
> her oblation-stone
> imménser hovers dark-ápse her. (*A*, 140)

The imagery here, strongly reminiscent of Hopkins, transforms the storm into a Mass, as the beleaguered ship becomes the "vessel" containing the wine, and the waves form a church around it.

Another entry into the imagery of the Passion and the Mass occurs when Elen observes that the *Mary* came from waters neighboring Jerusalem, "the Hill and navel of the world," and briefly narrates the transcendent events that took place there. The remarkable passage describing the Crucifixion employs unconventional devices to project meaning in many directions. Snatches of the nursery rhyme "Sing a Song of Sixpence" identify the Hill of Calvary, where the gold of Christ's redemptive suffering was found, with the song's "counting house." Using the song's imagery, the poet declares that Mary shared his suffering ("whose queen was in her silent parlour / on that same hill of dolour") and that his sacrifice was her "bread and honey" and nourished the faith of humanity (*A*, 157). Subtle echoes of Chaucer and T. S. Eliot produce further significant intertextual effects. This portion of Elen's recital ends with an inventory of the seamen who will profit from Christ's suffering ritualized by repetitions of the liturgical *dona eis requiem* (give them rest), an appropriate effect, for here, as elsewhere, Jones is emphasizing that the ritual based on the Crucifixion is central in human history.

The sixth section, "Keel, Ram, Stauros," answers the question asked at the end of "Middle-Sea and Lear-Sea" three parts earlier: "Did he berth her? And to schedule?" (*A*, 108). It affirms that the ship linking north and south, whose "vine-juice skipper" embodies both Christ and Dionysus, is about to arrive at salvation. (Among the epithets used for him earlier are "pickled, old, pelagios" and "bacchic pelasgian.") The anticipated landing is preceded by a transformation of the ship into a scene of ritual. It becomes a church—"the plank-built walls converge / to apse his leaning nave" (*A*, 181)—and the captain "asperges" the ship's deck with the remains of the wine in a ceremonial chalice as a priest sprinkles holy water in blessing, a ceremony performed earlier in this section by a priest blessing the Ram, the length of wood used in antiquity as a battering weapon. But the action has pagan as well as Christian significance, for it is also a "libation" that is "laid up to the gods."

The body of "Keel, Ram, Stauros," which has only an indirect connection with the Eucharist, is organized according to the modernist principle that a long poem can be unified by symbols rather than a theme. In his preface, Jones used "wood" to illustrate the contention that artists depend on the potential associations a particular concept may have. His idea is put to use in this section, where wood, made sacred by its presence in the Cross, is a sort of central axis around which the development of the text turns. It makes up the mast of the ship, the "trembling tree" that is the "Spine / for her barrelling ribs" (*A*, 174). The poem then moves on to other constructions of wood, both upright and horizontal. The first is the keel of the ship, whose "timber of foundation" forms its churchlike "inverted vaults," and the second the battering ram of Roman warfare. The return to wood in a vertical form comes in a celebration of the Cross, before a reversion to the ship and the conclusion of the section with its approach to the landing at Athens. Through its association with the Cross, the wood symbolism sustains the ongoing allegory of the wooden ship as a vessel of faith, rendering every part of it sacred.

"Mabinog's Liturgy," whose title presents it as a ritual, has a prominent theme, Christmas and the Nativity, but it is nevertheless the most disjointed and most digressive section of *The Anathemata.* Contrasting passages succeed each other without transitions and with many digressions, discussing the celebration of the Nativity in disparate, often incongruous types of language. The section is characterized by allusions and parallels displaying Jones's usual reckless disregard of anachronism, and also by a steady sprinkling of liturgical language in Latin and English from the Christmas service and other rites. The illustration facing page 219 includes one passage of this kind, a quotation from Chapter 2 of St. Luke that forms the Gospel for the Christmas Mass, in the form of a Latin "inscription." The margin connects the Christian text with pagan sources as the inscription in "Rite and Fore-Time" does, this time with words from Virgil's Messianic Fourth Eclogue, which run along the side and top of the page. The point that Christianity and its rites are rooted in earlier traditions is inherent throughout the section, where pagan deities and their worship seem interchangeable with Christian ones. The theme appears at what may be considered the ritual climax of the section, the Mass attended by Guinevere (the "column"), and also where Jones suggests, in exceptionally compact language, both the agricultural origin of the sacrament and its predecessor in the "Two Lands" of Egypt:

> even before the Magian handling and the Apollinian word
> that shall make of the waiting creatures, in the vessels on the
> board-cloths over the Stone, his body who said, DO THIS
> > for my Anamnesis.
> > By whom also this column was.
> He whose fore-type said, in the Two Lands
> > I AM BARLEY. (*A,* 204-205)

This "fore-type," according to Jones's note, was an Egyptian king whose coffin-text declared his divinity in this way.

Christian concepts are mingled with the Eleusinian tradition in another account of the Mass:

> Lar of Lares Consitivi. . . .
> that whets his weapon acute at both edges.
> Out from the mother (coronate of the daughter)
>   bearing the corn-stalks.
> Exact Archon (by whom Astráea on Themis)
>   Lord-Paraclete of the Assize
> Yet who alone is named MISERICORS. (*A,* 209)

Here Christ is connected with no fewer than three pagan deities. He is identified with "Lar," the household god of the Romans, in his aspect as a sower ("consitivi") through an allusion in Revelation, "he which hath the sharp sword with two edges." This ambiguous figure is then said to be the issue of Demeter, who with Persephone presides over the fertility of the soil. The "Archon," according to Jones's note, is Triptolemus, the foster-son of Demeter, a grain-god and the founder of agriculture, whose memory, Jones maintains, is "reasserted" in the Mass (*A,* 230n.). He is identified with Christ through MISERICORS—"the merciful one"—and through a passage in "Sherthursdaye and Venus Day" where Christ is called "Our chrism'd Triptolemus," using a Greek word meaning "anointed" that is related to the word "Christ."

By identifying the day of the Last Supper with its pagan equivalent, the title of "Sherthursdaye and Venus Day" reintroduces the eclecticism that has appeared throughout *The Anathemata* in support of the belief that the Mass embodies all other worships. It presents Abraham's sacrifice as a forerunner of Christ's sacrifice by saying that it took place at the future site of the Crucifixion, "the hill of the out-cry / the hill of dereliction" (*A,* 233). However, Jones declares that the Christian sacrament supersedes the rites descended from Abraham's sacrifice: "Levites! the new rite holds / is here / before your older rites begin" (*A,* 230). This contention is supported by an allusion to Melchisedek as the founder of a rite superior to that of Abraham's descendants that Christ, presumably, renewed. Among the rituals assimilated in the Eucharist is that of Eleusis, which is seen as a primary source: "from dear and grave Demeter come / germ of all: / of the dear arts as well as bread" (*A,* 230).

As wood became sacred in "Keel, Ram, Stauros" because of its presence in the Cross, water is given an even more prominent place in "Sherthursdaye and Venus Day" because of its role in Christian ritual. On the ground that it is "the material stuff without which the sacraments could not be" (*A,* 236n.), Jones (who speaks in his own voice in this final section) celebrates it as a symbol of salvation, with Christ as its master. The climax of the passage is

"SITIO," Christ's cry from the Cross, complaining of his thirst, and, symbolically, of the absence of grace. The scene of the Nativity—"in Bedlem byre onde his bed"—is merged with an image of the Mass ("into both hands / he takes the stemmed dish" [A, 242]), and these lead up to the final question about Christ's death and its answer, that it is the condition of our union with him ("How else be coupled of this Wanderer" [A, 243]). The poem returns to its beginning with an image of a celebrant whom we are free to identify with the one in the first lines of "Rite and Fore-Time," and concludes, characteristically, with two questions suggesting the now familiar doctrine that the Crucifixion was the fulfillment of a ritual initiated by Christ at the Last Supper.

In 1822 the geologist William Buckland unearthed a Paleolithic skeleton on the Gower Peninusula. The remains were those of a young man, but because the bones were stained with red and it was accompanied by ornaments, the find was popularly known as "The Red Lady of Paviland." In "Rite and Fore-Time" Jones confers an "aureole" on this man, and in a long explanatory note, he recalls that "He had been buried with rites." (A, 76n.) In "The Sleeping Lord," where he is called "the first of the sleepers of / Pritenia," he is identified with the lost sheep that is found in the parable in Luke 15:4-7 and receives the gifts of the deity who was "his Proserpine." In this way, Jones accepts the prehistoric youth into the community of those, Christian and pagan alike, who express faith through ritual. His reason appears in his note for the passage; the Eucharist consecrates other rites retroactively: ". . . there are those many, of all times and places, whose lives and deaths have been made acceptable by the same Death on the Hill of which every Christian breaking of bread is an epiphany and a recalling" (A, 76n.).

It is clear that Jones feels that ritual itself, whether pagan or Christian, is the means of gaining grace. Jones, like the Eliot of the Harvard seminar, the theorists of Chinese ritual, Ezra Pound, and many anthropologists, finds that its central value lies not in the doctrines it may imply, but in the performance itself. He often emphasizes the value of concrete embodiment, but the importance of physical things rests on their capacity for evoking the transcendental. The Latin quotation from a Christmas Mass in the inscription facing page 77 says, "as we see God in visible form, we are caught up in love of things invisible." Such material things as the objects used in the Mass are capable of embodying sacred mysteries, but the mysteries remain hidden.

Regardless of its success as a poem, and as a work which fulfills Jones's aim of establishing traditional beliefs in the contemporary world, it might be said that *The Anathemata* brings ritual and experiment together in a positive way. What seems like strain and division in the *Cantos* has the effect, in Jones's poem, of exhibiting certain affinities between the view of the world implied by ritual and that implied by experimentation. Its treatment of time, its violations of linguistic decorum, and its development of multiple meanings through analogies and homologies are the methods of myth, and Jones defended them on that basis: ". . . collective myth cares nothing for discrepancies of time or circumstance" (*A,* 168n.). But as we have seen, his departures from conventional style must also be attributed, at least in part, to his awareness of contemporary science.

In his preface, Jones laments the possibility that words might lose their power of association and connotation. This power is heavily exploited in *The Anathemata,* as when the word "wood" relates the wood of the Cross to ship's timbers and the Roman battering ram. Such expansions of the suggestive force of words are characteristic of the "patterning language" of religion and ritual. But in Jones's case, as in that of other modern poets, the conflation of unfamiliar and widely separated historical or legendary events owes something to the scientific revisions of our ideas of time, space, and personal identity. At least one critic, Stuart Piggott, has felt that these effects are comparable to concepts that modern science has made familiar: "As you read, the simple-seeming syllables in the context of their deposits, explode in a radiant and beneficent blast of highly charged meanings . . . the words are radio-active with history. . . . enough hit their target to start up in ourselves a chain reaction of generated excitement."[43]

Jones insisted that his poem should be read aloud (which would sacrifice the effects of visual spacing), and David Blamires finds that his text follows the "antiphonal structure and parallelism" of liturgy and the Psalms.[44] It is, in fact, often difficult to tell whether the unconventional aspects of *The Anathemata* arise from a spirit of traditional ritualism or modern experimentation. Many passages correspond to both as when, for example, a Latin phrase from a church service interrupts the modern English text, or when Christ, in science-generated language, shows his "ichthyic" sign "among the palaeo-zoe." It is part of *The Anathemata's* success that in conjunctions of this kind, the secular or scientific is not negated by the sacred but rather embraced and exalted by it.

In his preface, Jones compares his poem to "a longish conversation between two friends" that would seem enigmatic if heard only in parts. It is a constructive version of the dialogue between the archaic and the modern that Mircea Eliade noted as a feature of modern culture. The two world views that compete within the modern consciousness meet in the poem's general structure as well as in its diction. Dilworth conveys this in an excellent image when he says that its diverse elements can be seen moving like electrons in the four dimensions of space and time, a literary galaxy of moving parts in which the meaning of each part involves its symbolic resonance with the other parts. The poem's meditative awareness moves inward, often in the interrogative mood, towards the nucleus of these orbiting images. That nucleus is the Eucharist . . . the great Symbol, synonymous with time's central redemptive event.[45]

Jones declared that "what goes before conditions what comes after and *vice versa*" (A, 33). Thus, the form of the poem is analogous to the scientific concept of a unified force field, but it is centered on ritual, with all of its intuitive and traditional implications.

10

Conclusion

Physicists sound like mystics when they discuss relativity.
—Leonard Shlain, *Art and Physics*

Nearly half a century has passed since the modern poets did their work, but the controversy about the state of knowledge continues. Scientific dogmatism has not been abandoned by everyone. In 1986, Harold Osborne could adhere to the traditional dichotomy by saying ". . . all scientists are aware that the dividing line between scientific theory and non-scientific speculation is that between a theory which is testable against the actuality of experience and that which is not."[1] But Oliver Sacks, writing in the *New York Review of Books* in 1993, continued the powerful antipositivist tradition by asserting that "There is not necessarily any contradiction between a mystical or transcendental philosophy and a rigorously empirical mode of experiment and observation."[2]

Paul Feyerabend, in his widely ranging criticism of conventional science, maintains that science is incapable of producing value-free, universally applicable knowledge because it responds to various competing sources of authority, a condition that he willingly characterizes as one of "epistemological anarchy."[3] Feyerabend's belief supports the view that every attempt to express what we know, through language or other means, invariably mingles objective and subjective elements. This, he says, "removes the apparent difference between the sciences and the arts."[4] Arthur I. Miller agrees, although he is somewhat less absolute: "There is a domain of thinking where distinctions between conceptions in art and science become meaningless."[5]

In a book devoted to parallels between modern art and physics Leonard Shlain has defined the relationship in this way: ". . . revolutionary art anticipates visionary physics. . . . The artist introduces a new way to see the world, then the physicist formulates a new way to think about the world," an observation that supports Pound's argument that artists are "the antennas of the race."[6]

According to Feyerabend, this erosion of the barrier between forms of cognition will lead to "the language of the future" in which *one must learn to argue with unexplained terms and to use sentences for which no clear rules of usage are as yet available.*" Such language, he acknowledges, will be vague, because new concepts are insufficiently understood. It does not predicate but rather indicates the need for further research. Its importance rests not on specific findings but on what Feyerabend calls its "grammatical habit," that is, a manner of thought and expression that signals a radically different intellectual orientation from the ordinary rational one. According to Lyndall Gordon, Eliot's *Little Gidding* functions in this way. "Eliot," she says, "does not state truth. He simply points toward it by arriving at places where truth is manifest."[7] Such statements are not understood at first, says Feyerabend. The inventor of a new hypothesis "must be able to talk nonsense until the amount of nonsense . . . is big enough to give sense to all its part." When that happens, "Madness turns into sanity."[8] We recall that Roger Grainger also described the "alternative language" of ritual as "nonsense" employed to convey certain exceptional truths to the world of sense.

Support for such views as those of Feyerabend have come from Jacques Lacan, who, in a document originating as early as 1953, asserted that there is no opposition between the "exact sciences" and those he calls "conjectural." What he means by the "conjectural sciences," which, of course, include psychoanalysis, are those in which the scientist accepts intimations arising from the lowest levels of the unconscious, "where the diaphragm functions" and where it is in touch with the Freudian primary process. These insights are not mere guesses; they yield "certainty," for this region of the mind is not unstructured or chaotic. *"It must,"* says Lacan, citing the authority of Freud, *"have a relation with causality."*

Lacan acknowledges that the conjectural scientist's work does not yield exact results, because the structure of the unconscious is unknowable. When he declares that there is no necessary opposition between such *sciences humaines* as psychoanalysis and the physical sciences, he no doubt means that the latter have recognized indeterminacy—if indeterminacy is what he means by "the trenchant, decisive crystallization that has already been produced in the physical sciences."[9] Lacan's belief in the wisdom of the diaphragm, "Without 'chaos,' no knowledge. Without a frequent dismissal of reason, no progress," corresponds to Feyerabend's idea that the growing edge of scientific knowledge is formed by intuitive ideas that ignore the rules, and invalidate accepted standards of truth.[10]

Again, the role of language is at issue. According to Lacan, the signifiers generated in the preconscious that the scientist uses in his thinking reflect this causal relation. Lacan attributes the evocative power of language to its correspondence with the structure of the unconscious, a characteristic that is also displayed in the kinship structures Lévi-Strauss has found in primitive societies. To briefly sketch (and somewhat oversimplify) his explanation, this structure is the basis of such "primordial Law" as the Oedipus prohibition; such law depends upon language's ability to name kinship relationships. Lacan, therefore, in an exceptional (though indirect) reference to the transcendental, eloquently declares that the word has a definitive effect on human life: "Symbols in fact envelop the life of man in a network so total that . . . they bring to his birth . . . the shape of his destiny."[11]

We must note this assertion that unconscious structures are fundamental and inborn. "Nature," says Lacan, "provides . . . signifiers, and these signifiers organize human relationships in a creative way."[12] Syntax, and the comparisons and relationships corresponding to metaphor and metonymy, are among the resources of the unconscious, as dreams show. Further, the symbolic power of language properly addresses the feelings and emotions: "The function of language is not to inform but to evoke."[13] These assertions parallel, on an entirely different plane, David Jones's contention that man is a sign-making animal and that the sacraments are "absolutely central and inevitable and inescapable to us."

Lacan's critique of current language, like that of the modern poets, springs from a sense that the scientific environment of modern life has had the effect of depriving language of its symbolic function. It leads the subject to speak of himself as if he were an aspect of the objective world and to forget his own existence in such impersonal activities as the practice of exact science. Under these conditions, the speaker articulates, not his own feelings, but those forced on him by what we would call "the media" of modern life. Lacan quotes a stanza of Eliot's "Hollow Men" who have "Headpieces filled with straw" to show what he means. The effect, as I observed in my discussion of Eliot's poem, is to trivialize the ritual forms with which the poem ends. Lacan is not without hope, however. He feels that the evocative power of language may be restored, for "creative subjectivity has not ceased in its struggle to renew the never-exhausted power of symbols."[14]

That is, of course, the struggle our poets undertook a generation before Lacan. They wrote at a time when art was thought to achieve its ends autonomously, on the basis of esthetic value alone. Walter Pater's ideas and those of the French Symbolists were still influential, and Formalist critical doctrines were developing on the Continent. Ezra Pound could praise his sculptor friend, Jacob Epstein, as someone who could discuss "form not *the form of anything,*" and Clive Bell argued for the dominance in art of "significant form." The modernist revolution was, to a great extent, a crusade in defence of the independence of art, following Pater's claim that art was not a reflection of life but itself a mode of life.

The use of ritual and experiment by the modern poets can be seen as an effort to counteract the isolation of the autonomous poem entailed in their symbolist and Formalist allegiances. Each procedure is in its own way, an interrogation of nature; it is rooted in the extensional world and in turn exerts an influence on it. The modern poets, motivated by a new seriousness and sense of responsibility, meant to use ritual and experiment as ways of bringing poetry to bear on the problems of modern life. However, religion and science have their own claims to autonomy, and in invoking their authority, modern poetry ran the risk of suffering new introversions.

Poems grappling with a cultural and linguistic situation divided by many contradictions cannot be said to have coherent themes. They seem instead to correspond to those fields of discourse, like medicine, in which Foucault can find no unifying principle. Like those studies, such poems as the *Cantos*, H. D.'s *Trilogy*, and Jones's *The Anathemata* may best be seen as instances of the "discursive object" that Foucault sees as governed by "systems of dispersion" that "permit the activation of incompatible themes."[15] As an "object" of that kind, the poem cannot be read either as a personal expression or as a referential mimesis of the outside world, but only as an autonomous artifact suggestive of horizons of consciousness that escape immediate definition.

Mircea Eliade has predicted that humanity, when confronted by the threat of a final catastrophe, will turn from dangerous innovative actions to those that reflect sacred archetypes. While the modern poets considered innovation to be essential for solving the spiritual problems inherited from the past, Eliade's study convincingly shows that the lasting power of tradition is not to be underestimated and helps us to understand why the "dialogue between archaic man and modern man" that he describes became one of the major themes of modern poetry.[16]

The effect of this dialogue in the work of our poets is illuminated by the analysis of Mikhail Bakhtin, the theorist of dialogism. According to his chapter "Discourse in the Novel" in *The Dialogic Imagination*, the vocabulary of the modern novel is alive with the reflections of "heteroglossia," the social influences that generate words and color their meanings. In such works, the varying ideological backgrounds of the words spring into significant relations with each other, creating a subliminal "dialogue" that the reader can tune into through his knowledge of social and ideological conditions.[17]

Bakhtin denies that dialogism can occur in poetry, which, he maintains, employs "by convention" a monologic, authoritative discourse expressing the individual views of the poet, not those of social groups. But this is a convention that much modern poetry has shed. As we have seen in the long poems of Pound and Jones, for example, the voice of the poet is often absent, the idiom often displays radical shifts, and the differing vocabularies may indeed be rooted in social and historical heteroglossia. If heteroglossia are defined as ideologies that give rise to their own forms of speech, the ideologies of ritual and experiment would seem to qualify. Bakhtin enables us to see that poetry which plays forms of language derived from ritual and experimental orientations against each other is genuinely "dialogic" (though not exactly in his sense), and his analytic methods usefully describe what we might expect poetry of this kind to do.

In such poetry we should look not for some final meaning but for what Bakhtin sees as the fruit of the dialogic discourse: "ever newer ways *to mean*." A poem of this kind achieves the effects that Bakhtin attributes to what he calls "the internally persuasive word," that is, an expression that reflects the historical flexibility of language. These include: "its capacity for further creative life in the context of our ideological consciousness, its unfinishedness, and the inexhaustibility of our further dialogic interaction with it. We have not yet learned from it all it might tell us; we can take it into new contexts, attach it to new material, put it in a new situation in order to wrest new answers from it."[18]

Reiss, we recall, considered the "analytico-referential" and "patterning" forms of discourse to be absolutely incompatible and even incapable of mutually comprehending each other. From this point of view, it would seem impossible to achieve a poetic of dialogue, and the failures of coherence in much modern poetry would seem to confirm this. But Reiss does acknowledge that there are certain relationships between the two forms of discourse; he shows that the analytico-referential discourse of modernism grew out of the efforts of patterning discourse to assert its authority in the face of scientific discoveries and also finds that the modes of thought they represent can, under certain conditions, be regarded as complementary rather than contradictory.[19]

While acknowledging that patterning discourse cannot regain the dominance it had in earlier times, Reiss does find in texts extending from the mid-nineteenth century and growing more numerous and more cogent in the twentieth, significant deviations from the dominant analytico-referential discourse. He offers two interpretations of this: they may be continuations of the undertone of skepticism that has always accompanied the dominant discourse, or they may be preliminary indications that the limit of analytico-referential discourse has been reached and that an alternative mode must be found.[20] That alternative may spring from the paradoxical joining of ritualizing and experimental language that we have been examining.

For it is clear that by bringing the apparently contradictory idioms of religion and contemporary science together, the modern poets achieved a genuine renewal and expansion of the resources of poetry. "In one sense" wrote Alfred North Whitehead in 1925, "the conflict between science and religion is a slight matter. . . What one side sees, the other misses; and vice versa."[21] In their effort to see both sides, the modern poets failed to achieve a resolution of the conflict, for they were unconvincing as theorists of the rational and irrational, and the early notion that poetry could be a science was fortunately doomed. While modern poetry did not resolve the nineteenth-century conflict of science and theology or close the gap between the two cultures pointed out by C. P. Snow in the twentieth, it did serve as an eloquent witness of the continuing effort to end the discord between rational and intuitive forms of thought. In this role, it brought about the transformation of poetry that has been universally recognized as a poetic revolution. The invention of expressive resources that confronted contraries with each other in a mutually shaping and correcting relation was one of its contributions to the reconstruction of existing concepts that was going on everywhere else in the early twentieth century. This effort is the source of much of the irony, ambiguity, and self-reflexiveness that characterizes modern poetry, as well as the motive of its experimentation.

Thus, the most significant effects of the juxtaposition of ritual and experiment were those it had on poetry itself, enabling it to overcome traditional limitations without rejecting tradition, and to exploit scientism without surrendering to science. Whatever ambitions the poets may have had toward making their art the vehicle of some grand union of science and religion, their work survives as a poetic revolution rather than an ideological one. Their place is in the line of poets who successively enlarged the field of sensibility available to poetry, such as the seventeenth-century metaphysicals, Wordsworth, Coleridge, Browning, and Hopkins, and, if we turn to French literature, such figures as Baudelaire, Rimbaud, Laforgue, and Mallarmé. Whitehead called the science-religion dispute "a mere logical contradiction," and added: "In formal logic a contradiction is the signal of a defeat: but in the evolution of real knowledge it marks the first step in progress towards a victory."[22] The progress of modern poetry was an advance in poetry rather than knowledge, but it seems fair to say that our poets were taking a first step toward the victory that Whitehead envisioned by showing that logically contradictory forms of expression could be joined to present a more complete view of human beings and their world than science or religion alone can reveal.

Notes

Notes to Chapter 1:
Ritual, Experiment, Poetry

1. Bryher, *The Heart to Artemis: A Writer's Memoirs* (New York: Harcourt, Brace and World, 1962), 203-204.

2. Alfred North Whitehead, *Science and the Modern World* (Reprint. New York: New American Library, 1964), 162, 165, 166. Whitehead's book, which consists of the Lowell Lectures delivered in 1925, reflects thinking contemporaneous with the modern period. Decades later, C. P. Snow lamented a similar division, this one between science and the humanities, in his Rede Lecture, *The Two Cultures and the Scientific Revolution* (Cambridge: Cambridge University Press, 1959), which generated a flood of controversy.

3. Whitehead, *Science and the Modern World*, 166.

4. Catherine Bell, *Ritual Theory, Ritual Practice* (New York: Oxford University Press, 1992), 7-8.

5. For details about these relations, see Lillian Feder, *Ancient Myth in Modern Poetry* (Princeton, N.J.: Princeton University Press, 1971), chap. 4, "Myth and Ritual," 181-269, and John B. Vickery, *The Literary Impact of The Golden Bough* (Princeton, N.J.: Princeton University Press, 1973).

6. For postdeconstructionist defenses of "presence" in poetry, see George Steiner, *Real Presences* (Cambridge: Cambridge University Press, 1986) and Murray Krieger, "Poetic Presence and Illusion, I," in *Poetic Presence and Illusion*, ed. Murray Krieger (Baltimore, Md. and London: Johns Hopkins University Press, 1979), 3-27.

7. Jane Ellen Harrison, *Themis* (Cambridge: Cambridge University Press, 1927), 16, and Harrison, *Prolegomena to the Study of Greek Religion* (Cambridge: Cambridge University Press, 1903. Reprint. New York: Meridian Books, 1957), 28-30. See also

her _Ancient Art and Ritual_ (New York: Holt, 1913), 138, where the function of restoring the efficacy of ritual is attributed to the drama.

8. Mircea Eliade, _Birth and Rebirth_, trans. Willard R. Trask (New York: Harper and Torchbook, 1958. Originally published as _Naissances mystiques_, Paris: Gallimard, 1959), xiii, 6.

9. Owen Barfield, _Saving the Appearances_ (London: Faber and Faber, 1957), 31-32.

10. Mircea Eliade, _The Myth of the Eternal Return or, Cosmos and History_, trans. Willard R. Trask (Princeton, N.J.: Princeton University Press,1954. Originally published as _Mythe de l'éternel retour_, Paris: Gallimard, 1949), 20.

11. Ibid., 34.

12. Albert Einstein, "Relativity and the Problem of Space," _Ideas and Opinions_ (New York: Crown, 1954), 364; and Gerald Holton, "Thematic Presuppositions and the Direction of Scientific Advance," in _Scientific Explanation_, ed. A. F. Heath (Oxford: Oxford University Press, 1981), 1-27, and _The Scientific Imagination: Case Studies_ (Cambridge: Cambridge University Press, 1979), 7-11. In his book, Holton gives the number of _themata_ in the physical sciences as "less than 100," but in the lecture he makes it about fifty.

13. Karl R. Popper, _The Logic of Scientific Discovery_ (London: Hutchinson, 1959); Thomas Kuhn, _The Structure of Scientific Revolutions_ (1962. Chicago: University of Chicago Press, 1970); and Stephen Toulmin, _The Philosophy of Science_ (London: Hutchinson, 1953) illustrate the numerous twentieth-century positions developed from this view. See also "Alternatives to the Received View," in _The Structure of Scientific Theories_, ed. Frederick Suppe, 2nd ed. (Urbana: University of Illinois Press, 1977), 119-232 .

14. James Wayne Dye, "The Poetization of Science," in _The Languages of Creativity_, ed. Mark Amsler (Newark: University of Delaware Press, 1986), 100-l01. This excellent essay sketches the way in which the principles of scientific cognition have changed and attributes scientific advance to constructive or inventive energies rather than to mere investigation.

15. Paul Feyerabend, _Against Method_ (Atlantic Highlands, N.J.: Humanities Press, 1975), 32. See also, for one of many similar opinions, Imre Lakatos, "Falsification and the Methodology of Scientific Research Programmes," in _Criticism and the Growth of Knowledge_, Proceedings of the International Colloquium in the Philosophy of Science, London, 1965, Vol. 4, ed. Imre Lakatos and Alan Musgrave (Cambridge: Cambridge University Press, 1970), 4:187-88.

16. Eliade, _The Myth of the Eternal Return_, 147, 153. Should Eliade have included Yeats as a supporter of the archaic religious myth? In _Rites and Symbols of Initiation_, trans. Willard R. Trask (New York: Harper and Row, 1965), Eliade is critical of occultism, which exhibits the need for spiritual renewal but nevertheless is evidence of "deplorable spiritual poverty." He says that _Ulysses_ and _The Waste Land_ are among the few modern works that contain "initiatory themes" by authors who did not partici-

pate in occult activities. The distinction may explain his failure to mention Yeats in this connection.

17. See Northrop Frye, *Anatomy of Criticism* (Princeton, N.J.: Princeton University Press,1957. Reprint. New York: Athenaeum, 1966), 105-108, 119-22. Arguing that it is not necessary to relate the ritual elements of drama to actual historical rituals, Frye maintains that in drama, "ritual, as the content of action, and more particularly of dramatic action, is something continuously latent in the order of words, and is quite independent of direct influence" (109). A similar point might be made about many lyric poems, though "direct influence" is also very prominent in modern poetry.

18. Julian Huxley, "A Discussion of Ritualization of Behaviour in Animals and Man," in *Philosophic Transactions of the Royal Society* (Series B, Vol. 251), 259.

19. " . . . the earliest phases of kinds seem often to have been ritualistic, if not actually part of the religious rites associated with common situations." Alastair Fowler, *Kinds of Literature: An Introduction to the Theory of Genres and Modes* (Cambridge, Mass.: Harvard University Press, 1982), 149.

20. Ellen Dissanayake, *What is Art For?* (Seattle: University of Washington Press,1988), 152, 156.

21. Victor Turner, "Social Dramas and Stories About Them," *Critical Inquiry* 7 (Autumn 1980):161.

22. Ibid., 165.

23. Victor Turner, "Variations on a Theme of Liminality," in *Secular Ritual*, ed. Sally F. Moore and Barbara G. Myerhoff (Assen: Van Gorcum, 1977), 40, 42. This volume consists of papers read at a conference held in 1974. See also Turner's *The Ritual Process* (Chicago: Aldine Publishing Company, 1969).

24. Turner, "Variations on a Theme of Liminality," 45. See also "Liminal and Liminoid in Play, Flow, and Ritual" in Turner's *From Ritual to Theatre* (New York: Performing Arts Journal Publications, 1982), 20-60.

25. T. S. Eliot, review of *The Growth of Civilization* and *The Origin of Magic and Religion*, both by W. D. Perry in the *Criterion* 2 (July 1924): 490.

26. W. H. Auden, "Making, Knowing and Judging," in *The Dyer's Hand* (New York: Random House, 1962), 27, 57-59.

27. Geoffrey H. Hartman, "Structuralism: The Anglo-American Adventure," in *Beyond Formalism* (New Haven and London: Yale University Press, 1970), 20-23.

28. Peter Bürger, *Theory of the Avant-Garde*, trans. Michael Shaw (Minneapolis: University of Minnesota Press, 1984. Originally published in 1974 and 1979 under various titles by Suhrkamp Verlag, Frankfurt), 28.

29. Stéphane Mallarmé, "Catholicisme" and "De Même," in *Oeuvres Complètes* (Paris: Bibliothèque de la Pléiade, 1965), 390-97. The quotation appears on p. 397. "The hour is right to undertake excavations in it [that is, religion], with the necessary objectivity, in order to exhume ancient and magnificent purposes."

30. Mallarmé, "Le Livre, instrument spirituel," in *Oeuvres Complètes*, 378-82.

31. Jacques Scherer, *Le "Livre" de Mallarmé* (Nouvelle édition. Paris: Gallimard, 1978), 37.

32. David Jones, "A Christmas Message," in *The Dying Gaul and Other Writings*, ed. Harman Grisewood (London: Faber and Faber,1978), 167.

33. For ritual elements in modern drama and the novel, see Edwin M. Mosely, "Religion and the Literary Genres," in *Mansions of the Spirit*, ed. George A. Panichas (New York: Hawthorn Books,1967), 87-103.

34. David Ward, *T. S. Eliot Between Two Worlds*, (London and Boston: Routledge and Kegan Paul, 1973): 277.

35. Renato Poggioli, *The Theory of the Avant-Garde*, trans. Gerald Fitzgerald (Cambridge, Mass., and London: Belknap Press, 1968. Originally published as *Teoria dell'arte d'avanguardia*, Società editrice il Mulino, 1962), 131-40.

36. Gillian Beer, *Darwin's Plots* (London: Routledge and Kegan Paul, 1983), 159.

37. Cleanth Brooks, "Organic Theory in Poetry," in *Literature and Belief*, English Institute Essays,1957, ed. M. H. Abrams (New York and London: Columbia University Press, 1958), 65. Charles B. Wheeler has outlined an experimental procedure for *reading* an unconventional poem. To discover its "implicit rules," the reader "frames a general hypothesis . . . builds a tentative conclusion. . . . This conclusion is then tested carefully against the poem itself. . . . The first decision must be revised in the light of this additional knowledge, then tested again, until the accumulation of experimental data points steadily to one interpretative pattern. But at no time is the reader dealing with anything like certainty." *The Design of Poetry* (New York: W. W. Norton, 1966), 67.

38. Lyndall Gordon, *Eliot's New Life* (New York: Farrar, Straus, Giroux,1988), 142.

39. Whitehead, *Science and the Modern World*, 162.

Notes to Chapter 2:
The Language of Ritual and Experiment

1. Ruth apRoberts, *Arnold and God* (Berkeley: University of California Press, 1983), 216.

2. Timothy J. Reiss, *The Discourse of Modernism* (Ithaca, N.Y.: Cornell University Press, 1982), 41-42.

3. This and the following accounts of scientific theory are drawn from *The Structure of Scientific Theories*, ed. with an intro. Frederick Suppe, 2nd ed. (Urbana: University of Illinois Press, 1977), 6-56.

4. Reiss, *The Discourse of Modernism*, 164.

5. Ernst Cassirer, *Language and Myth*, trans. Susanne Langer (New York and London: Harper and Bros., 1946. Originally published as *Sprache und Mythos*), 58. See also pp. 32 ff. for the process by which words acquire a fixed meaning in a way that is analogous to myth-formation.

6. Owen Barfield, *Saving the Appearances* (London: Faber and Faber, 1985), 85.

7. Brian Vickers, "Analogy versus Identity: The Rejection of Occult Symbolism, 1580-1680," in *Occult and Scientific Mentalities in the Renaissance,* ed. Brian Vickers (Cambridge: Cambridge University Press, l984), 95-163. Vickers quotes Aristotle's observation that an entire poem written in metaphor without any literal language would be "a riddle" (115). This would seem to be the method used in the enigmatic poems of Hart Crane and Dylan Thomas.

8. Quoted in *The Poems of Dylan Thomas,* ed. with an intro. Daniel Jones (New York: New Directions, 1971), 265.

9. Roger Grainger, *The Language of the Rite* (London: Darton, Longman and Todd, 1974), 91.

10. Ibid., 122.

11. Ibid., 51, 57. Grainger's authority is Freud's "Obsessive Acts and Religious Practices" (1907) in *The Standard Edition of the Complete Psychological Works of Sigmund Freud,* vol. 9, ed. James Strachey (London: Hogarth Press, 1953), 9:115-28.

12. Grainger, *The Language of the Rite,* 47, 11.

13. Karl Pearson, *The Grammar of Science* (1892. Reprint. London: A and C. Black, 1900), 60-62, 82-87, 179-81.

14. Thomas Henry Huxley, "The Evolution of Theology," in *Selected Works,* vol 4. ([l886] New York and London: D. Appleton and Co., n.d.), 4:372.

15. Ernst Cassirer, *The Philosophy of Symbolic Forms,* vol. 2, trans. Ralph Manheim (New Haven: Yale University Press, 1955. Originally published as *Philosophie der Symbolischen Formen,* Oxford: Oxford University Press, 1953-57), 2:26.

16. Northrop Frye, *Anatomy of Criticism* (Princeton. N.J.: Princeton University Press, 1957. Reprint. New York: Athenaeum, l966), 350.

17. Geoffrey Cantor, "The Rhetoric of Experiment," in *The Uses of Experiment,* ed. David Gooding, Trevor Pinch and Simon Schaffer (Cambridge: Cambridge University Press, 1989), 159-80.

18. Huxley, "The Evolution of Theology," 4: 357.

19. Jacques Derrida, "White Mythology: Metaphor in the Text of Philosophy," in *Margins of Philosophy,* trans. Alan Bass (Chicago: University of Chicago Press, 1982. Originally published as *Marges de la philosophie,* Paris: Éditions de minuit, 1972), 210, 270-71, and 246.

20. Max Black, "Metaphor," in *Models and Metaphors* (Ithaca, N.Y.: Cornell University Press, 1962), 46. See also *Darwin's Plots* (London: Routledge and Kegan Paul, 1983), where Gillian Beer reiterates Black's "interaction" idea and adds that the contrast between the metaphoric terms is capable of embodying apparent contradiction, so that "metaphor is a means both of initiating and of controlling novelty . . . a means to recognizable discovery" (96).

21. Paul Ricoeur, "Metaphor and the Central Problem of Hermeneutics," in *Hermeneutics and the Human Sciences,* ed. and trans. John B. Thompson (Cambridge and New York:

Cambridge University Press, 1981. Originally published in Paris by Éditions de la Maison des sciences de l'homme, 1981),171-74.

22. Ibid., 243. In another passage, Ricoeur says of metaphor: "The imagination operates here on the verbal level to produce new configurations of meaning, at the cost of extending the polysemy characteristic of natural languages" (39).

23. Barry Barnes, *Scientific Knowledge and Sociological Theory* (London and Boston: Routledge and Kegan Paul, 1974), 87, 53, 57.

24. Ibid., 54, 92.

25. Claude Bernard, *An Introduction to the Study of Experimental Medicine*, trans. Henry Copley Greene (New York: Macmillan, 1927. Originally published as *Introduction á l'ètude de la mèdecine expèrimentale*, Paris: J.B. Baillière et fils, 1865): 222.

26. Bernard I. Duffey, "The Experimental Lyric in Modern Poetry: Eliot, Pound, Williams," *Journal of Modern Literature*, 3 (July 1974), 1101, 1087-88. This is an excellent and suggestive discussion of the subject.

Notes to Chapter 3:
William Butler Yeats

1. William Butler Yeats, *Autobiographies* (New York: Macmillan, 1927), 313-14. A detailed account of the rituals Yeats devised is given in Virginia Moore, *The Unicorn* (New York: Macmillan, 1954), 73-81.

2. Moore, *The Unicorn*, 73-81. See also M. C. Flannery, *Yeats and Magic* (New York: Harper and Row, 1978). Photographs of the ritual implements made by Yeats appear in Kathleen Raine, *Yeats the Initiate: Certain Themes in the Work of W. B. Yeats* (Mountrath and London: The Dolmen Press and George Allen & Unwin, 1986), Illustration No. 64 and No.196.

3. Morton I. Seiden, *William Butler Yeats: The Poet as Mythmaker* (East Lansing: Michigan State University Press, 1962), 219.

4. Helen Hennesy Vendler, *Yeats' Vision and the Later Plays* (Cambridge, Mass.: Harvard University Press, 1963), 37.

5. Yeats, *Per Amica Silentia Lunae* in *Mythologies* (London: Macmillan, 1959), 334.

6. Ibid., 331.

7. Yeats, *A Critical Edition of Yeats's A Vision*, ed. George Mills Harper and Walter Kelly Hood (London: Macmillan, 1978), 18. In the following passages, Yeats's poems are quoted from *The Collected Poems of W. B. Yeats* (New York: Macmillan, 1963).

8. Yeats, *A Critical Edition of Yeats's A Vision*, 331-35, and Jacques Lacan, *The Four Fundamental Concepts of Psychoanalysis*, trans. Alan Sheridan (New York and London: W. W. Norton and Company, 1977. Originally published as *Les quatre concepts fondamentaux de la psychanalyse*, ed. Jacques-Alain Miller. Paris: Éditions du Seuil, 1973), 198-99, 203-204.

9. Yeats, *Autobiographies*, 372.

10. Yeats, *The Variorum Edition of the Plays of W. B. Yeats*, ed. Russell K. Alspach and Catharine C. Alspach (New York: Macmillan, 1968), 970. Yeats's plays and the notes to his plays will be cited from this edition. For details about Yeats's experience with automatic writing, see the "Editorial Introduction" to *A Critical Edition of Yeats's A Vision*, xi-l.

11. Yeats, *A Critical Edition of Yeats's A Vision*, 9-11. For the significance of the dancer image, see Frank Kermode, *Romantic Image* (New York: Vintage Books, 1964), chap. 4, "The Dancer."

12. Yeats, *A Critical Edition of Yeats's A Vision*, 191.

13. Richard Ellmann, *Yeats: The Man and the Masks* (New York: Macmillan, 1948), 239. For extended discussions of the ritual element in Yeats's poetry, see Ellmann's *Identity of Yeats* (New York: Oxford University Press, 1954), 170-79 ("Ritualizing"); and Lillian Feder, *Ancient Myth in Modern Poetry* (Princeton, N.J.: Princeton University Press, 1971), 185-200.

14. For an analysis of the Frazerian imagery in this poem, see John B. Vickery, *The Literary Impact of The Golden Bough* (Princeton, N.J.: Princeton University Press, 1973), 226-29. Further comment appears in Kathleen Raine, *Yeats, the Tarot and the Golden Dawn*, 2nd ed. (Dublin: Dolmen Press, 1976).

15. Vickery identifies as Yeats's source for this scene Frazer's account of the ritual of Adonis. See Vickery, *The Literary Impact of The Golden Bough*, 221-26.

16. Yeats, *A Critical Edition of Yeats's A Vision*, 69-71.

17. René Girard, *Violence and the Sacred*, trans. Patrick Gregory (Baltimore and London: Johns Hopkins University Press, 1977. Originally published as *Le Violence et le sacré*. Paris: Éditions Bernard Grasset, 1972), 283.

18. Quoted from Yeats's "The Theatre" in the theater journal *Beltaine* in Liam Miller, *The Noble Drama of W.B. Yeats* (Dublin: Dolmen Press, 1977), 38.

19. Andrew Parkin, *The Dramatic Imagination of W. B. Yeats* (Dublin: Gill and Macmillan, 1978), 98. Noh was not ritualistic in its origins, but it developed into fixed ceremonial performances, some of which were actual rituals. Some were sponsored by Buddhist and Shinto temples to teach religion and stimulate prayer; the secular plays often retain links with the religious history of the form.

20. Seiden, *William Butler Yeats: The Poet as Mythmaker*, 227-28.

21. Parkin, *The Dramatic Imagination of W. B. Yeats*, 146.

22. Yeats, Letter of 17 April 1929, *W. B. Yeats and T. Sturge Moore: Their Correspondence 1901-1937*, ed. Ursula Bridge (New York: Oxford University Press, 1953), 154 .

23. Yeats, *Autobiographies*, 224-26.

24. Moore, *The Unicorn*, 126-27, 218-19.

25. Yeats, Letter of 17 April 1929, *W. B. Yeats and T. Sturge Moore: Their Correspondence 1901-1937*, 154 .

26. Yeats, Notes to "The Resurrection," *The Variorum Edition of the Plays of W. B. Yeats*, 934.

27. Yeats, *Essays and Introductions* (London and New York: Macmillan, 1961), 202.

Notes to Chapter 4:
T. S. Eliot's Early Poems

1. Cf. Carol T. Christ, *Victorian and Modern Poetics* (Chicago and London: University of Chicago Press, 1984): 134-35: "This desire [for a unifying structure] results paradoxically in both the most radical experiments in discontinuity of poetic forms and a conservative social orthodoxy" (135).

2. Some of the sources of this conflict and their influence on Eliot's thinking are lucidly covered in William Skaff, *The Philosophy of T. S. Eliot: From Skepticism to A Surrealist Poetic, 1909-1927* (Philadelphia: University of Pennsylvania Press, 1985).

3. A. D. Moody, *Thomas Stearns Eliot: Poet* (Cambridge: Cambridge University Press, 1979), 197.

4. T. S. Eliot, to Norbert Wiener, 6 January 1915, *The Letters of T. S. Eliot: 1898-1922*, vol. 1 (San Diego, Calif., New York, London: Harcourt, Brace, Jovanovich,1988), 79-81.

5. T. S. Eliot, "Literature, Science and Dogma," *Dial* 82 (March 1927): 240. The earlier review, of *The Growth of Civilisation* and *The Origin of Magic and Religion*, both by W. J. Perry, appeared in the *Criterion* 2 (July 1924): 489-91.

6. T. S. Eliot, "Tradition and the Individual Talent," in *Selected Essays* (New York: Harcourt, Brace and World, 1964), 3.

7. Ibid., 5.

8. Carol Christ, *Victorian and Modern Poetics*, 134-35.

9. Eliot, *Selected Essays*, 6-7.

10. Ibid., 22.

11. Skaff, *The Philosophy of T. S. Eliot*, 104. The three poems are *The Waste Land, Ash Wednesday* and *Four Quartets.* By "ritualistic structure" Skaff means patterns involving rhythm, abstraction, and stylization.

12. Compare Freud's assertion: "In all believers . . . the motives which impel them to religious practices are unknown to them or are represented in consciousness by others which are advanced in their place." "Obsessive Acts and Religious Practices," (*The Standard Edition of the Complete Psychological Works of Sigmund Freud*, vol. 9, ed. James Strachey, London: Hogarth Press, 1953), 122-23.

13. T. S. Eliot, "Philosophical Essays and Notes" (a manuscript in the library of King's College, Cambridge, consisting of notes for a talk delivered at a seminar conducted by Josiah Royce at Harvard University on December 9, 1913). See also Harry Todd Costello, *Josiah Royce's Seminar*, ed. Grover Smith (New Brunswick, N.J.: Rutgers

University Press, 1963). For Eliot's attitudes toward primitive religion, see William Harmon, "T. S. Eliot: Anthropologist and Primitive," *American Anthropologist*, 78 (December 1976): 797-811, and Marc Manganaro, "Dissociation in 'Dead Land': The Primitive Mind in the Early Poetry of T. S. Eliot," *Journal of Modern Literature*, 13 (March 1986): 97-110.

14. F. R. Leavis, *New Bearings in English Poetry* (1932. Reprint. Ann Arbor: University of Michigan Press,1960), 93. According to Peter Ackroyd, Eliot remembered his anthropological studies; its ideas frequently turn up in his later writings. Ackroyd feels that Eliot depended on ritual as a way of resisting the chaos of absolute subjectivity and observes that "the notion of ritual permeates both Eliot's work and the meticulous routines of his adult life." *T. S. Eliot: A Life* (New York: Simon and Schuster, 1984), 49.

15. T. S. Eliot, "London Letter," *Dial* 71 (October 1921): 453; and Eliot, "Marianne Moore," *Dial* 75 (December 1923): 597.

16. "In 'Prufrock' the 'taking of a toast and tea' is a symbolic food ritual, a debasement of the Eucharist." Marjorie Perloff, *The Poetics of Indeterminacy* (Princeton, N.J.: Princeton University Press, 1981), 119. Quotations from Eliot's poems are from *The Complete Poems and Plays*, 1909-1950 (New York: Harcourt, Brace and World, Inc., 1962), and will be followed in the text by their page numbers in this edition.

17. David Ward, *T. S. Eliot Between Two Worlds* (London and Boston: Routledge and Kegan Paul, 1973), 17.

18. See Lyndall Gordon, *Eliot's Early Years* (Oxford and New York: Oxford University Press, 1977), chaps. 3 and 4.

19. Hugh Kenner sees an even more sinister implication in this passage: "Some rite, not innocent, unites these persons. . . . the lurid malaise of some cosmopolitan Black Mass." Kenner, *The Invisible Poet: T. S. Eliot* (1959. Reprint. New York: The Citadel Press, 1964), 130.

20. Ward, *T. S. Eliot Between Two Worlds*, 73. For differing opinions of the ritual status of the poem, see Moody, *Thomas Stearns Eliot: Poet*, 111 and 262 ff., and Calvin Bedient, *He Do the Police in Different Voices* (Chicago and London: University of Chicago Press, 1986), 121-22 .

21. Mircea Eliade, *The Myth of the Eternal Return or, Cosmos and History*, trans. Willard R. Trask (Princeton, N.J.: Princeton University Press, 1954. Originally published as *Mythe de l'éternel retour*, Paris: Gallimard, 1949), 7-11, 153.

22. Gordon, *Eliot's Early Years*, 61. For Eliot's feeling that murder is a release from spiritual oppression, see Moody, *Thomas Stearns Eliot: Poet*, 116-17.

23. René Girard, *Violence and the Sacred*, trans. Patrick Gregory (Baltimore and London: Johns Hopkins University Press, 1977. Originally published as *Le Violence et le sacré*, Paris: Éditions Bernard Grasset, 1972), 78-85, 206, and *passim*. Girard has developed an elaborate "nonsacrificial" reading of the Gospels intended to correct the misin-

terpretation of the Crucifixion as an instance of generative violence. He maintains that the Crucifixion was not a sacrifice, but on the contrary, a dramatic demand for an end to the pattern of conflict and violence on which religion had been based. According to Girard, the New Testament, especially the Gospels, repudiates sacrifice and presents the death of Jesus as an exposure of the fact that violence is demanded by religious institutions and not by God, thus offering "a kind of practical atheism." *Things Hidden Since the Foundation of the World,* trans. Stephen Bann and Michael Metteer (Palo Alto: Stanford University Press, 1987. Originally published as *Des choses cachées depuis la fondation du monde*), 183.

24. Girard, *Violence and the Sacred,* 135.

25. Ibid., 103; Jakobson is quoted in Ann Jefferson, "Russian Formalism," in *Modern Literary Theory,* ed. Ann Jefferson and David Robey (New York: Barnes and Noble, 1982), 29; Wallace Stevens, "The Noble Rider and the Sound of Words," in *The Necessary Angel: Essays on Reality and the Imagination* (1942. Reprint. New York: Vintage Books, 1951), 35-36.

26. T. S. Eliot, "Ulysses, Order and Myth," *Dial* 75 (November 1923): 480-83.

27. A later comment is even more emphatic. Artistic creation, said Eliot, in response to a correspondent who had criticized one of his reviews, "is a sacrifice of the man to the work, it is a kind of death." *The Letters of T. S. Eliot,* 387, reprinted from *The Athenaeum* of June 25th, 1920.

28. T. S. Eliot, "The Death of Saint Narcissus," in *Poems Written in Early Youth* (London: Faber and Faber, 1967), 34-35. Early drafts of this poem, together with reproductions of the manuscript appear in *The Waste Land: A Facsimile and Transcript of the Original Drafts Including the Annotations of Ezra Pound,* ed. Valerie Eliot (New York: Harcourt Brace Jovanovich Inc., 1971), 90-97.

29. Girard, *Violence and the Sacred,* chap. 2. The quotations appear on 51 and 67.

30. For interesting comment on ritual aspects of the buried corpse and the first part of "A Game of Chess," see John T. Mayer, *T. S. Eliot's Silent Voices* (New York and Oxford: Oxford University Press, 1989), 261, 263-65.

31. Girard, *Violence and the Sacred,* 34-35.

32. "The regulations governing marriage resemble the regulations governing the choice of sacrificial victims." Ibid., 220. See also ibid., chap. 9, "Lévi-Strauss, Structuralism and Marriage Laws," in which Girard argues that in these ceremonies, "the ritual violence that accompanies the exchange of women serves a sacrificial purpose for each group. In sum, the groups agree never to be completely at peace, so that their members may find it easier to be at peace among themselves" (249).

33. A canceled sentence that appears in the early draft shows that this couple is the same as the one in the hyacinth garden. See *The Waste Land: A Facsimile and Transcript of the Original Drafts,* 13. The final text also links the two scenes through the repeated "nothing." When the husband answers his wife's question about the wind with this

word, and when she asks him whether he remembers "nothing," both are referring to the hyacinth garden, where, he says, he knew "nothing."

34. T. S. Eliot, "Conclusion," in *The Use of Poetry and the Use of Criticism* (1933. Reprint. London: Faber and Faber, 1967), 155.

35. Graham Hough, *Reflections on a Literary Revolution* (Washington, D.C.: Catholic University Press, 1960), 4.

36. Ward, *T. S. Eliot Between Two Worlds*, 144.

37. Or, as George Williamson has said of this quatrain: " . . . the most devastating irony is formal; the extension of game ritual into liturgical form." *A Reader's Guide to T. S. Eliot* (1953. Reprint. New York: Farrar, Straus and Giroux, 1966),160-61.

38. Ward, *T. S. Eliot Between Two Worlds*, 140. For an analysis of the two voices in "Ash Wednesday," see Jacob Korg, "Ritual and Experiment in Modern Poetry," *Journal of Modern Literature* 8 (February 1979): 142-46.

39. Grover Smith, *T. S. Eliot's Poetry and Plays* (Chicago and London: University of Chicago Press, 1956), 144.

40. See ibid., 46, but also Moody, who feels that the passage echoes the arrival of the Israelites in the Promised Land. *Thomas Stearns Eliot: Poet*, 145. This view leads him to discount the pessimism of the following section. My reasons for regarding the "inheritance" as ironic are based mainly on the foregoing lines, but also on the poem's denial of the "division" enjoined by the Biblical passage.

41. Bernard I. Duffey, "The Experimental Lyric in Modern Poetry: Eliot, Pound, Williams," *Journal of Modern Literature* 3, no. 5 (July 1974): 1085-1103.

42. Bachelard, *Le nouvel esprit scientifique*, 2nd ed. (Paris: Presses Universitaires, 1968). The quotations appear on 172: "The very essence of reflection is to understand that one did not understand," and on 171: "Tomorrow I shall know."

Notes to Chapter 5:
Four Quartets

1. Ronald Bush, *T. S. Eliot: A Study in Character and Style* (New York and Oxford: Oxford University Press, 1983), 199.

2. Quoted in "Ideology and Poetry" by Kathleen Nott in *The Waste Land in Different Voices*, ed. A. D. Moody (New York: St. Martin's Press, 1974), 204.

3. Helen Gardner, *The Composition of Four Quartets* (New York: Oxford University Press, 1978), 29.

4. Lillian Feder, *Ancient Myth in Modern Poetry* (Princeton, N.J.: Princeton University Press, 1971), 236.

5. A. D. Moody, *Thomas Stearns Eliot: Poet* (Cambridge: Cambridge University Press, 1979), 228.

6. Derek Traversi, *T. S. Eliot: The Longer Poems* (New York and London: Harcourt, Brace, Jovanovich, 1976), 103.

7. Mircea Eliade, *The Myth of the Eternal Return or, Cosmos and History*, trans. Willard R. Trask (Princeton, N.J.: Princeton University Press, 1954. Originally published as *Mythe de l'éternel retour*, Paris: Gallimard, 1949), 12 ff.

8. Bush, *T. S. Eliot: A Study in Character and Style*, 202. Bush's comment that the lines are "incantatory" suggests their ritual quality. His criticism that they are not sufficiently precise or rigorous is, of course, accurate, but that vagueness is inherent in patterning language.

9. David Ward, *T. S. Eliot Between Two Worlds* (London and Boston: Routledge and Kegan Paul, 1973), 277.

10. Eliot, like Yeats, associated the disciplined rhythms of dance with both art and ritual and once wrote, ". . . ritual, consisting of a set of repeated movements, is essentially a dance." "The Beating of a Drum," *Nation and Athenaeum* 34 (October 6 1923):12.

11. T. S. Eliot, "The Music of Poetry," in *On Poetry and Poets* (New York: Noonday Press, 1957), 26, 22-23, 30.

12. Cf. Bush summarizing Eliot's view: "The poet, if he is a poet, cannot turn language inside out for his own purposes. . . . he is bound to the journalist: the poet's duty is to rehabilitate the language they share." *T. S. Eliot: A Study in Character and Style*, 159.

13. Moody, *Thomas Stearns Eliot: Poet*, 262. Eliot is nearly consistent in muting references to the events of the Passion. Note his statement, in "Religion and Literature," that overtly devotional poetry is bound to be minor poetry. *Selected Essays* (New York: Harcourt, Brace and World, 1964), 345-46.

14. W. H. Auden, *The Dyer's Hand* (New York: Random House, 1962), 27.

15. Gardner, *The Composition of Four Quartets*, 183, 111, 157, 206-207.

16. Ibid., 112.

17. Traversi, *T. S. Eliot: The Longer Poems*, 114.

18. Robert Browning, "Essay on Shelley," in *Browning: Poetry and Prose*, selected by Simon Nowell-Smith (London: Rupert Hart-Davis, 1950), 674.

19. T. S. Eliot, "Shakespeare and the Stoicism of Seneca," in *Selected Essays*, 117.

Notes to Chapter 6:
Ezra Pound's Early Poems

1. Quoted from an interview by Donald Hall in "Ezra Pound" in *Writers at Work: The Paris Review Interviews*, Second Series (New York: The Viking Press, 1963), 38.

2. Ezra Pound, to Henry Hope Shakespear, 16 February 1914, *Ezra Pound and Dorothy Shakespear: Their Letters, 1909-1914*, ed. Omar Pound and A. Walton Litz (New York: New Directions, 1984), 217.

3. Carroll F. Terrell, "Preface," *A Companion to the Cantos of Ezra Pound*, 2 vols. (Berkeley, Los Angeles, and London: University of California Press, 1984), 2: 7. One religion that Pound rejected, however, was Judaism.

4. Akiko Miyake, *Ezra Pound and the Mysteries of Love* (Durham, N.C. and London: Duke University Press, 1991), especially chap. 2, "Pound's Earlier Attempt at Ascension," 22-45; and Demetres P. Tryphonopoulos, *The Celestial Tradition* (Waterloo, Ont.: Wilfrid Laurier University Press, 1992), which contains an excellent sketch of the background of this aspect of Pound's thinking in chap. 2, "The Occult Tradition," 23-58. Tryphonopoulos feels, however, that the link with Rossetti came much later than Miyake's date suggests.

5. Jane Harrison, *Prolegomena to the Study of Greek Religion* (Cambridge: Cambridge University Press, 1903. Reprint. New York: Meridian Books, 1957), 164.

6. Ezra Pound, *Selected Prose, 1909-1965*, ed. William Cookson (New York: New Directions, [1973]), 49-52. Further references to this source will appear in the text as *SP*.

7. Pound, unpublished letter quoted in Henry Swabey, "A Page Without Which . . . ," *Paideuma* 5 (Fall 1976): 334.

8. Miyake, *Ezra Pound and the Mysteries of Love*, 180.

9. Ezra Pound, "Psychology and Troubadours," in *The Spirit of Romance* (Norfolk, Conn.: New Directions, n.d.), 89. Boris de Rachewiltz notes that "Pound approves of church ritual in so far as it retains traces of the older pagan meaning." See "Pagan and Magic Elements in Ezra Pound's Works," in *New Approaches to Ezra Pound*, ed. Eva Hesse (Berkeley and Los Angeles: University of California Press, 1969), 194-95.

10. For discussion of the ritual poems of *Lustra* see Hugh Witemeyer, *The Poetry of Ezra Pound: Forms and Renewal* (Berkeley and Los Angeles: University of California Press, 1969), 122-34.

11. Miyake, *Ezra Pound and the Mysteries of Love*, chap. 1. Miyake acknowledges that Pound's only direct reference to Rossetti's book is a casual one in *Carta da Visita* as late as 1942. But she offers enough indirect evidence to make a convincing case for his early knowledge of it and for its immediate influence on his ideas. She also points out allusions to the Eleusinian ceremonies and their gods in his early poems. See 30-39.

12. Gabriele Rossetti, *Il Mistero dell'Amor platonico del Medio Evo derivato da' Misteri antichi*, 5 vols. (London: Richard and John E. Taylor, 1840), 1: 202. The work he cites is *Esprit du dogme de la Franche-Maçonnerie* (1825) by Reghellini.

13. Ezra Pound, "Interesting French Publications," *Book News Monthly* 25 (September 1906): 31-34. Péladan also influenced Denis De Rougemont, who acknowledged that he followed Péladan in tracing courtly love through the Albigensian heresy and back to Manicheanism.

14. Pound, *The Spirit of Romance*, 90.

15. Ezra Pound, to Henry Swabey, 31 October 1939, *The Letters of Ezra Pound 1907-1941*, ed. D. D. Paige (New York: Harcourt, Brace and World, 1950), 327. In a letter

written on 3 November 1939 to Douglas McPherson, Pound says: "The minute you proclaim that the mysteries exist *at all* you've got to recognize that 95% of yr. contemporaries will not and cannot understand *one* word of what you are driving at. And you can *not* explain. The SECRETUM stays shut to the vulgo." Ibid., 328-29. Major parts of Rossetti's and Pound's theory about medieval love poetry were confirmed in Denis de Rougemont's *Love in the Western World* (first published in 1939 as *L'amour et l'occident*), which exerted a strong influence on H. D.

16. See Ronald Bush, *The Genesis of Ezra Pound's Cantos*, 105-106, 110-11. "The Noh play's structure . . . could not be separated from its ritual function."

17. Ezra Pound, untitled review of Upward's *The Divine Mystery. New Freewoman* 1 (15 November 1913): 207-208. Pound's source here is *The Divine Mystery* (1907. Reprint. Santa Barbara, Calif.: Ross-Erikson Inc., 1976), xxxiv, 3. Upward's view of the order of history resembles that of Yeats. "History," he says, "is a great ritualist" (222).

18. Bush attributes some of Pound's basic religious ideas to Upward's influence, including the identification of art as a kind of ritual. See *The Genesis of Ezra Pound's Cantos*, 99-100.

19. Upward, *The Divine Mystery*, 56.

20. Tryphonopoulos argues that Pound's interest in the occult began before he left the United States but was greatly augmented by his London connections. See *The Celestial Tradition*, chap. 3, "Pound's Occult Education," 59-100.

21. For a thorough study of this relation, see James Longenbach, *Stone Cottage: Pound, Yeats and Modernism* (New York and Oxford: Oxford University Press, 1988).

22. Quotations are from Pound, *The Spirit of Romance*, 7, and "The Serious Artist," in *Literary Essays of Ezra Pound*, ed. with an introduction by T. S. Eliot (New York: New Directions, 1968), 48.

23. For the influence of Ford's scientific emphasis on Pound, see Stanley K. Coffman, Jr., *Imagism: A Chapter for the History of Modern Poetry* (Norman: University of Oklahoma Press, 1951), 139-40; and Ian F.A. Bell, *Critic as Scientist: The Modernist Poetics of Ezra Pound* (London and New York: Methuen and Co., 1981), 89-94.

24. Hudson Maxim, *The Science of Poetry and the Philosophy of Language* (New York and London: Funk and Wagnalls, 1910), ix-x.

25. Bell, *Critic as Scientist*, 27-37.

26. Ibid., 206-209. Also: "The conjunction of mathematics and magic . . . was to be the centre of Pound's aesthetics, and the means whereby he gave modernity to areas of experience customarily understood to be 'arcane, mysterious'" (39). Martin A. Kayman, more generally, argues that Pound sought to maintain an audience by the "scientific technique" of Imagism while preserving "the spiritual basis of art." He identifies his modernism as a synthesis of "subjective and objective realism" and says that his interest in alchemy "appears to lend itself, on a wider level, to a particular

and global synthesis of the mystical and the scientific." Kayman, *The Modernism of Ezra Pound: The Science of Poetry* (London: Macmillan, 1986), 17, 18, 71.

27. Robert Casillo, *The Genealogy of Demons: Anti-Semitism, Fascism, and the Myths of Ezra Pound* (Evanston, Ill.: Northwestern University Press, 1988), 330.

28. Bell, *Critic as Scientist*, 207.

29. Ezra Pound, *Guide to Kulchur* (New York: New Directions, n.d., 1952), 291.

30. Ibid., 252.

31. "Past History," in *Pound/Joyce*, ed. Forrest Read (New York: New Directions, 1965), 251.

32. Renato Poggioli, *The Theory of the Avant-Garde*, trans. Gerald Fitzgerald (Cambridge, Mass. and London: Belknap Press, 1968. Originally published as *Teoria dell'arte d'avanguardia* [Società editrice il Mulino, 1962]), 137. Poggioli is skeptical of the value of experimentation throughout his study.

33. William Pratt, *The Imagist Poem* (New York: E. P. Dutton, 1963), 29; Christine Froula, *To Write Paradise: Style and Error in Pound's Cantos* (New Haven: Yale University Press, 1984), 20.

34. Ezra Pound, "Fan-Piece, For Her Imperial Lord" from *Lustra*, in *Personae: the Collected Shorter Poems of Ezra Pound* (New York: New Directions, 1971), 108. Further citations from this collection will be identified parenthetically in the text by page numbers marked *Personae*.

35. Witemeyer, *The Poetry of Ezra Pound*, 32.

36. John T. Gage, *In the Arresting Eye: The Rhetoric of Imagism* (Baton Rouge and London: Louisiana State University Press, 1981), 156.

37. Longenbach, *Stone Cottage*, 31-33.

38. See Bell, *Critic as Scientist*, 14-15, and chap. 4, "The vortex: shapes ancient and modern"; and Miyake, *Ezra Pound and the Mysteries of Love*, 22-26.

39. M. L. Rosenthal and Sally M. Gall, *The Modern Poetic Sequence* (New York and Oxford: Oxford University Press, 1983), 9, 6-7, 11.

40. Witemeyer, *The Poetry of Ezra Pound*, 103.

41. John Espey, *Ezra Pound's Mauberley* (Reprint. Berkeley, Los Angeles and London: University of California Press, 1974), 44. This study is indispensable as a source of information about the sources of *Mauberley*.

Notes to Chapter 7:
The Cantos

1. Ezra Pound, *The Cantos of Ezra Pound* (New York: New Directions, 1973), 795. All citations from cantos that appear in this chapter are taken from this source and are identified by canto number.

2. Ezra Pound, *Guide to Kulchur* (New York: New Directions, n.d., 1952), 223.

3. This interview with Donald Hall is reprinted from the *Paris Review*, no. 28 (1962) in *Writers at Work*, 2nd ser. (New York: The Viking Press, 1963), where the quotation appears on 57.

4. Christine Froula connects subject-rhyme to Pound's historical views and success-fully argues that it is based on abstract patterns reflecting beliefs that Pound considered universal. See Froula, *To Write Paradise: Style and Error in Pound's Cantos* (New Haven: Yale University Press, 1984), 22-33. This study is an excellent guide to Canto 4. The drafts Froula includes show Pound moving from the verbose Browningesque style of the early *Three Cantos* to the over-elliptical telegraphese of the final Canto 4; they also expose the links among the images that Pound had in mind and give more space to the wedding ritual. Froula shows how undependable Pound's history and use of his sources can be and makes it clear that his errors present a constant hazard to close readers of the text. See especially her chap. 3, "The Pound Error," 139-170.

5. Jean-Michel Rabaté, *Language, Sexuality and Ideology in Ezra Pound's Cantos* (London: Macmillan, 1986), 289.

6. Pound, *Selected Prose 1905-1965*, ed. William Cookson (New York: New Directions, [1973]), 398. The quotation is from "Prefatio aut Cimicium Tumulus," an essay first published in 1933.

7. This is a much debated topic in Pound criticism. Demetres P. Tryphonopoulos, in *The Celestial Tradition: A Study of Ezra Pound's The Cantos*, says that the *Cantos* as a whole is a guide to Pound's "syncretic rite." The poems "take us a certain distance along Pound's palingenetic ritual: but they stop short of . . . full revelation" (162). On the other hand, Anthony Woodward, in *Ezra Pound and The Pisan Cantos* (London: Routledge and Kegan Paul, 1980), is especially conscious of the interplay of skepticism and conviction that makes Pound a representative modernist, and this perhaps accounts for the limitation Tryphonopoulos has noted (29 ff). Some of the other works that examine the relation of the *Cantos* to the Eleusinian rite are: Leon Surette, *A Light from Eleusis* (Oxford: Clarendon Press, 1979); Akiko Miyake, *Ezra Pound and the Mysteries of Love* (Durham, N.C. and London: Duke University Press, 1991); Lillian Feder, *Ancient Myth in Modern Poetry* (Princeton, N.J.: Princeton University Press, 1971), 200-19; Rabaté, *Language, Sexuality and Ideology in Ezra Pound's Cantos*, 90 ff; and Helen M. Dennis, "The Eleusinian Mysteries as an Organizing Principle in *The Pisan Cantos*," *Paideuma* 10 (Fall 1981): 273-82.

8. Daniel D. Pearlman, *The Barb of Time* (New York: Oxford University Press, 1969), 22, 37, and *passim*, and Surette, *A Light from Eleusis*, 55, 67.

9. Miyake, *Ezra Pound and the Mysteries of Love*, xi.

10. Information about the Eleusinian ritual is based mainly on George E. Mylonas, *Eleusis and the Eleusinian Mysteries* (Princeton, N.J.: Princeton University Press, 1961); and C.

Kerenyi, *Eleusis: Archetypal Image of Mother and Daughter,* trans. Ralph Manheim (New York: Pantheon Books, 1964).

11. Mylonas, *Eleusis and the Eleusinian Mysteries,* 281.

12. Pound, *Guide to Kulchur,* 294, 144-45.

13. Mylonas, *Eleusis and the Eleusinian Mysteries,* 311-16. Rossetti, in *Il Mistero,* says that the *participants* married the goddess and that their souls then passed to heaven temporarily until they were fully transported to it .

14. Pound, "Terra Italica," in *Selected Prose,* 55, 59, 56. The words mean, literally, "comb" and "pudenda" and form a euphemism for the *mons Veneris.* Mylonas, emphatically denying that this image could be included among the sacred objects, speculates that the idea may have been derived from an Egyptian custom in which women exposed themselves. See Mylonas, *Eleusis and the Eleusinian Mysteries,* 293 ff.

15. Ezra Pound, to Homer L. Pound, 11 April 1927, *The Letters of Ezra Pound, 1907-1941,* ed. D. D. Paige (New York: Harcourt, Brace and World, 1950), 210.

16. For Eleusis, see Kerenyi, *Eleusis: Archetypal Image of Mother and Daughter,* 121. Pound's reference is in *The Cantos of Ezra Pound* (New York: New Directions, 1973), 217.

17. Pound, *Guide to Kulchur,* 299.

18. Rabaté, *Language, Sexuality and Ideology in Ezra Pound's Cantos,* 90; Woodward, *Ezra Pound and The Pisan Cantos,* 28. Rabaté offers an intriguing explanation of Pound's objection to usury, supported by a passage in "Addendum for C": "The endless increase of money implied infinity, a concept disruptive of the Greek conception of a closed and orderly cosmos" (188).

19. Noel Stock, *The Life of Ezra Pound* (New York: Pantheon, 1970), 450.

20. Lawrence S. Rainey, *Ezra Pound and the Monument of Culture: Text, History and the Malatesta Cantos* (Chicago and London: University of Chicago Press,1991), 48-49, 182. Miyake argues that the many female deities represented in the Tempio show that the building as a whole is dedicated to Isotta, which, together with its use of zodiacal and other pagan iconography, means that it commemorates the "love mystery" descended from the Eleusinian rite. Rainey, while acknowledging that the theme is important in the *Cantos,* rejects this view of the Tempio as an error on Pound's part, but Miyake accepts the associations with Eleusis proposed by Rossetti and accepted by Pound. See Miyake, *Ezra Pound and the Mysteries of Love,* chap. 4, "The Lady Temple: A Defense of the Builder."

21. Pound, *Guide to Kulchur,* 145.

22. M. L. Rosenthal, *Sailing into the Unknown: Yeats, Pound and Eliot* (New York: Oxford University Press, 1978), 210. Rosenthal follows this comment by specifying the areas of experimentation: "Romantic absorption in the reciprocities of subjective and objective . . . the possibilities implicit in the open sequences of Whitman and other forerunners. . . . the adaptation of lyric technique and Symbolist preoccupations to longer structures. . . . rhythmic improvisations; assimilation of more and more

supposedly unpoetic words and modes of expression; visual arrangements . . . the use of casual or purely functional cultural objects and technological devices . . . as objects of direct contemplation" (210-11).

23. Froula, *To Write Paradise: Style and Error in Pound's Cantos*, 37. For a detailed discussion of the drafts of Canto 4, see ibid., chap. l. Ronald Bush's account of Pound's indecision about the last cantos confirms the impression of experimentation. See Bush, "'Unstill, ever turning': The Composition of Ezra Pound's *Drafts & Fragments*," in *Ezra Pound and Europe*, ed. Richard Taylor and Claus Melchior (Amsterdam and Atlanta, Ga.: Rodopi, 1993), 223-41.

24. Froula, *To Write Paradise: Style and Error in Pound's Cantos*, 51.

25. Alfred North Whitehead, *Science and the Modern World* (1925. Reprint. New York: New American Library, 1964), 97.

26. See Hugh Kenner's chapter, "Fields of Force," in *The Poetry of Ezra Pound*, ed. Hugh Kenner (New York: New Directions, 1951).

27. N. Katherine Hayles, *The Cosmic Web* (Ithaca, N.Y. and London: Cornell University Press, 1984), 10. See the preface and chap.1 for a discussion of field theory and literature. Pound used electromagnetism, with its capacity to exert energy at a distance, as an analogy for sexual attraction in "Psychology and Troubadours," chap. 5 of *The Spirit of Romance* (Norfolk, Conn.: New Directions, n.d., 1910). Ian F. A. Bell comments: "Pound's essay . . . combines the discourses of alchemy, cosmic consciousness and electromagnetism to sustain his view of the tensile and sexual mysteries of Provence." *Critic as Scientist: The Modernist Poetics of Ezra Pound* (London and New York: Methuen and Co., 1981), 147. The reaction of H. D. is from *End to Torment: A Memoir of Ezra Pound*, ed. Norman Holmes Pearson and Michael King (New York: New Directions, 1979), 30.

28. Bell, *Critic as Scientist: The Modernist Poetics of Ezra Pound*, 145.

29. Ibid., 156.

30. Woodward, *Ezra Pound and The Pisan Cantos*, 68.

31. Guy Davenport, "Persephone's Ezra," in *New Approaches to Ezra Pound*, ed. Eva Hesse (Berkeley and Los Angeles: University of California Press, 1969), 150.

32. Tryphonopoulos, *The Celestial Tradition: A Study of Ezra Pound's The Cantos*, 147. See his excellent explication of the sexual and mythic elements of this canto, ibid., 142-52.

33. Pearlman, *The Barb of Time*, 177.

34. In the myth, Adonis is killed by a boar, and flowers (rather than fruit) grow from the drops of his blood after Aphrodite sprinkles them with nectar. Espey's phrase is from *Ezra Pound's Mauberley* (1955. Reprint. Berkeley, Los Angeles and London: University of California Press, 1974), 110.

35. For Bride Scratton, see Stock, *The Life of Ezra Pound*, 243-44; and Wendy S. Flory, *Ezra Pound and the Cantos* (New Haven and London: Yale University Press, 1980), 114-15. It is possible that by referring to Stefano's painting as "Madonna in hortulo,"

Pound is linking the Virgin to the bride of Catullus's poem. The word "hortulo," a diminutive of the Latin "hortus," meaning garden, is perfectly appropriate to the foliage in the painting, but it is also found in Catullus's poem in the strophe following the one naming Aurunculeia. It reads: "Talis in vario solet / Divitis domini hortulo" ("The little garden of the master is accustomed to such varied riches").

36. See chap. 8 of Miyake, *Ezra Pound and the Mysteries of Love*. This chapter develops a parallel between Pound's neo-Platonic mystique of love and the teaching of the Ta Hio or "Great Learning." See also Surette, *A Light from Eleusis*, 71-78 ("The translation of 'Dona mi Prega' then, incorporates into the *Cantos* a philosophical expression of Pound's Eleusis").

37. Ezra Pound, *Literary Essays of Ezra Pound*, ed. with an introduction by T. S. Eliot (New York: New Directions, 1968), 149, 159.

38. See Tryphonopoulos, *The Celestial Tradition: A Study of Ezra Pound's The Cantos*, 108-27, for a thorough analysis of this canto, with speculations about its sources and discussion of other commentators. Jane Harrison points out that Dionysos was called "Iacchos" at Eleusis and "Zagreus" in other rites and observes that "Zagreus is a god of ritual rather than poetry, Iacchos is of poetry rather than ritual." *Prolegomena to the Study of Greek Religion* (Cambridge: Cambridge University Press, 1903. Reprint. New York: Meridian Books, 1957), 543. The fact that the two forms of expression are applied to the same deity suggests that the attributes they embody were considered to be closely related.

39. See Ernest Fenollosa's *The Chinese Written Character as a Medium for Poetry* (San Francisco, Calif.: City Lights Books, 1936); and Jacques Derrida's *Of Grammatology*, trans. Gayatri Chakravorty Spivak (Baltimore and London: Johns Hopkins University Press, 1976. Originally published as *De la Grammatologie*, Paris: Éditions de Minuit, 1967), 76. The quotation is from Michael André Bernstein, *The Tale of the Tribe: Ezra Pound and the Modern Verse Epic* (Princeton, N.J.: Princeton University Press, 1980), 158.

40. Information about the Chinese ritual tradition is based mainly on David McMullen, "The Ritual Code of T'ang China," in *Rituals of Royalty*, ed. David Cannadine and Simon Price (Cambridge: Cambridge University Press, 1987), 181-236.

41. J. M. Callery, "Introduction," to *Li Ki ou Mémorial des Rites* (Paris: Imprimerie Royale, 1853), xiii. "Ceremony sums up the whole Chinese spirit. . . . Its loves (of this nation), if it has any, are satisfied by ceremony; its duties are fulfilled through the medium of ceremony; virtue and vice are recognized in ceremony; the natural relationships of created beings are essentially linked in ceremony; in a word, for it, ceremony is man, moral man, political man, religious man, in his multiple relations with family, society, the state, morality and religion!"

42. Pearlman, *The Barb of Time*, 43; Feder, *Ancient Myth in Modern Poetry*, 205; Clark Emery, *Ideas into Action: A Study of Pound's Cantos* (Coral Gables, Fla.: University of Miami Press, 1958), 5; Carroll F. Terrell, *A Companion to the Cantos of Ezra Pound*, 2 vols. (Berkeley, Los Angeles, and London: University of California Press, 1984), I: 201; William Tay, "Between Kung and Eleusis," *Paideuma* 4 (Spring 1975): 54.

43. Miyake, *Ezra Pound and the Mysteries of Love*, 177-80.

44. Ezra Pound, trans., *Confucius* (New York: New Directions, 1969), 262, 203, 288. What is meant by "the rites" encompasses an enormous body of activities, ranging from the sacrifice of such animals as dogs, fowls, pigs, and sheep (meant to nourish the dead, as in the Greek offer of blood to the spirits in Hades) to the appropriate dress for certain occasions.

45. For a discussion of the treatment of sacrifice in the *Cantos*, see Robert Casillo, *The Genealogy of Demons: Anti-Semitism, Fascism, and the Myths of Ezra Pound* (Evanston, Ill.: Northwestern University Press, 1988), 253-60. Casillo supports his book's general argument that anti-Semitism is basic to Pound's thinking by using evidence from Pound's broadcasts and in the work of writers he knew, such as Céline and Upward, to show that Pound viewed the Jews as scapegoats in the sacrificial ritual. Casillo also implies that Pound believed the enduring myth that they performed ritual murder. He concludes, "To ignore the darker and concealed significance of Pound's ritualism is also to accept bondage to 'Nature,' sacrifice and unrecognized scapegoating" (276). This argument fails to recognize the fact that rituals which are primitive and violent in their origins may evolve into civilized religious ceremonials. There is no doubt, however, that Pound's anti-Semitism was violent and all-consuming, as Casillo's study amply shows.

46. John J. Nolde, *Blossoms from the East: The China Cantos of Ezra Pound* (Orono, Maine: The National Poetry Foundation,1938), 81-82.

47. Pound, *The Classic Anthology Defined by Confucius*, trans. Ezra Pound (Cambridge, Mass.: Harvard University Press, 1954), 162. Typical passages from the temple odes are:

> Think to thine art, Lord Grain
> By thy power to drink down
> cup for cup of heaven's own
> stablish thou us by damp and heat. (Ode 275)

> Speed, speed the plow
>   on south slopes now
> grain is to sow
> lively within. (Ode 291)

These ritual actions correspond to two parts of the Eleusinian rite: the drinking of the *cyceon*, the sacred mint mixture demanded by Demeter, and the ceremonial plowing.

48. For a genealogy of the history De Mailla translated, see Nolde, *Blossoms from the East: The China Cantos of Ezra Pound*, 25-26. I have relied on this source for most of my information about De Mailla and Pound's use of Chinese history.

49. See Rabaté, *Language, Sexuality and Ideology in Ezra Pound's Cantos*, 97-101, for an analysis of the varied "voices" heard in the Chinese cantos.

50. Ibid., 103-104.

51. For Pound's views, see William Harmon, *Time in Ezra Pound's Work* (Chapel Hill: University of North Carolina Press, 1977), especially 1-15.

52. Woodward, *Ezra Pound and The Pisan Cantos*, 16.

53. Ezra Pound, to Homer L. Pound, 11 April 1927, *The Letters of Ezra Pound, 1907-1941*, 210.

54. Quoted from the Preface to *The Anathemata* by Rabaté, *Language, Sexuality and Ideology in Ezra Pound's Cantos*, 141.

55. Miyake, *Ezra Pound and the Mysteries of Love*, 178. See also Hugh Kenner, *The Pound Era* (Berkeley and Los Angeles: University of California Press, 1971), 143-44.

56. H. D., *End to Torment*, 17. She identifies Pound with the lynx again on 27 in speculating that he displayed the tendency to adopt the attributes of a wolf, observing that the Greek for wolf, "lykos," recalls "the Lynx, so poignantly invoked in the famous section of the Pisan Canto LXXIX" (17).

57. Janice S. Robinson, *H. D.: The Life and Work of an American Poet* (Boston, Mass.: Houghton Mifflin Company, 1982), 423-24.

58. Dennis, "The Eleusinian Mysteries as an Organizing Principle in *The Pisan Cantos*," 273-82. "The *Pisan Cantos* re-enact in modern terms the ritual reassurance of the natural life which flows through all things . . . whatever the fate of the individual poet" (281).

59. Pound, "Deus est Amor," in *Selected Prose*, 70.

60. Woodward, *Ezra Pound and The Pisan Cantos*, 90-91.

61. Victor Turner, *The Ritual Process* (Chicago: Aldine Publishing Company, 1969), 106-107.

62. The translation is from Dante Alighieri, *The Divine Comedy: Paradiso*, trans. with introductions by Allen Mandelbaum (New York: Bantam Books, 1986), 7. The original reads: "Trasumanar significar *per verba* non si poria . . . col tuo lume mi levasti."

63. H. D., *End to Torment*, 30.

64. Massimo Bacigalupo, *The Forméd Trace: The Later Poetry of Ezra Pound* (New York: Columbia University Press, 1980), 305, 307-308. See this passage for a detailed account of the sources in this prayer.

65. Terrell, *Companion*, 2, 565. "Pitié," like "Le Paradis" of Canto 90, echoes François Villon. It seems to allude to the first line of "Épistre à ses amis," written in prison ("Aiez pitié, aiez pitié de moi"), and "Le Paradis" may allude to the "Ballade pour prier Nostre Dame," where the speaker sees in her church "Paradis paint."

66. Bacigalupo, *The Forméd Trace: The Later Poetry of Ezra Pound*, 348.

67. Casillo, *The Genealogy of Demons: Anti-Semitism, Fascism, and the Myths of Ezra Pound*, 101-102.

68. Pound's main source was the third rendering of K'ang Hsi's rules. It was published as *The Sacred Edict*, edited and translated by F. W. Baller (Shanghai: American Presbyterian Missionary Press, 1892). Pound used the English translation, the notes,

and the preface to this edition, as well as the untranslated Chinese second version of the *Edict*, which also appears in the volume, and quoted some of the ideograms.

69. Bacigalupo, *The Forméd Trace: The Later Poetry of Ezra Pound,* 382-83.

70. Different authorities list these Confucian rites differently. In "Thought Built on Sagetrieb," *Paideuma* 3 (Fall 1974):169-90, David Gordon gives a list of six derived from Couvreur's *Li Ki,* 1: 238, but James Legge and J. M. Callery give a list of seven: (1) capping (the son is given three caps in succession to show that he is mature and can adopt a complete costume, a symbol of harmonious relationships), (2) marriage, (3) "drinking in the Districts" (the custom of welcoming visitors), (4) archery, (5) banquets, (6) visits (Legge calls this an "interchange of signs"), (7) mourning or funerals.

71. Pound made use of three of Rock's works: *The Ancient Na-khi Kingdom of Southwest China* Vols. 8 and 9, Monograph Series of the Harvard-Yenching Institute (Cambridge, Mass.: Harvard University Press, 1947); *The Romance of $^2K'a$-$^2Mä$-^1Gyu-^3Mi-$^2Gkui, a Tribal Love Story (Bulletin de l'École Française d'Extréme-Orient,* 1939); and *The ^2Muan ^1bpo Ceremony or the Sacrifice to Heaven as Practiced by the Na-khi* (Reprint. *Annali Lateranensi,* vol. 16, Città del Vaticano: Tipografia Poliglotta Vaticana, 1952). The edition of the last actually used by Pound is given in Terrell's *Companion* as vol. 13 of *Monumenta Serica* (1948). My citations, however, are from the Vatican reprint.

72. John Peck, "Landscape and Ceremony in the Later *Cantos," Agenda,* 9 (Winter 1971): 26-69; the quotation appears on 38. Pound took liberties with his source, as usual, and often altered its text.

73. See ibid., and Carroll F. Terrell, "The Na-khi Documents I," *Paideuma,* 3 (Spring 1947): 91-122. The pine-branch fire appears in Rock's text, but Rock's "him," of course, is mistaken, for the deity of the mountain is female.

74. Rock, *The ^2Muan ^1bpo Ceremony,* 46.

75. For a detailed analysis of this canto, see Bacigalupo, *The Forméd Trace,* chap. 15, "A Late Mythologem: Canto 106" (425-43). Wendy S. Flory takes the view that the prayer invokes a woman loved by Pound who is addressed by the names of the various goddesses. See *Ezra Pound and the Cantos,* 264-67.

76. See Bacigalupo's detailed explication of this canto in *The Forméd Trace,* chap. 17, "A Quiet House," 461-80, and the explication and story of the suicide-myth in James J. Wilhelm, *The Later Cantos of Ezra Pound* (New York: Walker and Company, 1977), 172-78.

77. Derrida, *Of Grammatology,* 87. Derrida follows the premise that nonlinear writing—which must correspond to Reiss's "patterning discourse"—preceded the linear and encompassed a unity that was gradually fragmented by scientific progress. However, he does not expect regression to the past, but rather a new state of consciousness that will envelop and transcend the scientific. For some thorough investigations of Pound's new way of rereading the past, see Rainey, *Ezra Pound and the Monument of Culture: Text, History and the Malatesta Cantos,* chap. 5, and Herbert N. Schneidau, chap.

5, "Ezra Pound: Archaeology of the Immanent" in *Waking Giants* (New York: Oxford University Press, 1991). Although it does not mention Derrida in this connection, Michael André Bernstein's *Tale of the Tribe,* whose subtitle is "Ezra Pound and the Modern Verse Epic," can be seen as a direct reply to his view that the epic is wedded to linearity. Bernstein finds that the *Cantos* lacks an identifiable narrative source, that its uses of myth and history remain disunified, that it employs contradictory structural principles, and yet that it strives to perform the essential epic function of treating the past as a source of valuable exempla.

78. Bell, *Ritual Theory, Ritual Practice* (New York: Oxford University Press, 1992), 105-106.
79. Woodward, *Ezra Pound and The Pisan Cantos,* 95-96, 84, 86, 56.
80. Richard Sieburth, "Dada Pound," *South Atlantic Quarterly,* 83 (Winter 1984): 56-57.
81. Octavio Paz, *Children of the Mire,* trans. Rachel Phillips (Cambridge, Mass.: Harvard University Press, 1974), 114-15, 136.
82. Bell, *Ritual Theory, Ritual Practice,* 114-15.
83. Woodward, *Ezra Pound and The Pisan Cantos,* 97.

Notes to Chapter 8:
H. D.

1. Hilda Doolittle, *Collected Poems 1912-1944,* ed. Louis L. Martz (1983. Reprint. New York: New Directions, 1986), 127. Further quotations from this volume will be annotated parenthetically in the text by page numbers marked *CP.*
2. Susan Stanford Friedman, *Penelope's Web* (Cambridge: Cambridge University Press, 1990), 19.
3. Friedman, *Psyche Reborn* (Bloomington: Indiana University Press, 1981), 210.
4. H. D., *Tribute to Freud* (Reprint. New York: New Directions, 1956). H. D. notes that her first chapter, "Writing on the Wall," was published in a London periodical in 1945-46 and that the second chapter, "Advent," is composed of material written in 1933 and "assembled" in 1948. For Freud's influence on H. D. as a poet, see Friedman, *Psyche Reborn,* especially chaps. 1 and 2, and Dianne Chisholm, *H. D.'s Freudian Poetics* (Ithaca, N.Y. and London: Cornell University Press, 1992).
5. H. D., *Tribute to Freud,* 145, 93, 102, 99.
6. Quoted in Barbara Guest, *Herself Defined: the Poet H. D. and Her World* (Garden City, N.Y.: Doubleday and Company, 1984), 227.
7. See Friedman, *Psyche Reborn,* 110, for critical accounts of H. D.'s "patterns."
8. H. D., *Tribute to Freud,* 145.
9. Ibid., 37.
10. H. D., *HERmione* (1927. Reprint. New York: New Directions, 1981), 25; H. D., *Tribute to Freud,* 176.

11. Ibid., 50-51.

12. Cyrena N. Pondrom, "H. D. and the Origins of Imagism," in *Signets: Reading H. D.*, ed. Susan Stanford Friedman and Rachel Blau DuPlessis (Madison: University of Wisconsin Press, 1990), 85-109.

13. Eileen Gregory, "Rose Cut in Rock: Sappho and H. D.'s Sea Garden," in *Signets: Reading H. D.*, 129-54. The quotation is on140.

14. Janice S. Robinson, *H. D.: The Life and Work of an American Poet* (Boston, Mass.: Houghton Mifflin Company, 1982), 121, 52. Robinson makes an amusing error in the surname assigned to the Pound character in *HERmione*. H. D. calls him "Lowndes," but Robinson has him as "Lowdnes," an unexpectedly appropriate name for the aggressive character.

15. Peter Bürger, *Theory of the Avant-Garde*, trans. Michael Shaw (Minneapolis: University of Minnesota Press, 1984. Originally published in 1974 and 1979 under various titles by Suhrkamp Verlag, Frankfurt), 28.

16. H. D., *HERmione*, 211.

17. M. L. Rosenthal and Sally M. Gall, *The Modern Poetic Sequence: The Genius of Modern Poetry* (New York and Oxford: Oxford University Press, 1983), 6-7, 15.

18. Alicia Ostriker, "No Rules of Procedure," in *Signets: Reading H. D.*, 344.

19. Julia Kristeva confirms H. D.'s argument in an essay on the "borderline" idioms of postmodernism by observing that writing carried out with a sense of limits "individuates." She goes on to say that this expression of "primary narcissism" performs the function of psychoanalysis, an interesting connection in view of H. D.'s mental history, and her claim that her work would prepare "the patient for the Healer." See Kristeva, "Postmodernism?" in *Romanticism, Modernism, Postmodernism* (Lewisburg, Pa.: Bucknell University Press, 1980), 137-38.

20. Guest, *Herself Defined: the Poet H. D. and Her World*, 157-58.

21. L. S. Dembo, *Conceptions of Reality in Modern American Poetry* (Berkeley, Calif.: University of California Press, 1966), 28.

22. Adalaide Morris, "The Concept of Projection," in *Signets: Reading H. D.*, 289-91. One instance of this, the transmutation of the Hebrew word *marah* into the Christian Mary, is prepared with the commands, "polish the crucible / and set the jet of flame / under," so that the verbal transformation is introduced as an alchemical procedure performed for a religious end.

23. H. D., *Helen in Egypt* (Reprint. New York: New Directions, 1974), 1. Further references to this edition will be cited by page numbers in the text.

24. Joseph Riddel, "H. D.'s Scene of Writing: Poetry as (And) Analysis," *Studies in the Literary Imagination* 12 (Spring 1979): 41-59.

25. For detailed readings and analyses of *Helen in Egypt*, see Friedman, *Psyche Reborn*, 253-72, 286-96; and Friedman, "Creating a Women's Mythology" in *Signets: Reading H. D.*, chap. 20; and Angela DiPace Fritz, *Thought and Vision* (Washington, D.C.:

Catholic University Press, 1988), chap. 6, "Invariance and Transformation: Helen in Egypt (1951-1954)," 140-85.

26. H. D., *End to Torment: A Memoir of Ezra Pound,* ed. Norman Holmes Pearson and Michael King (New York: New Directions, 1979), 32.

27. H. D.'s comment in *Helen,* "Theseus had been successful in his Quest of the Symbolic Golden Fleece" (181), is not an error. Jason was the leader of this Quest, and while Theseus is not usually mentioned among the heroes who accompanied him, it is one of the many exploits attributed to him in legends. Plutarch even quotes a saying, "Nothing without Theseus."

28. There is a parallel episode in H. D.'s novel, *Palimpsest,* whose third section is based on her Egyptian visit. The heroine puts her hand on the temple carvings, but is disturbed when the man she is with *presses* it against the hieroglyphics. She is tempted to respond to this "Theseus," this "protective god-like presence," but she instead pulls her hand away and moves off. In both examples, the touching of the mysterious writing embodies a direct, intuitive relation with something beyond actual knowledge.

29. Many of H. D.'s critics feel that this renewal is primarily an assertion of female ascendancy. The revival of interest in her work is largely due to feminist criticism. See, for example, Friedman, *Penelope's Web* and *Psyche Reborn,* and essays by Rachel Blau Du Plessis, Susan Gubar, Albert Gelpi, and Friedman in Friedman and DuPlessis, ed., *Signets: Reading H. D.*

30. H. D., *End to Torment,* 56.

Notes to Chapter 9:
David Jones

1. W. H. Auden, "A Contemporary Epic," *Encounter* 2 (February 1954): 67-71.

2. David Jones, "Religion and the Muses," *Epoch and Artist* (London: Faber and Faber, 1959), 98.

3. David Jones, *The Anathemata* (London: Faber and Faber, 1952. Reprint, 1979), 15.

4. Neil Corcoran, *The Song of Deeds* (Cardiff: University of Wales Press, 1982), 76.

5. Jones, preface to *In Parenthesis* (London and Boston: Faber and Faber, 1937. Reprint, 1987), xiv. Further references to this source will be annotated parenthetically in the text by page numbers.

6. Elizabeth Ward tells us: "He was himself inclined to attribute his breakdowns to the difficulties he experienced attempting to practise his art within an historical situation marked by a disjunction of values so great . . . as to threaten imaginative paralysis and almost justify despair." The pressure he felt, she says was "that of the artist in a technological age, deriving less from history than from the impossibly

demanding world of myth." *David Jones, Mythmaker* (Manchester: Manchester University Press, 1983), 66.

7. The radiance of particulars is mentioned in Jones's preface to *Epoch and Artist*, 16. The allusions to geology and water are in David Jones, Letter to H. S. E., 27 March 1943, *Dai Greatcoat*, ed. René Hague (London and Boston: Faber and Faber, 1980), 122.

8. Ezra Pound, *Gaudier-Brzeska: A Memoir* (London: The Bodley Head, 1916), 20.

9. Jones, *Epoch and Artist*, 148, 149, 275. For an analysis of the relations between Jones's ideas and those of two Catholic thinkers who influenced him, Maritain and Maurice de la Taille, see Ward, *David Jones, Mythmaker*, 66, 34-40.

10. Jones, *Epoch and Artist*, 157.

11. David Jones, "Art in Relation to War," *The Dying Gaul and Other Writings*, ed. Harman Grisewood (London: Faber and Faber, 1978), 136.

12. Ernst Cassirer, *The Philosophy of Symbolic Forms*, trans. Ralph Manheim, vol. 2 (New Haven: Yale University Press, 1955. Originally published as *Philosophie der Symbolischen Formen*, Oxford: Oxford University Press, 1953-57), 2, 39.

13. Jones, *Epoch and Artist*, 156, 155, 158.

14. Corcoran, *The Song of Deeds*, 83.

15. William Blisset, *The Long Conversation. A Memoir of David Jones* (Oxford: Oxford University Press, 1981), 45-46.

16. Jones, *Epoch and Artist*, 210; and Jones, Letter to H. J. G., 22 May 1862, *Dai Greatcoat*, 188.

17. Jones, *Epoch and Artist*, 166-67. Also: "the sacraments are . . . absolutely central and inevitable and inescapable to us as creatures with bodies, whose nature is to *do this* or that, rather than *think* it." Jones, Letter to R. H., 16 June 1966, *Dai Greatcoat*, 222.'

18. ". . . it becomes obvious," Elizabeth Ward says, that he had been working "within an artistic and intellectual climate which, dominated theoretically by the practice and criticism of Eliot, naturally encompassed also the formal experimentation of Joyce, and beyond him, of Pound." *David Jones, Mythmaker*, 80.

19. Jones, *Epoch and Artist*, 30.

20. Compare, for example, this passage from a translation of Filippo Marinetti's *Zang Tumb Tuuum* (1914):

> no no nausea . . . San Giovanni tumbling of 8 electric lights into the sea
> to the right Reggio 2nd cascade of white fire
> beneath my feet bulkhead-keel 1,000 m. depth center of the straits volcanic
>   sewer opened 5 years ago
> possible stretchings of the terrestrial intestine.

in *Stung by Salt and War*, trans. by Richard J. Pioli (New York: Peter Lang, 1987).

21. Jones, "Art in Relation to War," *The Dying Gaul*, 134, 132. Jones observes that in his time, "the art most practised is that of war."

22. Jones, *Epoch and Artist*, 159-60.

23. Thomas Dilworth, *The Liturgical Parenthesis of David Jones*, and Dilworth, *The Shape of Meaning in the Poetry of David Jones*. In the latter, see chap. 4, "Sacred Mythos," for a discussion of ritual in *In Parenthesis*. Initiation ritual is treated on 125-26. For an earlier treatment of this theme, see Jeremy Hooker, *David Jones: An Exploratory Study of the Writing* (London: Enitharmon Press, 1975), which offers an exploration of "the archetypal pattern of initiation and its associated symbols" in both *In Parenthesis* and *The Anathemata*.

24. David Jones, Letter to R. H., 9-15 July 1973, *Dai Greatcoat*, 248-49.

25. Blamires, *David Jones: Artist and Writer* (Manchester: Manchester University Press, 1971), 101.

26. Dilworth, *The Shape of Meaning in the Poetry of David Jones*, 135-37.

27. Ibid., 139-46. The quotations appear on 141.

28. Hooker, *David Jones: An Exploratory Study of the Writing*, 20.

29. *The Anathemata*, 29. Further citations from this source will be identified parenthetically in the text by page numbers marked *A*.

30. Corcoran, in an ingenious defense of the notes, suggests that they are meant to display the raw factual material that has been transformed into verse in a process of "transubstantiation." See *The Song of Deeds*, 91.

31. Jones, *Dai Greatcoat*, 161. The oft-noted resemblances between *The Anathemata* and Pound's *Cantos* are certainly remarkable. Thomas Dilworth places both in a special genre he calls "displaced epic"—poems that aim at an epic effect by implying, instead of narrating, epic action. (*The Shape of Meaning*, 152-53). See also 361-62 for a brief survey of Jones's poetic innovations and 365-67 for a detailed comparison of the two poems. Since I am concerned primarily with the interplay of ritual and experiment, I do not offer a general interpretation of *The Anathemata*. Excellent detailed exegeses can be found in Dilworth's two chapters on *The Anathemata* in *The Shape of Meaning*, in René Hague's *Commentary on the Anathemata of David Jones* (Toronto and Buffalo: University of Toronto Press, 1977), and in Neil Corcoran's *The Song of Deeds*, and I am indebted to these for guidance.

32. Saunders Lewis, Letter to Saunders Lewis, "Saunders Lewis Introduces Two Letters from David Jones," *Agenda*, 11 (Autumn-Winter 1973/4): 20.

33. Corcoran, *The Song of Deeds*, 49.

34. Dilworth, *The Shape of Meaning*, 156-57.

35. Jonathan Miles, *Backgrounds to David Jones: A Study in Sources and Drafts* (Cardiff: University of Wales Press, 1990), 97.

36. Corcoran, *The Song of Deeds*, 45.

37. For geological information behind Jones's text, see Miles, *Backgrounds to David Jones: A Study in Sources and Drafts*, 99-109.

38. The inscription is translated in *The Small Roman Missal* (Leeds: Laverty and Sons, Ltd., 1936) as: "for through the mystery of the Word made flesh the new light of Thy glory hath shone upon the eyes of our mind."

39. Some of the technical terms are copied directly from the textbook Jones was using as a source of geological information. See Thomas Dilworth, "David Jones' Use of a Geology Text for *The Anathemata*," *English Language Notes* 15 (December 1977): 115-19. The sequences of periods are copied nearly *verbatim* from tables appearing in this book. The reading "sub-species" in post-1972 editions of the poem is an erroneous editorial change that I have corrected in my quotation. Some of the genuine misprints in the text, however, have never been corrected.

40. The *Small Roman Missal:* "The Holy Mass is the unbloody Sacrifice of the New Law in which the Body and Blood of Jesus Christ is offered to God under the species of bread and wine. The Holy Mass is the Sacrifice of the Cross without blood-shedding" (vii). Jones, from a letter to Harman Grisewood, 22 May 1962: "Even the old 'penny catechism' was nearer the mark as 'art criticism' when it says that the Mass is the showing again in an unbloody manner what was done once and for all in a bloody manner. . . . I am sure that some such concept is the inner secret and nodal point of *all* the arts." *Dai Greatcoat*, 190.

41. James Joyce, *Finnegans Wake* (New York: The Viking Press, 1939. Reprint, 1964), "Allalivial, allalluvial!" (213). The inscription facing page 55 of *The Anathemata* is quoted from the same chapter of the *Wake*, the one part of Joyce's work with which Jones was familiar. He mentions it in explaining another *Wake* echo in his note on page 145.

42. See Dilworth's *Shape of Meaning*, 246-54, for an analysis of the allegorical aspects of the voyage.

43. Stuart Piggott, "David Jones and the Past of Man," *Agenda* 5 (Spring/Summer 1967), 78. Jones mentioned this article as a piece "which I much value."

44. Blamires, *David Jones: Artist and Writer*, 137-39.

45. Dilworth, *The Shape of Meaning in the Poetry of David Jones*, 153-54.

Notes to Chapter 10:
Conclusion

1. Harold Osborne, "Interpretation in Science and Art," *British Journal of Aesthetics* 26 (Winter 1986): 3-15. The quotation is from 12.

2. Oliver Sacks, "The Poet of Chemistry," *New York Review of Books* 40 (November 4, 1993): 56. See also the exchange headlined "Does Ideology Stop at the Laboratory Door?" *New York Times*, News in Review, October 22, 1989, 24.

3. Paul Feyerabend, *Farewell to Reason* (London and New York: Verso, 1987), 84-89.

4. Ibid., 15. His discussion of creativity in chap. 4 of this book does not seem consistent with some of the ideas in the earlier *Against Method* (Atlantic Highlands, N.J.: Humanities Press, 1975). In the latter, he attributes progress in science to a

willingness to break with previous knowledge and recommends the invention of fanciful and irrational theories as a critical approach to theories based on induction.

5. Arthur I. Miller, "Visualization Lost and Regained: The Genesis of the Quantum Theory in the Period 1913-27," in *On Aesthetics in Science*, ed. Judith Wechsler (Cambridge, Mass., and London: MIT Press, 1978), 73.

6. Leonard Shlain, *Art and Physics: Parallel Visions in Space, Time, and Light* (New York: William Morrow, 1991), 427.

7. Lyndall Gordon, *Eliot's Early Years* (Oxford and New York: Oxford University Press, 1977), 139-40.

8. Feyerabend, *Against Method*, 256, 269-70. Interestingly, in this book, Feyerabend borrows a term from the arts to describe his position, and terms it "Dadaism" in preference to "anarchism."

9. Jacques Lacan, *The Four Fundamental Concepts of Psychoanalysis*, trans. Alan Sheridan (Reprint. New York and London: W. W. Norton and Company, 1977. Originally published as *Les quatre concepts fondamentaux de la psychanalyse*, ed. Jacques-Alain Miller, Paris: Éditions du Seuil, 1973), 43. Lacan is not friendly to experiment. His view encapsulates the belief that it is incompatible with intuitive thinking. He believes that trust in the arbitrary or "fictitious" principles of experiment, whose relation to nature is "problematic" obstructs the development of psychoanalysis as a conjectural science with its trust in intuitive insights. *Écrits: A Selection*, trans. Alan Sheridan (New York and London: W. W. Norton and Company, 1977), 72-74.

10. Feyerabend, *Against Method*, 179. Among his many arguments along this line, see chap. 15, 171-80, for an assertion of the merits of "anarchistic epistemology" that does not exclude "unreason."

11. Lacan, *Écrits*, 68.

12. Lacan, *The Four Fundamental Concepts of Psychoanalysis*, 20.

13. Lacan, *Écrits*, 86.

14. Ibid., 71.

15. Michel Foucault, *The Archaeology of Knowledge* (New York: Pantheon, 1972), 37.

16. Mircea Eliade, *The Myth of the Eternal Return*, trans. Willard R. Trask (Princeton, N.J.: Princeton University Press, 1954. Originally published as *Mythe de l'éternel retour*, Paris: Gallimard, 1949), 159.

17. M. M. Bakhtin, "Discourse in the Novel," in *The Dialogic Imagination*, trans. Caryl Emerson and Michael Holquist; ed. Michael Holquist (Austin: University of Texas Press, 1981), 259-422.

18. Ibid., 346.

19. Timothy J. Reiss, *The Discourse of Modernism* (Ithaca, N.Y.: Cornell University Press, 1982), 166. For discussions of the relation between such pre-scientific studies as alchemy and modern science, see *Reason, Experiment and Mysticism*, ed. M. L. Righini Bonelli and William R. Shea (New York: Science History Publications, 1975). In

222 RITUAL AND EXPERIMENT IN MODERN POETRY

their introduction, the editors accept "the experimental method" as a convenient abbreviation for the principles of thinking introduced by the scientific revolution but maintain that it is not a uniform method, and propose the term "hypothetico-deductive," an interesting augmentation of Reiss's "analytico-referential."

20. Reiss, *The Discourse of Modernism*, 379-85.
21. Alfred North Whitehead, *Science and the Modern World*, (1925. Reprint. New York: New American Library, 1964), 165.
22. Ibid., 167.

Bibliography

Ackroyd, Peter. *T. S. Eliot: A Life*. New York: Simon and Schuster, 1984.

Alexander, Michael. *The Poetic Achievement of Ezra Pound*. Berkeley and Los Angeles: University of California Press, 1970.

Alighieri, Dante. *The Divine Comedy*. 3 Vols. Translated with introductions by Allen Mandelbaum. New York: Bantam Books, 1986.

apRoberts, Ruth. *Arnold and God*. Berkeley: University of California Press, 1983.

Auden, W. H. "A Contemporary Epic." *Encounter* 2 (February 1954): 67-71.

————. *The Dyer's Hand*. New York: Random House, 1962.

Bachelard, Gaston. *Le nouvel esprit scientifique*. 2nd ed. Paris: Presses Universitaires, 1968.

Bacigalupo, Massimo. *The Forméd Trace: The Later Poetry of Ezra Pound*. New York: Columbia University Press, 1980.

Bakhtin, M. M. *The Dialogic Imagination*. Translated by Caryl Emerson and Michael Holquist; ed. Michael Holquist. Austin: University of Texas Press, 1981.

Baller, F. W., ed. and trans. *The Sacred Edict*. Shanghai: American Presbyterian Missionary Press, 1892.

Barfield, Owen. *Saving the Appearances*. London: Faber and Faber, 1957.

Barnes, Barry. *Scientific Knowledge and Sociological Theory*. London and Boston: Routledge and Kegan Paul, 1974.

Bedient, Calvin. *He Do the Police in Different Voices*. Chicago and London: University of Chicago Press, 1986.

Beer, Gillian. *Darwin's Plots*. London: Routledge and Kegan Paul, 1983.

Bell, Catherine. *Ritual Theory, Ritual Practice*. New York: Oxford University Press, 1992.

Bell, Ian F. A. *Critic as Scientist: The Modernist Poetics of Ezra Pound*. London and New York: Methuen and Co., 1981.

Bernard, Claude. *An Introduction to the Study of Experimental Medicine*. Translated by Henry Copley Greene. New York: Macmillan, 1927. Originally published as *Introduction à l'étude de la médecine expérimentale* (Paris: J. B. Baillière et fils, 1865).

Bernstein, Michael André. *The Tale of the Tribe: Ezra Pound and the Modern Verse Epic.* Princeton, N.J.: Princeton University Press, 1980.

Black, Max. *Models and Metaphors.* Ithaca, N.Y.: Cornell University Press, 1962.

Blake, William. *The Four Zoas,* in *The Prophetic Writings of William Blake,* Vol 1, ed. D. J. Sloss and J. P. R. Wallis. 1926. Reprint. Oxford: the Clarendon Press, 1969.

Blamires, David. *David Jones: Artist and Writer.* Manchester: Manchester University Press, 1971.

Blisset, William. *The Long Conversation: A Memoir of David Jones.* Oxford: Oxford University Press, 1981.

Brook-Rose, Christine. *A ZBC of Ezra Pound.* Berkeley and Los Angeles: University of California Press, 1971.

Brooks, Cleanth. "Organic Theory in Poetry." In *Literature and Belief,* English Institute Essays, 1957, ed. M. H. Abrams, 53-69. New York and London: Columbia University Press, 1958.

Bryher. *The Heart to Artemis: A Writer's Memoirs.* New York: Harcourt, Brace and World, 1962.

Bürger, Peter. *Theory of the Avant-Garde.* Translated by Michael Shaw. Minneapolis: University of Minnesota Press, 1984. Originally published in 1974 and 1979 under various titles by Suhrkamp Verlag, Frankfurt.

Bush, Ronald. *The Genesis of Ezra Pound's Cantos.* Princeton, N.J.: Princeton University Press, 1976.

———. *T. S. Eliot: A Study in Character and Style.* New York and Oxford: Oxford University Press, 1983.

———. "'Unstill, ever turning': The Composition of Ezra Pound's *Drafts & Fragments.*" In *Ezra Pound and Europe,* ed. Richard Taylor and Claus Melchior, 223-41. Amsterdam and Atlanta, Ga.: Rodopi, 1993.

Cantor, Geoffrey. "The Rhetoric of Experiment." In *The Uses of Experiment,* ed. David Gooding, Trevor Pinch, and Simon Schaffer. Cambridge: Cambridge University Press, 1989.

Carpenter, Humphrey. *A Serious Character: The Life of Ezra Pound.* Boston, Mass.: Houghton Mifflin Company, 1988.

Casillo, Robert. *The Genealogy of Demons: Anti-Semitism, Fascism, and the Myths of Ezra Pound.* Evanston, Ill.: Northwestern University Press, 1988.

Cassirer, Ernst. *Language and Myth.* Translated by Susanne Langer. New York and London: Harper and Bros., 1946. Originally published as *Sprache und Mythos.*

———. *The Philosophy of Symbolic Forms.* Translated by Ralph Manheim. Vol. 2. New Haven: Yale University Press, 1955. Originally published as *Philosophie der Symbolischen Formen* (Oxford: Bruno Cassiver, 1953-57).

Chisholm, Dianne. *H. D.'s Freudian Poetics.* Ithaca, N.Y. and London: Cornell University Press, 1992.

Christ, Carol T. *Victorian and Modern Poetics.* Chicago and London: University of Chicago Press, 1984.

Coffman, Stanley K., Jr. *Imagism: A Chapter for the History of Modern Poetry.* Norman: University of Oklahoma Press, 1951.

Corcoran, Neil. *The Song of Deeds.* Cardiff: University of Wales Press, 1982.

Costello, Harry Todd. *Josiah Royce's Seminar,* ed. Grover Smith. New Brunswick, N.J.: Rutgers University Press, 1963.

Dasenbrock, Reed Way. *The Literary Vorticism of Ezra Pound and Wyndham Lewis.* Baltimore, Md. and London: Johns Hopkins University Press, 1985.

Davenport, Guy. "Persephone's Ezra." In *New Approaches to Ezra Pound,* ed. Eva Hesse, 145-73. Berkeley and Los Angeles: University of California Press, 1969.

Davie, Donald. *Ezra Pound: The Poet as Sculptor.* New York: Oxford University Press, 1964.

Davis, Kay. *Fugue and Fresco: Structures in Pound's Cantos.* Orono, Maine: National Poetry Foundation, 1984.

Dembo, L. S. *Conceptions of Reality in Modern American Poetry.* Berkeley, Calif.: University of California Press, 1966.

Dennis, Helen M. "The Eleusinian Mysteries as an Organizing Principle of The Pisan Cantos." *Paideuma* 10 (Fall 1981): 273-82.

De Rachewiltz, Boris. "Pagan and Magic Elements in Ezra Pound's Works." In *New Approaches to Ezra Pound,* ed. Eva Hesse, 174-97. Berkeley and Los Angeles: University of California Press, 1969.

Derrida, Jacques. *Of Grammatology.* Translated by Gayatri Chakravorty Spivak. Baltimore and London: Johns Hopkins University Press, 1976. Originally published as *De la Grammatologie* (Paris: Éditions de Minuit, 1967).

———. "White Mythology: Metaphor in the Text of Philosophy." In *Margins of Philosophy,* 209-71. Translated by Alan Bass. Chicago: University of Chicago Press, 1982. Originally published as *Marges de la philosophie* (Paris: Éditions de minuit, 1972).

Dilworth, Thomas. "David Jones' Use of a Geology Text for *The Anathemata.*" *English Language Notes* 15 (December 1977): 115-19.

———. *The Liturgical Parenthesis of David Jones.* Ipswich: Golgonooza Press, 1979.

———. *The Shape of Meaning in the Poetry of David Jones.* Toronto: University of Toronto Press, 1988.

DiPace Fritz, Angela. *Thought and Vision.* Washington, D.C.: Catholic University Press, 1988.

Dissanayake, Ellen. *What is Art For?* Seattle: University of Washington Press, 1988.

Doolittle, Hilda. *Bid Me To Live, A Madrigal.* 1960. Reprint. New York: Dial Press, [1983].

———. *Collected Poems 1912-1944,* ed. Louis L. Martz. 1983. Reprint. New York: New Directions, 1986.

———. *End to Torment: A Memoir of Ezra Pound,* ed. Norman Holmes Pearson and Michael King. New York: New Directions, 1979.

———. *Helen in Egypt.* 1961. Reprint. New York: New Directions, 1974.

———. *HERmione.* 1927. Reprint. New York: New Directions, 1981.

————. *Notes on Thought and Vision and The Wise Sappho*. San Francisco: City Lights Books, 1982.

————. *Tribute to Freud*. 1974. Reprint. New York: New Directions, 1956.

Duffey, Bernard I. "The Experimental Lyric in Modern Poetry: Eliot, Pound, Williams." *Journal of Modern Literature* 3, no. 5 (July 1974): 1085-1103.

Dye, James Wayne. "The Poetization of Science." In *The Languages of Creativity*, ed. Mark Amsler, 92-108. Newark: University of Delaware Press, 1986.

Einstein, Albert. "Relativity and the Problem of Space." In *Ideas and Opinions*, 360-77. New York: Crown, 1954.

Eliade, Mircea. *Birth and Rebirth*. Translated by Willard R. Trask. New York: Harper and Torchbook, 1958. Originally published as *Naissances mystiques*. (Paris: Gallimard, 1959).

————. *The Myth of the Eternal Return or, Cosmos and History*. Translated by Willard R. Trask. Princeton, N.J.: Princeton University Press, 1954. Originally published as *Mythe de l'éternel retour* (Paris: Gallimard, 1949).

————. *Rites and Symbols of Initiation*. Translated by Willard R. Trask. New York: Harper and Row, 1965. First published as *Birth and Rebirth*, (1923): 11-12.

Eliot, Charlotte. *Savonarola, a Dramatic Poem*. Introduction by T. S. Eliot. London: Cobden-Sanderson, 1926.

Eliot, T. S. "The Beating of a Drum." *Nation and Athenaeum* 34 (October 6, 1923): 11-12.

————. *The Complete Poems and Plays, 1909-1950*. New York: Harcourt, Brace & World, Inc., 1952.

————. *The Letters of T. S. Eliot: Vol. 1, 1898-1922*, ed. Valerie Eliot. San Diego, Calif., New York, London: Harcourt, Brace, Jovanovich, 1988.

————. "Literature, Science and Dogma." *Dial* 82 (March 1927): 239-43.

————. "London Letter." *Dial* 71 (October 1921) [452]-455.

————. "London Letter." *Dial* 75 (December 1923) [594]-597.

————. *On Poetry and Poets*. New York: Noonday Press, 1957.

————. *Poems Written in Early Youth*. London: Faber and Faber, 1967.

————. *Selected Essays*. New York: Harcourt, Brace and World, 1964.

————. "Ulysses, Order and Myth." *Dial* 75 (November 1923): 480-83.

————. *The Use of Poetry and the Use of Criticism*. 1933. Reprint. London: Faber and Faber, 1967.

————. *The Waste Land: A Facsimile and Transcript of the Original Drafts Including the Annotations of Ezra Pound*, ed. Valerie Eliot. New York: Harcourt Brace Jovanovich Inc., 1971.

Ellmann, Richard. *Identity of Yeats*. New York: Oxford University Press, 1954.

————. *Yeats: The Man and the Masks*. New York: Macmillan, 1948.

Emery, Clark. *Ideas into Action: A Study of Pound's Cantos*. Coral Gables, Fla.: University of Miami Press, 1958.

Espey, John. *Ezra Pound's Mauberley*. 1955. Reprint. Berkeley, Los Angeles and London: University of California Press, 1974.

Feder, Lillian. *Ancient Myth in Modern Poetry*. Princeton, N.J.: Princeton University Press, 1971.

Fenollosa, Ernest. *The Chinese Written Character as a Medium for Poetry*. San Francisco, Calif.: City Lights Books, 1936.

Feyerabend, Paul. *Against Method*. Atlantic Highlands, N.J.: Humanities Press, 1975.

———. *Farewell to Reason*. London and New York: Verso, 1987.

Flannery, M. C. *Yeats and Magic*. New York: Harper and Row, 1978.

Flory, Wendy S. *Ezra Pound and the Cantos*. New Haven and London: Yale University Press, 1980.

Foucault, Michel. *The Archaeology of Knowledge*. New York: Pantheon, 1972.

Fowler, Alastair. *Kinds of Literature: An Introduction to the Theory of Genres and Modes*. Cambridge, Mass.: Harvard University Press, 1982.

Freud, Sigmund. "Obsessive Acts and Religious Practices." 1907. In *The Standard Edition of the Complete Psychological Works of Sigmund Freud*, vol. 9, ed. James Strachey, 115-28. London: Hogarth Press, 1953.

Friedman, Susan Stanford. "Creating a Women's Mythology." In *Signets: Reading H. D.*, ed. Susan Stanford Friedman and Rachel Blau DuPlessis, 373-405. Madison: University of Wisconsin Press, 1990.

———. *Penelope's Web*. Cambridge: Cambridge University Press, 1990.

———. *Psyche Reborn*. Bloomington: Indiana University Press, 1981.

Friedman, Susan Stanford and Rachel Blau du Plessis, eds. *Signets: Reading H. D.* Madison: University of Wisconsin Press, 1990.

Froula, Christine. *To Write Paradise: Style and Error in Pound's Cantos*. New Haven: Yale University Press, 1984.

Frye, Northrop. *Anatomy of Criticism*. Princeton. N.J.: Princeton University Press, 1957. Reprint. New York: Athenaeum, 1966.

Gage, John T. *In the Arresting Eye: The Rhetoric of Imagism*. Baton Rouge and London: Louisiana State University Press, 1981.

Gardner, Helen. *The Composition of Four Quartets*. New York: Oxford University Press, 1978.

Girard, René. *Things Hidden Since the Foundation of the World*. Translated by Stephen Bann and Michael Metteer. Palo Alto: Stanford University Press, 1987. Originally published as *Des choses cachées depuis la fondation du monde*.

———. *Violence and the Sacred*. Translated by Patrick Gregory. Baltimore and London: Johns Hopkins University Press, 1977. Originally published as *Le Violence et le sacré* (Paris: Éditions Bernard Grasset, 1972).

Gordon, David. "Thought Built on Sagetrieb." *Paideuma* 3 (Fall 1974): 169-90.

Gordon, Lyndall. *Eliot's Early Years*. Oxford and New York: Oxford University Press, 1977.

———. *Eliot's New Life*. New York: Farrar, Straus, Giroux, 1988.

Grainger, Roger. *The Language of the Rite*. London: Darton, Longman and Todd, 1974.

Gregory, Eileen. "Rose Cut in Rock: Sappho and H. D.'s Sea Garden." In *Signets: Reading H. D.*, ed. Susan Stanford Friedman and Rachel Blau DuPlessis. 129-54. Madison: University of Wisconsin Press, 1990.

Guest, Barbara. *Herself Defined: the Poet H. D. and Her World.* Garden City, N.Y.: Doubleday and Company, 1984.

Hague, René. *Commentary on the Anathemata of David Jones.* Toronto and Buffalo: University of Toronto Press, 1977.

Harmon, William. *Time in Ezra Pound's Work.* Chapel Hill: University of North Carolina Press, 1977.

———. "T. S. Eliot: Anthropologist and Primitive." *American Anthropologist* 78 (December 1976): 797-811.

Harrison, Jane Ellen. *Ancient Art and Ritual.* New York: Holt, 1913.

———. *Prolegomena to the Study of Greek Religion.* Cambridge: Cambridge University Press, 1903. Reprint. New York: Meridian Books, 1957.

———. *Themis.* Cambridge: Cambridge University Press, 1927.

Hartman, Geoffrey H. "Structuralism: The Anglo-American Adventure." In *Beyond Formalism,* 3-23. New Haven and London: Yale University Press, 1970.

Hayles, N. Katherine. *The Cosmic Web.* Ithaca, N.Y., and London: Cornell University Press, 1984.

Heymann, C. David. *Ezra Pound: The Last Rower.* New York: Viking Press, 1976.

Holton, Gerald. *The Scientific Imagination: Case Studies.* Cambridge: Cambridge University Press, 1979.

———. "Thematic Presuppositions and the Direction of Scientific Advance." In *Scientific Explanation,* ed. A. F. Heath, 1-27. Oxford: Oxford University Press, 1981.

Hooker, Jeremy. *David Jones: An Exploratory Study of the Writing.* London: Enitharmon Press, 1975.

Hough, Graham. *Reflections on a Literary Revolution.* Washington, D.C.: Catholic University Press, 1960.

Huxley, Julian. "A Discussion of Ritualization of Behaviour in Animals and Man." *Philosophic Transactions of the Royal Society* (Series B), vol. 251 (1966).

Huxley, Thomas Henry. "The Evolution of Theology" [1886]. *Selected Works,* vol 4. New York and London: D. Appleton and Co., n.d.

Ismail, Jamila. "'News of the Universe: ^{2}Muan ^{1}bpö and the *Cantos.*" *Agenda* 9 (Winter 1971): 70-87.

Jackson, Thomas H. *The Early Poetry of Ezra Pound.* Cambridge, Mass.: Harvard University Press, 1969.

Jefferson, Ann, and David Robey, eds. *Modern Literary Theory.* New York: Barnes and Noble, 1982.

Jones, David. *The Anathemata.* 1952. Reprint. London: Faber and Faber, 1979.

———. *Dai Greatcoat,* ed. René Hague. London and Boston: Faber and Faber, 1980.

———. *The Sleeping Lord and Other Fragments.* London: Faber and Faber, 1974.

———. *The Dying Gaul and Other Writings,* ed. Harman Grisewood. London: Faber and Faber, 1978.

————. *Epoch and Artist*. London: Faber and Faber, 1959.

————. *In Parenthesis*. 1937. Reprint. London and Boston: Faber and Faber, 1987.

Joyce, James. *Finnegans Wake*. 1939. New York: Viking Press, 1964.

Kayman, Martin A. *The Modernism of Ezra Pound: The Science of Poetry*. London: Macmillan, 1986.

Kearns, George. *Guide to Ezra Pound's Selected Cantos*. New Brunswick, N.J.: Rutgers University Press, 1980.

Kenner, Hugh. *The Invisible Poet: T. S. Eliot*. 1959. Reprint. New York: The Citadel Press, 1964.

————. *The Poetry of Ezra Pound*. New York: New Directions, 1951.

————. *The Pound Era*. Berkeley and Los Angeles: University of California Press, 1971.

Kerenyi, C. *Eleusis: Archetypal Image of Mother and Daughter*. Translated by Ralph Manheim. New York: Pantheon Books, 1964.

Kermode, Frank. *Romantic Image*. 1957. Reprint. New York: Vintage Books, 1964.

Korg, Jacob. "Ritual and Experiment in Modern Poetry." *Journal of Modern Literature* 8 (February 1979): 127-46.

Krieger, Murray. "Poetic Presence and Illusion, 1." In *Poetic Presence and Illusion*, 3-27. Baltimore, Md. and London: Johns Hopkins University Press, 1979.

Kristeva, Julia. "Postmodernism?" In *Romanticism, Modernism, Postmodernism*. Lewisburg, Pa.: Bucknell University Press, 1980.

Kuhn, Thomas. *The Structure of Scientific Revolutions*. 1962. Chicago: University of Chicago Press, 1970.

Lacan, Jacques. *Écrits: A Selection*. Translated from the French by Alan Sheridan. New York and London: W. W. Norton and Company, 1977.

————. *The Four Fundamental Concepts of Psychoanalysis*. Translated by Alan Sheridan. Reprint. New York and London: W. W. Norton and Company, 1977. Originally published as *Les quatre concepts fondamentaux de la psychanalyse*, ed. Jacques-Alain Miller (Paris: Éditions du Seuil, 1973).

Lakatos, Imre. "Falsification and the Methodology of Scientific Research Programmes." In *Criticism and the Growth of Knowledge*, Proceedings of the International Colloquium in the Philosophy of Science, London, 1965, vol. 4, ed. Imre Lakatos and Alan Musgrave, 91-196. Cambridge: Cambridge University Press, 1970.

Leavis, F. R. *New Bearings in English Poetry*. 1932. Reprint. Ann Arbor: University of Michigan Press, 1960.

Lewis, Saunders. "Saunders Lewis Introduces Two Letters from David Jones." *Agenda* 11 (Autumn-Winter 1973/4): 17-29.

Li Ki ou Mémorial des Rites. Translated by J. M. Callery. Paris: Imprimerie Royale, 1853.

Longenbach, James. *Stone Cottage: Pound, Yeats and Modernism*. New York and Oxford: Oxford University Press, 1988.

Makin, Peter. *Provence and Pound*. Berkeley: University of California Press, 1978.

Mallarmé, Stéphane. *Oeuvres Complètes*. Paris: Bibliothèque de la Pléiade, 1965.

Manganaro, Marc. "Dissociation in 'Dead Land': The Primitive Mind in the Early Poetry of T. S. Eliot." *Journal of Modern Literature* 13 (March 1986): 97-110.

Maxim, Hudson. *The Science of Poetry and the Philosophy of Language.* New York and London: Funk and Wagnalls, 1910.

Mayer, John T. *T. S. Eliot's Silent Voices.* New York and Oxford: Oxford University Press, 1989.

McMullen, David. "The Ritual Code of T'ang China." In *Rituals of Royalty*, ed. David Cannadine and Simon Price, 181-236. Cambridge: Cambridge University Press, 1987.

Miles, Jonathan. *Backgrounds to David Jones: A Study in Sources and Drafts.* Cardiff: University of Wales Press, 1990.

Miller, Arthur I. "Visualization Lost and Regained: The Genesis of the Quantum Theory in the Period 1913-27." In *On Aesthetics in Science*, ed. Judith Wechsler, 73-102. Cambridge, Mass. and London: MIT Press, 1978.

Miller, Liam. *The Noble Drama of W.B. Yeats.* Dublin: Dolmen Press, 1977.

Miyake, Akiko. *Ezra Pound and the Mysteries of Love.* Durham, N.C. and London: Duke University Press, 1991.

Moody, A. D. *Thomas Stearns Eliot: Poet.* Cambridge: Cambridge University Press, 1979.

————, ed. *The Waste Land in Different Voices.* New York: St. Martin's Press, 1974.

Moore, Virginia. *The Unicorn: William Butler Yeats' Search for Reality.* New York: Macmillan, 1954.

Morris, Adalaide. "The Concept of Projection." In *Signets: Reading H. D.*, ed. Susan Stanford Friedman and Rachel Blau DuPlessis, 273-96. Madison: University of Wisconsin Press, 1990.

Mosely, Edwin M. "Religion and the Literary Genres." In *Mansions of the Spirit*, ed. George A. Panichas, 87-103. New York: Hawthorn Books, 1967.

Mylonas, George E. *Eleusis and the Eleusinian Mysteries.* Princeton, N.J.: Princeton University Press, 1961.

Nolde, John J. *Blossoms from the East: The China Cantos of Ezra Pound.* Orono, Maine: The National Poetry Foundation, 1938.

Osborne, Harold. "Interpretation in Science and Art." *British Journal of Aesthetics* 26 (Winter 1986): 3-15.

Ostriker, Alicia. "No Rules of Procedure." In *Signets: Reading H. D.*, ed. Susan Stanford Friedman and Rachel Blau DuPlessis, 336-51. Madison: University of Wisconsin Press, 1990.

Parkin, Andrew. *The Dramatic Imagination of W. B. Yeats.* Dublin: Gill and Macmillan, 1978.

Paz, Octavio. *Children of the Mire.* Translated by Rachel Phillips. Cambridge, Mass.: Harvard University Press, 1974.

Pearlman, Daniel D. *The Barb of Time: On the Unity of Pound's Cantos.* New York: Oxford University Press, 1969.

Pearson, Karl. *The Grammar of Science.* 1892. Reprint. London: A. and C. Black, 1900.

Peck, John. "Landscape and Ceremony in the Later *Cantos*: From 'The Roads of France' to 'Rock's World.'" *Agenda* 9 (Winter 1971): 26-69.

Perloff, Marjorie. *The Poetics of Indeterminacy*. Princeton, N.J.: Princeton University Press, 1981.

Perret, N. M. "'God's Eye Art 'Ou.' Eleusis as a Paradigm for Enlightenment in Canto CVI." *Paideuma* 13 (1984): 419-32.

Piggott, Stuart. "David Jones and the Past of Man," *Agenda* 5 (Spring/Summer 1967): 76-89.

Poggioli, Renato. *The Theory of the Avant-Garde*. Translated by Gerald Fitzgerald. Cambridge, Mass. and London: Belknap Press, 1968. Originally published as *Teoria dell'arte d'avanguardia* (Società editrice il Mulino, 1962).

Pondrom, Cyrena N. "H. D. and the Origins of Imagism."In *Signets: Reading H. D.*, ed. Susan Stanford Friedman and Rachel Blau DuPlessis, 85-109. Madison: University of Wisconsin Press, 1990.

Popper, Karl R. *The Logic of Scientific Discovery*. London: Hutchinson, 1959.

Pound, Ezra. *The Cantos of Ezra Pound*. New York: New Directions, 1973.

———, trans. *The Classic Anthology Defined by Confucius*. Cambridge, Mass.: Harvard University Press, 1954.

———, trans. and commentary. *Confucius*. New York: New Directions, 1969.

———. "D'Artagnan Twenty Years After," *Criterion* 16 (1937): 606-17.

———. *Ezra Pound and Dorothy Shakespear: Their Letters, 1909-1914*, ed. Omar Pound and A. Walton Litz. New York: New Directions, 1984.

———. *Gaudier-Brzeska: A Memoir*. London: The Bodley Head, 1916.

———. *Guide to Kulchur*. 1952. New York: New Directions, n.d.

———. "Interesting French Publications." *Book News Monthly* 25 (September 1906): 31-34.

———. *The Letters of Ezra Pound 1907-1941*, ed. D. D. Paige. New York: Harcourt, Brace and World, 1950.

———. *Literary Essays of Ezra Pound*, ed. with an introduction by T. S. Eliot. New York: New Directions, 1968.

———. *Personae: the Collected Shorter Poems of Ezra Pound*. New York: New Directions, 1971.

———. *Selected Prose, 1909-1965*, ed. William Cookson. New York: New Directions, [1973].

———. *The Spirit of Romance*. 1910. Norfolk, Conn.: New Directions, n.d.

———. *Three Cantos, Poetry* 10 (June 1917): 113-21.

———. *The Translations of Ezra Pound*. With an introduction by Hugh Kenner (New York: New Directions [n.d.])

———. Untitled review of Upward's *The Divine Mystery*. *New Freewoman* 1(15 November 1913): 207-208.

Pound, Ezra and Ernest Fenollosa. *Noh or Accomplishment: A Study of the Classical Stage of Japan*. New York: A. A. Knopf, 1917.

Pratt, William. *The Imagist Poem*. New York: E. P. Dutton, 1963.

Rabaté, Jean-Michel. *Language, Sexuality and Ideology in Ezra Pound's Cantos*. London: Macmillan, 1986.

Raine, Kathleen. *Yeats the Initiate: Certain Themes in the Work of W. B. Yeats*. Mountrath and London: The Dolmen Press and George Allen & Unwin, 1986.

————. *Yeats, the Tarot and the Golden Dawn.* 2nd ed. Dublin: Dolmen Press, 1976.

Rainey, Lawrence S. *Ezra Pound and the Monument of Culture: Text, History and the Malatesta Cantos.* Chicago and London: University of Chicago Press, 1991.

Read, Forrest, ed. *Pound/Joyce.* New York: New Directions, 1965.

Reiss, Timothy J. *The Discourse of Modernism.* Ithaca, N.Y.: Cornell University Press, 1982.

Ricoeur, Paul. *Hermeneutics and the Human Sciences: Essays on Language, Action and Interpretation.* Ed. and translated by John B. Thompson. Cambridge and New York: Cambridge University Press, 1981. Originally published in Paris by Éditions de la Maison des sciences de l'homme, 1981.

Riddel, Joseph. "H. D.'s Scene of Writing: Poetry as (and) Analysis." *Studies in the Literary Imagination* 12 (Spring 1979): 41-59.

Robinson, Janice S. *H. D.: The Life and Work of an American Poet.* Boston, Mass.: Houghton Mifflin Company, 1982.

Rock, Joseph. *The Ancient Na-khi Kingdom of Southwest China.* Vols. 8 and 9, Monograph Series of the Harvard-Yenching Institute. Cambridge, Mass.: Harvard University Press, 1947.

————. *The ^{2}Muan ^{1}bpo Ceremony or the Sacrifice to Heaven as Practiced by the Na-khi.* 1948. Reprint. *Annali Lateranensi,* vol. 16. Città del Vaticano: Tipografia Poliglotta Vaticana, 1952.

————. *The Romance of ^{2}K'a-^{2}Mä-^{1}Gyu-^{3}Mi-^{2}Gkui, a Tribal Love Story. Bulletin de l'École Française d'Extréme-Orient* (1939).

Rosenthal, M. L. *Sailing into the Unknown: Yeats, Pound and Eliot.* New York: Oxford University Press, 1978.

————, and Sally M. Gall. *The Modern Poetic Sequence: The Genius of Modern Poetry.* New York and Oxford: Oxford University Press, 1983.

Rossetti, Gabriele. *Il Mistero dell'Amor platonico del Medio Evo derivato da' Misteri antichi.* 5 vols. London: Richard and John E. Taylor, 1840.

Sacks, Oliver. "The Poet of Chemistry." *New York Review of Books* 40 (November 4, 1993): 50-56.

Scherer, Jacques. *Le "Livre" de Mallarmé.* Nouvelle édition. Paris: Gallimard, 1978.

Schneidau, Herbert N. *Waking Giants.* New York: Oxford University Press, 1991.

Scofield, Martin. *T. S. Eliot: The Poems.* Cambridge: Cambridge University Press, 1988.

Seiden, Morton I. *William Butler Yeats: The Poet as Mythmaker.* East Lansing: Michigan State University Press, 1962.

Shlain, Leonard. *Art and Physics: Parallel Visions in Space, Time, and Light.* New York: William Morrow, 1991.

Sieburth, Richard. "Dada Pound." *South Atlantic Quarterly* 83 (Winter 1984): 44-68.

Skaff, William. *The Philosophy of T. S. Eliot: From Skepticism to a Surrealist Poetic, 1909-1927.* Philadelphia: University of Pennsylvania Press, 1985.

Smith, Grover. *T. S. Eliot's Poetry and Plays.* Chicago and London: University of Chicago Press, 1956.

Snow, C. P. *The Two Cultures and the Scientific Revolution.* Cambridge: Cambridge University Press, 1959.

Steiner, George. *Real Presences.* Cambridge: Cambridge University Press, 1986.

Stevens, Wallace. *The Necessary Angel: Essays on Reality and the Imagination.* 1942. Reprint. New York: Vintage Books, 1951.

Stock, Noel. *The Life of Ezra Pound.* New York: Pantheon, 1970.

Suppe, Frederick., ed. *The Structure of Scientific Theories,* 2nd ed. Urbana: University of Illinois Press, 1977.

Surette, Leon. *A Light from Eleusis: A Study of Ezra Pound's Cantos.* Oxford: Clarendon Press, 1979.

Swabey. Henry. "A Page Without Which. . ." *Paideuma* 5 (Fall 1976): 329-37.

Swinburne, Algernon Charles. *Poems.* New York: Modern Library, n.d.

Tay, William. "Between Kung and Eleusis: Li Chi, The Eleusinian Rites, Erigena and Ezra Pound." *Paideuma* 4 (Spring 1975): 37-54.

Terrell, Carroll F. *A Companion to the Cantos of Ezra Pound.* 2 vols. Berkeley, Los Angeles, and London: University of California Press, 1984.

———. "The Na-khi Documents I: The Landscape of Paradise." *Paideuma* 3 (Spring 1974): 91-122.

The Small Roman Missal. Leeds: Laverty and Sons, Ltd., 1936.

Thomas, Dylan. *The Poems of Dylan Thomas,* ed. with an introduction by Daniel Jones. New York: New Directions, 1971.

Toulmin, Stephen. *The Philosophy of Science.* London: Hutchinson, 1953.

Traversi, Derek. *T. S. Eliot: The Longer Poems.* New York and London: Harcourt, Brace, Jovanovich, 1976.

Tryphonopoulos, Demetres P. *The Celestial Tradition.* Waterloo, Ont.: Wilfrid Laurier University Press, 1992.

Turner, Victor. "Liminal and Liminoid in Play, Flow, and Ritual." In *From Ritual to Theatre,* ed. Victor Turner, 20-60. New York: Performing Arts Journal Publications, 1982.

———. *The Ritual Process.* Chicago: Aldine Publishing Company, 1969.

———. "Social Dramas and Stories About Them." *Critical Inquiry* 7 (Autumn 1980): 141-68.

———. "Variations on a Theme of Liminality." In *Secular Ritual,* ed. Sally F. Moore and Barbara G. Myerhoff, 36-52. Assen: Van Gorcum, 1977.

Upward, Allen. *The Divine Mystery.* 1907. Reprint. Santa Barbara, Calif.: Ross-Erikson Inc., 1976.

Vendler, Helen Hennessy. *Yeats' Vision and the Later Plays.* Cambridge, Mass.: Harvard University Press, 1963.

Vickers, Brian. "Analogy versus Identity: The Rejection of Occult Symbolism, 1580-1680." In *Occult and Scientific Mentalities in the Renaissance,* ed. Brian Vickers, 95-163. Cambridge: Cambridge University Press, 1984.

Vickery, John B. *The Literary Impact of The Golden Bough.* Princeton, N.J.: Princeton University Press, 1973.

Ward, David. *T.S. Eliot Between Two Worlds.* London and Boston: Routledge and Kegan Paul, 1973.

Ward, Elizabeth. *David Jones, Mythmaker*. Manchester: Manchester University Press, 1983.

Weston, Jessie L. *From Ritual to Romance*. 1920. Reprint. New York: Peter Smith, 1941.

Wheeler, Charles B. *The Design of Poetry*. New York: W. W. Norton, 1966.

Whitehead, Alfred North. *Science and the Modern World*. 1925. Reprint. New York: New American Library, 1964.

Wilhelm, James J. *The Later Cantos of Ezra Pound*. New York: Walker and Company, 1977.

Williamson, George. *A Reader's Guide to T. S. Eliot*. 1953. Reprint. New York: Farrar, Straus and Giroux, 1966.

Witemeyer, Hugh. *The Poetry of Ezra Pound: Forms and Renewal*. Berkeley and Los Angeles: University of California Press, 1969.

Woodward, Anthony. *Ezra Pound and The Pisan Cantos*. London: Routledge and Kegan Paul, 1980.

Yeats, William Butler. *Autobiographies*. New York: Macmillan, 1927.

―――. *The Collected Poems of W. B. Yeats*. New York: Macmillan, 1963.

―――. *A Critical Edition of Yeats's A Vision*, ed. George Mills Harper and Walter Kelly Hood. London: Macmillan, 1978.

―――. *Essays and Introductions*. London and New York: Macmillan, 1961.

―――. *Per Amica Silentia Lunae*. In *Mythologies*. London: Macmillan, 1959.

―――. *The Variorum Edition of the Plays of W. B. Yeats*, ed. Russell K. Alspach and Catharine C. Alspach. New York: Macmillan, 1968.

―――. *W. B. Yeats and T. Sturge Moore: Their Correspondence 1901-1937*, ed. Ursula Bridge. New York: Oxford University Press, 1953.

Index

secular ritual, 2-3
in Yeats's poems and plays, 26-27, 30-35
ritualization, 2, 9, 45, 111-2
Ritual Theory, Ritual Practice (Catherine Bell), 2
Robinson, Janice S., *H. D., The Life and Work of
an American Poet*, 113, 139
Rock, The (Eliot), 52
Rock, Joseph F, *The Ancient Na-Khi Kingdom of
Southwest China*, 91, 124-5, 127, 128
Rock Drill, see Pound, *The Cantos*
Rosenthal, M. L. and Sally M. Gall, *The Mod-
ern Poetic Sequence*, 82, 83
on *The Anathemata*, 163
on *The Cantos*, 93
Rosicrucianism, 27, 28
Rossetti, Gabriele, *Il Mistero dell' Amor platonico
del Medio Evo*, 74-5, 84, 88
Russell, Bertrand, 40
Rutherford, Ernest, 50

Sacks, Oliver, 187
Sacred Edict, The (Shang Yu), 109, 120-4
sacred marriage (*hieros gamos*), 88-9, 90-1, 97,
98, 99, 114, 126; *see also* Eleusis, rituals or
mysteries of
sacrificial ritual, *see under* ritual
St. Elizabeth's Federal Hospital for the Insane,
71, 116, 119, 121
St. Victor, Richard, in *The Cantos*, 116
Sappho, 100
Savonarola (Charlotte Eliot), 41
science, scientific discourse, 20-2
in *The Anathemata*, 173-4, 176
in *The Cantos*, 132
Eliot on, 39-41
Feyerabend on, 6-7, 187-8
Mach on, 16
and metaphor, 22-3
Lacan on, 188-9
Yeats on, 36
science and poetry, *see* poetry and science
Science and Poetry (I. A. Richards), 15, 40
science and religion, 13
science, subjectivity of, 5-6
Scratton, Bride, 99
Science of Poetry and the Philosophy of Language, The
(Hudson Maxim), 76
Sea Garden (H. D.), 137-9, 140
Shlain, Leonard (*Art and Physics*), 187
Shih-Ching, see Confucius
Sieburth, Richard, 132
Seiden, Morton I., *William Butler Yeats: The Poet
as Mythmaker*, 26, 33

Serres, Michel, 39
Shakespear, Henry Hope, 71
Sidney, Sir Philip, 20
Skaff, William *The Philosophy of T. S. Eliot*, 41
Smith, Grover, *T. S. Eliot's Poetry and Plays*, 53
Snow, C. P., 192
Society for Psychic Research, 35
Socrates, *Cratylus*, 18
Sophocles, *Women of Trachis* (Pound's transla-
tion), 129-30
Sordello (Robert Browning), 96, 101
Spirit of Romance, The (Pound), 74, 76
Stevens, Wallace, 1, 45
Stravinsky, Igor, 42
Structure of Scientific Revolutions, The (Thomas
Kuhn), 6, 51
Surette, Leon, *A Light From Eleusis*, 87
subject-rhyme, 86
Swift, Jonathan, 31
Swinburne, Algernon Charles, 73, 84,
139
symbols
Lacan on, 189
in Yeats, 27
in science, 20, 123
Symbolists, 189

Tay, William, 107
Tempio Malatestiana, 92
Tennyson, Alfred Lord, *Maud*, 151
Terrell, Carroll F., *A Companion to the Cantos of
Ezra Pound*, 107, 120
Theosophy, Theosophical Society, 3, 25, 35
Theseus in *Helen in Egypt*, 150, 152
Thetis in *Helen in Egypt*, 149, 150, 153-4
Thomas, Dylan, 18
Tiresias, 96
Toulmin, Stephen, 6
Tractatus Logico-Philosophicus (Ludwig
Wittgenstein), 16
transubstantiation, in *In Parenthesis*, 168
Jones's view of, 161-2
in *Trilogy*, 148; *see also* Mass
Traversi, Derek, *T. S. Eliot: The Longer Poems*,
59, 69-70
Tribute to Freud (H. D.), 136
Trilogy, see H. D.
Trojan War in *Helen in Egypt*, 150-1
Tryphonopoulos, Demetres P., *The Celestial
Tradition*, 71, 86, 98, 101-2
Turner, Victor, *The Ritual Process*, 8-9, 115
Tyndall, John, 25
Tyro in *The Cantos*, 117